# THE
# INTERNATIONAL
# DIRECTORY OF

# Voluntary
# Work

THE
INTERNATIONAL
DIRECTORY OF

# Voluntary Work

*Edited by*
David Woodworth
*Assisted by Cynthia Millar*

*Published by Vacation Work, 9 Park End Street, Oxford*

First published 1979
Second Edition 1982
Third Edition 1985
Fourth Edition 1989

THE INTERNATIONAL DIRECTORY OF
VOLUNTARY WORK

ISBN 1 85458 000 0 (softback)
ISBN 1 85458 001 9 (hardback)
ISSN 0143 – 3474

Printed by Gibbons Barford Print, Centenary House,
Wednesfield Road, Wolverhampton

# Contents

# Non-Residential Work in the United Kingdom 135

# Introduction

Many people have a misguided view of voluntary work. One such is contained in the film "Airplane" in which a couple of earnest young American volunteers are seen "civilising" the natives in a jungle clearing in Africa: the man is teaching them to play basketball, while the woman holds a Tupperware party. We hope that the enormous range of opportunities in this, the fourth and largest edition of The International Directory of Voluntary Work, will enlighten anyone who holds such a view. Voluntary work can cover anything from spending a single Saturday afternoon helping a charity with its flag day in your home town to passing two years in Malawi as a librarian training a local to replace you. The common factor linking all the opportunities listed in this book is that they all call for people who possess an altruistic desire to help others and we hope that in doing so they may gain some benefit themselves.

Different types of voluntary work may attract people with different additional motives for "becoming involved": for example, a mother with young children may wish to keep her secretarial skills in trim by spending a few hours a week doing office work for a charity, a student may pass two weeks of his summer vacation on a conservation scheme in France at least partly because it is a cheap way of spending time abroad and practising his French, or a qualified engineer may spend two years working on a construction project in the third world in order to widen his practical experience. This book attempts to direct all these categories of people towards an organisation that requires their assistance.

An unfortunate recent development is that because of the rise in unemployment, young people may find that an involvement with voluntary work is their only opportunity of gaining some practical experience of work. While it can never be a direct substitute for a paid job, it can enable people to gain confidence in working with others and perhaps to develop abilities they did not know they had and can only serve to impress employers in future job interviews. At the other extreme voluntary work provides those who have retired with a way of continuing to make use of the skills they have acquired over their working lives and can help to soften the traumas that often accompany retirement.

The popular definition of a volunteer as an unpaid worker is not totally accurate, and many of the opportunities listed in this book actually offer remuneration of some kind. In cases of full-time work it would be unreasonable to expect anyone — however dedicated — to work for no payment at all, but an allowance of £10 a week or less obviously does not class as normal payment for a 40-hour week, even if board and lodging are thrown in. As the figures and fringe benefits increase, the work is more difficult to classify. When speaking of money in the third world it should be remembered that figures can be very misleading. While an allowance of £5 a week plus free accommodation may sound like a formula for starvation in Britain or North America, the same payment in many third world countries may even be higher than the wages of most local residents. In real terms, what seems like a paltry sum on paper could in fact represent a respectable wage when compared with the local cost of living.

Another problem with defining voluntary work is the decision as to what constitutes "work". If for instance, you do the weekly shopping for an elderly housebound neighbour, you are merely being a good neighbour. If, on the other hand, you offer your services to an organisation such as Age Concern, you may well be asked to do the weekly shopping for the same elderly housebound neighbour. In this case, you would probably call yourself a volunteer. Similarly, if you do research into the breeding habits of a rare species of butterfly in your area, you are just pursuing a hobby. As a member of the British Butterfly Conservation Society, your work might come into the category of voluntary work.

Many of these borderline cases have been included in this book, although a lot of organisations have had to be omitted, either because the terms of employment come close to normal rates of pay, or because the help they need is barely classifiable as "work". A large number of societies and associations that only seek help from their members have been omitted if their interests seem to be too narrow. Political parties — which rely very heavily on volunteer labour, especially at election times — have also been omitted because it is assumed that their members will make themselves aware of any work that has to be done (paid or unpaid). Other omissions include many of the organisations which only need help for fund-raising, campaigning or demonstrating. A few such organisations have been included, but a complete listing would be virtually endless.

The current image of the volunteer is no longer that of the elderly lady taking flowers to patients in geriatric hospitals, although such help is still welcome. Volunteers now cover all age groups, all nationalities and all religious, social and educational backgrounds. It is hoped that the trends will continue as more and more people discover the benefits, both to themselves and to others, of devoting at least a little time to some worthwhile cause. Bearing in mind that the profession of health visiting started as a voluntary work scheme run by the Manchester and Salford Ladies' Sanitary Reform Association in 1862, it is to be hoped that many of the volunteer opportunities listed in this Directory — such as marriage guidance counsellors and the staff at Citizens' Advice Bureaux — will become fully paid jobs when the economic climate improves. Some already receive financial help with overheads from local authorities. At the same time, new schemes will be created, new societies established, and more volunteers needed. We hope that this book will encourage the growth of the volunteer movement by putting potential volunteers in touch with the organisations that need them.

**The International Directory of Voluntary Work will be revised regularly, and any new information that you think should be included should be sent to David Woodworth at Vacation Work, 9 Park End Street, Oxford.**

# Residential Work Throughout the World

This section of the Directory examines the different types of voluntary work for which the volunteer is required to live and work away from home. This usually means a full-time commitment, ranging from a weekend to several years.

For the purposes of classification, organisations requiring resident volunteers have been divided between long term and short term. The organisations classed as "long term" require volunteers for periods of a year or more; "short term" denotes residential work for anything up to a year. The short term organisations are further sub-divided geographically.

Obviously, the dividing line between short and long term is indistinct and arbitrary and there are many organisations which actually fall into both categories. In such cases, these organisations will be fully described under the category in which they are most active. Cross references will then be found at the end of the chapter on the opposite category.

Applicants for voluntary work outside their own country are reminded that visas and work permits are sometimes necessary. The fact that voluntary work is unpaid does not always exempt them from these requirements. Regulations around the world change frequently, so volunteers going abroad are advised to check with the appropriate embassy before departure.

# Long Term

When originally compiling this book we found that some distinction had to be made between long and short term voluntary work. The obvious one is that many people, such as teachers, students and those with sympathetic employers, can leave home for a few weeks or even months without unduly upsetting their normal way of life. But those going away for a year or more may be damaging their studies or career prospects or even lose their job.

Another difference is that while many short term volunteers need no special skills or experience except fitness and enthusiasm, most recruiters of long term volunteers look for people with some particular ability to offer. This is true to the point that one charity, well known for sending volunteers abroad, asked not to be included in this section, as they are already flooded with applications from totally unqualified people who think that the mere fact that they are prepared to go abroad for a year or more will assure them of a placement. Many, if not most, long term volunteers work in a voluntary capacity in the same profession in which they are trained and normally employed. This is because the emphasis on voluntary work in the third world is now to help developing countries to help themselves wherever possible through guidance and example in such areas of medicine, teaching, engineering, etc. Lengths of long-term voluntary work abroad have tended to increase, as it has been found that volunteers are more effective if they have more time to settle down in their new environment and can get more deeply involved in a project. It is also more cost effective for the sending society obviously saves money if it has to pay less frequently for travel expenses and the recruitment of new volunteers.

Volunteers who devote a year or more of their lives to helping others require a considerable amount of dedication to the particular cause for which they are working. It is hardly surprising therefore, that many of the organisations requiring long term volunteers are religious foundations. Some of these, like the Missions to Seamen are overtly Christian and evangelistic in outlook, and their need is therefore for committed Christians. Other Christian organisations, like the Catholic Medical Mission Board, are less interested in the evangelical side of missionary work, and more interested in providing practical help (in this case, medical) to the third world.

Not all long term work is in the third world, and not all projects are concerned with long-term development programmes. ATD Fourth World Voluntariat specialises in the developed nations of the "first world"; the Tear Fund is an organisation that handles disaster relief programmes rather than the mainstream of third world development.

The long term volunteer stands to gain more from his period of service than his short-term counterpart. To begin with, he is likely to have all his travel and living expenses paid. More significantly, his deeper involvement gives him a greater insight into both the project and the country in which he is working, and he may find that his abilities may be stretched further than they would be if he was in his normal occupation. Thus a recently qualified teacher may suddenly find herself confronting a whole class of adults in a teacher training college, or a young staff nurse may be appointed chief nursing officer in a brand new hospital. Anyone who survives such challenges is likely to return more confident, more skilled, and with a completely new outlook on life. But not everyone is capable of bearing such pressure, and so applicants for long-term voluntary work must be prepared to undergo a rigorous selection process by the recruiting organisation.

The main organisations needing long term volunteers are described in the following pages. A number of the organisations concentrating on short term opportunities also offer varying amounts of long term work. These organisations are listed at the end of this chapter, but are described in full in the various sub-sections of the *Short Term* chapter, which follows.

## ATD Fourth World Voluntariat
48 Addington Square, London SE5 7LB, UK. Tel: (01) 703 3231

ATD Fourth World is an international movement working in eight European countries, the USA, Canada, Africa, Asia and Central America. The movement is concerned with the "Fourth World", a term referring to the part of any national population at the botton of the social scale which is excluded from social, economic and political life. Through long-term involvement with the most disadvantaged communities, the purpose of ATD Fourth World's work is to demonstrate the will and capacity of the very poorest individuals and families to fulfill their role as parents and citizens. Practical projects established with them include family centres, children's street libraries and learning clubs, youth clubs, literacy programmes, training workshops, family holidays and community programmes that reinforce cooperation between very disadvantaged families and the community they live in. Fourth World families are involved in the planning, implementation, and evaluation of these projects.

The core of the movement is formed by an international voluntariat, whose members are full-time workers from different professions and backgrounds concerned by the suffering of persistently disadvantaged families. Applicants wishing to stay for a minimum of two years enter into the voluntariat training programme, which begins with a period of service in his or her country of origin. The minimum age for participation in the voluntariat is 18. Good health and references are required and previous work experience is desirable, but no specific qualifications are needed. Food and accommodation are provided and pocket money is given, after three months' service. National insurance contributions are paid on the same basis, but general insurance should be obtained by the volunteers themselves for the first three months except for cover for accidents while at work. Normal visa requirements apply.

The movement organises working weekends from its national centre in London, a three-month Short Term Volunteer Scheme, summer workcamps in the UK and in France. They provide an opportunity to contribute practically to the development of ATD Fourth World and to discover how people can work together to change the situation of these families.

Information about these opportunities can be obtained from the Director at the above address.

## Agency for Personal Service Overseas
29 Fitzwilliam Square, Dublin 2, Eire

APSO's function is to sponsor Irish people wishing to serve on economic and social development projects in developing countries. Although development workers are trained, volunteers must have some special skill or experience to offer and be aged over 21. Assignments are usually for two years. Return fares, accident and sickness insurance, board, lodging and pocket money are normally provided.

Applications should be made to the Information Officer at the above address.

## Auxiliary Missionaries of the Assumption
914 South 49th Street, Philadelphia, PA 19143, USA. Tel: (215) 724 1504

A lay missionary association, Auxiliary Missionaries of the Assumption operate religious communities in Third World countries or their equivalent, which help the local people through education and self development programmes. Communities currently exist in Africa, the United States, Japan and countries in Central America. Around 15 volunteers a year are required for one to two years service as parish ministry workers, health or child care workers or teachers.

Volunteers must be single Catholic women aged 23 to 35 who have a college degree and are fluent in the language of the country they intend to visit. Training consists of a one week orientation course in Philadelphia. Board and lodging within the religious community, travel to the mission site and a monthly stipend are provided. The volunteer pays for medical expenses and insurance, and must obtain a visa for their period of stay as a lay missionary.

British applicants should apply to Sister Aquinas, 23 Kensington Square, London W8 before March of each year.

## Baptist Missionary Society
93-97 Gloucester Place, London W1H 4AA, UK. Tel: (01) 935 1482

The Society is looking for Baptist volunteers who possess certain skills and are prepared to use them for two years or more in Zaire, Bangladesh and Brazil. Both Zaire and Bangladesh need doctors and nurses (RGN and RM) for work on community health and in hospitals and nursing schools. Zaire also requires graduate teachers for secondary schools, builders and engineers in the above institutions, and ministers to teach theology in theological schools. Bangladesh needs ministers or teachers of religious knowledge for pastoral training; Brazil also needs ministers.

A driving licence is almost always necessary in this work, and a knowledge of French is vital for communications in Zaire. Volunteers receive accommodation and a living allowance. The length of service varies from a "short term" of two years to an indefinite period.

Those interested should write to the Personnel Secretary at the above address.

## Benedictine Lay Volunteers

Mother of God Priory/Harmony Hill Center, RR 3, Box 254, Watertown, SD 57201, USA. Tel: (605) 886 6777

Sponsored by the Mother of God Benedictine Priory this programme provides volunteers with the opportunity to serve American people. Volunteers provide the community with whatever skills they have—teacher, cook, gardener, nurse, etc.

Approximately 20 one year placements are available to single people or married couples with no dependents provided they are at least 21 years old, in good health and speak English. Appropriate qualifications are required for holding professional positions within the community.

Board, lodging, liability and health insurance, stipend, transportation on-site and other benefits are provided.

Depending on the site, short term placements of one week to three months are also possible. The above restrictions for volunteers apply but only board, lodging and local educational outings are provided.

Apply to the Director at the above address for further information.

## Brethren Service

150 Route de Ferney, 1211 Geneva 20, Switzerland. Tel: 91 63 30

Brethren Service is an American based organisation, sponsored by the Church of the Brethren, whose primary activity relates to the exchange of personnel between America and other countries. After a brief period of orientation volunteers are assigned to a project related to social work, community development, youth leadership in churches etc. Most of those taking part in the scheme are American, but Brethren Service in Geneva does also send Europeans to projects in America. The number of participants from each European country is kept to a quota in order to maintain a balance.

Most volunteers are in their twenties, but the scheme is open to anyone over 18 who is in good health. Although Brethren Service is a church-sponsored agency, as are most of their projects, applicants need not be Christian in the orthodox sense but they must be motivated primarily by spiritual and humanitarian concern. The more skills the applicant has the better, although none are essential. However, most properties request persons with some training experience or interest in "social-type" work. A knowledge of foreign languages, for example, may increase the applicant's chances of being accepted. Volunteers going to the USA must pay for their own travel, but once there room, board and pocket money are provided. Normal term of service is one year.

Those interested should write to the Director at the above address for further details.

**Brethren Volunteer Service**
1451 Dundee Avenue, Elgin, Illinois 60120, USA. Tel: (312) 742-5100

The goals of the BVS programme are peacemaking, advocating social justice and meeting human needs. Volunteers serve in community-based organisations or national offices working on grass roots needs as well as systemic structural changes leading toward these goals. Projects include counselling of delinquent youth, community development work, care of the elderly, office work, and refugee work. Volunteers serve a minimum of one year in the States or two years abroad.

Volunteers must be at least 18 and in good health. Specific requirements may apply to some placements. The volunteers' experience begins with one month of orientation in preparation for service. Participants receive living expenses and $35.00 per month pocket money, as well as medical and accidental death insurance.

Contact the Recruitment Officer at the above address for further information.

**Bureau for Overseas Medical Service**
Africa Centre, 38 King Street, London WC2E 8JT. Tel: (01) 836 5833

The Bureau maintains a register for all types of health workers who wish to work in developing countries and acts as a co-ordinating body for the sending agencies it services. Around 60 placements are made each year for periods of six months to two years. The Bureau also produces a newsletter which lists posts available and conducts short training courses to prepare health workers for work in Third World countries.

All members of the register must have the appropriate medical qualifications.

For further information contact the Director at the above address.

**CUSO**
135 Rideau Street, Ottawa, Ontario, Canada K1N 9K7. Tel: (613) 563 1264

CUSO, an independent, non-profit organisation, has since 1961 sent more than 8,000 volunteers to fill manpower gaps in developing countries. Originally, recruitment was aimed at young graduates for teaching positions, but the needs have expanded to include health personnel and people of all ages skilled in trades, technology, business, community development and agriculture. At any one time CUSO has about 400 volunteers in the field, and is at present operating in thirty countries in Asia, Africa, Latin America, the Caribbean and the South Pacific. The annual intake of volunteers is about 200 and contracts are for two years.

Recruitment is carried out within Canada and is aimed at Canadian citizens and landed immigrants. There are no age limits, but all applicants must be suitably qualified (eg teacher's diploma, medical or paramedical qualifications) and in good health. For business or agricultural posts, experience may be a more valuable asset than formal qualifications. CUSO pays travel costs to and from the posting, also medical, dental and life insurance, and for any language training or orientation that may be necessary. Housing is either subsidised or provided free, and volunteers are also paid settlement and resettlement allowances. In principle, the employer is the overseas government or agency requesting CUSO's services, so volunteers are in most cases paid the same wage as local employees.

Enquiries should be sent to the Ottawa office, above, or to one of the 80 local or regional committees across the country. CUSO also hold regular recruitment and information meetings within Canada.

**The Catholic Institute for International Relations**
22 Coleman Fields, London N1 7AF. Tel: (01) 354 0883

At the request of governments and community organisations overseas, CIIR recruits professionally or technically qualified people with a minimum of two years work experience to work in development projects. By sharing skills with local counterparts, in agriculture, education, health, and other fields, they contribute to improving local conditions and promoting self-reliance. CIIR currently has programmes in Central and South America, Somalia, North Yemen and Zimbabwe. Contracts are for two years. A salary adequate for a single person is provided together with a return flight, language training, various allowances and extensive briefings. Write to the above address for a copy of the current vacancy list.

**Catholic Medical Mission Board (CMMB)**
10 West 17th Street, New York, New York 10011, USA. Tel: (212) 242 7757

The Board's "middle man" program places volunteer medical doctors, registered nurses, dentists and, far less frequently, A.S.C.P. certified medical technologists, licensed practical nurses, optometrists and physical therapists at independently operated medical mission institutions in Africa, the Caribbean, Central and South America, India, Mexico and Oceania. The duration of service may be short-term (more than one month and less than one year) or long-term (at least one year, preferably two). Board and lodging are provided free of charge. Long-term volunteers receive a modest monthly honorarium. Applicants must be fully qualified members of the medical, nursing and dental professions. Degree/certification/licence is required. (Health care specialists in other professions listed above must be certified in their respective specialities). Experience is necessary.

Applicants should contact the Rev. Joseph J. Walter, S. J., President and Director, at the above address.

**Centro Studi Terzo Mondo**
Via G.B. Morgagni 39, 20129 Milano, Italy. Tel: (02) 2719041

This organisation recruits and sends volunteers of all nationalities to various countries in Asia, Africa and America. About 100 volunteers are needed for social work, community development and teaching at different levels. Placements vary but are for between three months and two years long.

Accommodation is provided and applicants' expenses are paid.
Those interested should apply to the Director at the above address.

### Christians Abroad
11 Carteret Street, London SW1H 9DL, UK. Tel: (01) 222 2165

Christians Abroad is an ecumenical body which exists to help those who are thinking about long or short term work overseas. They provide an information service about opportunities abroad for different occupations and ages. Their individual information leaflets include several on volunteer work. Individual leaflets are available free of charge (cost of postage is appreciated) but bulk orders cost 5p per leaflet. They also recruit teachers on behalf of overseas employers and can sometimes place accountants, agriculturalists, civil engineers and others with skills relevant to development. Christians who will be working or travelling abroad are invited to contact them if they would like an introduction sent ahead of them to the church abroad or help in preparation.

Further information and a list of publications can be obtained from the Information Secretary.

### Christian Outreach
34 St. Mary's Crescent, Leamington Spa, Warwickshire. Tel: (0926) 315301

Christian Outreach functions chiefly as a child care agency working in the Far East and Africa. Its current projects include: running mother and child health clinics in refugee camps in Thailand and Sudan, working in a home for handicapped children in Bangkok and supporting a children's home in the Philippines. At any one time between 30 and 40 skilled volunteers help Christian Outreach with its work abroad for periods of between one and two years. They are needed mainly to work abroad as either midwives or paediatric nurses, but there are occasional needs for engineers, nursery nurses and administrators.

All volunteers must be at least temporarily resident in Britain, aged over 21, usually unmmarried, and qualified for the job they have applied for. They should also be regular attenders of a church of some Christian denomination and be prepared to live and work as part of a team. All expenses are paid, including air fares, accommodation, food, some pocket money and a resettlement allowance on return to the UK.

Those interested should contact the Director at the above address.

### Church Missionary Society
Partnership House, 157 Waterloo Road, London SE1 8UU, UK. Tel: (01) 928 8681

The Society sends long-term and short-term missionaries to 26 countries in Africa and Asia, in particular to Nigeria, Kenya, Uganda, Sierra Leone and Pakistan. Short-term missionaries go for two years and usually help local communities in a specific area such as medicine, education, administrative or construction work. Long-term missionaries commit themselves to a minimum of two three-year tours. There are, at any time, about 150 vacancies for long-term and 40-50 vacancies for short-term missionaries.

Both long-term and short-term missionaries must be practising Christians though not necessarily Anglican. Short-term missionaries should have had technical or professional training, and be qualified in their field. There is a minimum age for them, but no maximum age is specified; retired people are accepted. Long-term missionaries, however, must be able to do a full term before retiring (retiring age differs according to circumstances prevailing in the country concerned), so should not apply if past the early fifties. Applicants may be of any nationality if applying in the UK. Missionaries receive grants related to the cost of living in the country they work in, fares are paid, and there is a pension scheme. Visa and work permit requirements vary from country to country.

Those interested should apply to the Society at the above address.

## Concern
1 Upper Camden Street, Dublin 2, Eire. Tel: 681237

Concern is an Irish non-denominational organisation devoted to the relief, assistance and advancement of peoples in need in less developed areas of the world. Concern is working in Bangladesh, Thailand, Ethiopia, Mozambique, Somalia, Sudan and Tanzania. There are over 100 volunteers passing on their skills to locally employed staff. The type of professions that Concern recruit are: nurses, civil engineers, agriculturalists, horticulturalists, foresters, primary school teachers, social workers, accountants, home economic teachers and home farm advisors.

Assignments are for two years and all living expenses, including return airfare, are covered by Concern. There is a lower age limit of 21 years.

For further information contact the Head of Overseas Volunteer Department at the above address.

## Direct Relief International
PO Box 41929, Santa Barbara, CA 93140-1929, USA. Tel: (805) 687 3694

Direct Relief International is a non-profit organisation which arranges short and long term assignments for volunteer medical and dental personnel at hospitals and other health care facilities serving the needy in medically less-developed areas of the world; Africa, Latin America, the Caribbean, South Asia, the Far East, the Pacific Basin and the United States. It responds to requests from those in need provided that assurances are given that anyone who requests medical care will be serviced without discrimination. Over 100 volunteers are needed annually with most requests being for doctors, nurses, physical therapists, laboratory technicians, dental hygienists, pharmacists and other health professionals although there are some opportunities for junior and senior medical and dental students. Short term assignments are for up to one year while long term assignments are for a year or more.

Volunteers must be at least 18 years old and if not a student, qualified in their home country. Some locations may not accept certain degrees or may require varying standards of fluency in the language of that area. Work permits are usually sent by the requesting centre for completion by the volunteer and submission to the country's medical council. On short term assignments, most locations will furnish room and board while for long term assignments some locations will pay travel costs, some compensation and furnish room and board. Only some locations also accommodate the spouse or family of volunteers.

Write to the Assignment Officer at the above address for further information.

### Eirene, International Christian Service for Peace
Engerser Strasse 74b, D-5450 Neuwied 1, Germany

Eirene organizes three voluntary programmes which are complementary to each other; the north programme is operating in Europe and USA, the south programme in Nicaragua, Nigeria, Chad and Morocco and the solidarity and learning programme in Africa, Latin America and Asia. 1. In the north programme untrained volunteers work together with conscientious objectors, migrant workers, handicapped and youth groups. 2. In the south programme professionally qualified and experienced volunteers collaborate with projects in agriculture, irrigation, handicrafts, community development, co-operatives, health and vocational training. 3. In the solidarity and learning programme volunteers are invited to propose to Eirene a project in the Third World in which they want to collaborate. This scheme is financially and morally supported by basis groups in Europe; it provides a real link on the grassroot level between the Third World and Europe.

Approximately 20 volunteers are needed each year; most of them are recruited from Germany. Those wishing to work in Europe and the USA must be at least 20 and those going to Africa or Latin America must be at least 21. All volunteers are expected to know the language of the country to which they are being sent, and to have some previous involvement in social Christian and nonviolent activities. In the north programme the minimum duration of service is one year, in the south programme it is three years. Board, lodging, a monthly allowance, insurance and travel costs are all paid for, although volunteers are asked to find a support group to give some financial contribution as well as to support the service of the volunteer.

Applications should be made to the above address.

### Frontier Apostolate
PO Box 7000, Prince George, BC, V2N 3Z2, Canada. Tel: (604) 964 4424

Frontier Apostolate aims to promote Catholic Education in the Diocese of Prince George in British Columbia, Canada. Around 50 volunteers are needed annually to staff 13 elementary and two secondary Catholic schools in this region. The greatest need is for elementary and secondary school teachers but Frontier Apostolate also recruits secretaries, houseparents, bus drivers, kitchen staff, maintenance workers and Parish workers. Placements are for two years.

Canadian, American, Irish and English volunteers are accepted. Teachers need to be qualified and secretaries need general secretarial skills. It is desirable to have a driving licence. Medical coverage, room, board and a stipend of around £60 for first year volunteers and about £80 for further years are provided but there is only limited accommodation for married couples with children. Applicants are interviewed in their home country before being accepted for a position, but once accepted will be given the necessary employment authorisation.

Those interested should apply to the Director at the above address.

**Habitat for Humanity**
Habitat and Church Street, Americus, GA 31709, USA. Tel: 912 924 6935

Habitat for Humanity is an ecumenical Christian housing ministry whose objective is to eliminate poverty housing from the world. Habitat has 250 house building projects in North America and 50 projects at third world sites including Africa, Asia, the Pacific Islands and Latin America. Thousands of volunteers are needed for the North American programmes, 300 at the International office in Americus, Georgia and 75 for third world programmes. In North America there are openings for accounting, child care, administration, book keeping, construction, clerical work, graphic arts, shipping, maintenance, photography and public relations, while in third world countries volunteers are responsible for construction, administration and community development. Volunteers are needed year round for periods of one month or longer for all jobs in North America but volunteers for overseas projects must be prepared to serve for three years.

Volunteers to work in North America must be at least 18 years old and English speaking while volunteers for overseas projects need to be flexible and non-judgmental of other cultures, English speaking, at least 23 years old and define themselves as Christians. Construction and office skills are desirable.

Accommodation and pocket money to cover basic expenses are provided but volunteers must pay for their own transport, support and organise their own visas, etc. Volunteers for overseas projects receive 11 weeks of training in Americus, work permits for the assigned country, and once abroad housing, health insurance and a monthly stipend.

Contact the Director of Recruitment at the above address for more details.

**Innisfree Village**
Route 2, Box 506, Crozet, Va. 22932, USA

Approximately 18 volunteers who are experienced in working with mentally handicapped adults are required to act both as houseparents and co-workers in the bakery, weavery, woodshop and garden at the village in Crozet, Virginia. Volunteers of all nationalities are welcome provided that they are fluent in English, over 21 and in excellent health. The only other requirements are patience, an interest in community living, and an ability to cook. Board and lodging are provided, medical expenses and $130 a month pocket money. Volunteers are required to stay for one year and are given three weeks holiday with $28 per day spending money. They also accumulate $25 a month for severance.

Those interested should apply to the above address.

**International Liaison of Lay Volunteers in Mission (Catholic Network of Lay Mission Programs)**
P.O. Box 29149, 4121 Harewood Road N.E., Washington, D.C. 20017-9149, USA. Tel: (202) 529 1100

International Liaison acts as a reference centre for various agencies and programmes and potential volunteer personnel. Lay volunteers from all walks of life with many different skills and qualifications are referred to organisations which then send them on programmes which take place all over the world. Volunteers are usually aged between 25 and 65, but some are younger. Most programmes last for one to three years, but a few are for the summer only.

Those interested should contact International Liaison at the above address, who will refer them to an agency that seems to suit their interests, qualifications etc.

### IVS Overseas
3 Belvoir Street, Leicester LE1 6SL. Tel: (0533) 541862

IVS Overseas was until recently part of International Voluntary Service, the British branch of Service Civil International. Its activities involve the placement of qualified and skilled personnel in Botswana, Lesotho, Mozambique and Swaziland in response to requests from their governments or local communities for a minimum of two years. Recent requests have included those for people skilled in agriculture, civil, mechanical and water engineering, medicine, architecture, planning, construction, forestry, English language teaching and community development.

Applicants should have at least two years' relevant experience, be aged between 21 and 65, either be single or have a partner who can be placed in an IVS Overseas post and be eligible for permanent right of residence in the UK or Ireland. Volunteers receive a briefing, language training, return airfares, accommodation and an allowance based on the local going rate for the job. In addition their national insurance contributions are covered in their absence and they receive a resettlement grant on their return. It is imperative that volunteers support IVS' objective of tackling the causes of deprivation and underdevelopment by promoting self reliance and reducing dependency on the west.

Those interested should enquire initially by sending a short C.V. to the Recruitment/Selection Unit at the above address. Those shortlisted will be invited to apply and provided with detailed job descriptions.

### Jesuit Volunteer Corps: California-Southwest
1427 Twelfth Street, Oakland, California 94607, USA. Tel: (415) 465 5016

The Jesuit Volunteer Corps is a service organisation which offers women and men an opportunity to work full-time for justice and peace. Jesuit Volunteers work in the United States by serving the poor directly and working for structural change. The challenge for the volunteer is to integrate Christian faith by working and living among the poor and marginated, by living simply and in community with other Jesuit Volunteers and by examining the causes of social injustice. Since 1956, Volunteers have worked in collaboration with Jesuits, whose spirituality they incorporate in their work, community lives, and prayer. The JVC seeks to develop persons whose year or more of service challenges them to live always conscious of the poor, devoted to the promotion of justice and service of faith.

Applicants should be 21 years or older, or have a college education and have a firm Christian outlook, be in good physical condition, adaptable, and have a sense of humour. A one year commitment beginning in August is expected; room and board are provided, plus a small monthly stipend.

Applications should be made to the above address.

## Lalmba Association
7685 Quartz Street, Golden, CO 80403, USA. Tel: (303) 420 1810

The Lalmba Association operated medical clinics and other health programmes in Sudan, Kenya and Mexico. Between 20 and 40 volunteers are needed annually to staff these projects. Most opportunities are for medical staff, (physicians, nurses and midwives), but occasionally volunteers with managerial or administrative skills are needed to act as project directors. Placements in Sudan are for one year while placements in Kenya and Mexico are for two years.

Applicants must be at least 25 years old, qualified in either the United States of America or certain European countries and have some experience in their field. Round trip transportation, board, lodging, health and life insurance and pocket money are provided.

Contact the Medical Director at the above address for more information.

## Lay Volunteers International Association
Corso 4 Novembre, 28 - 12100 Cuneo, Italy. Tel: (0171) 62558 - 56975

This association organises rural development, primary health care and technical training projects in the following African countries: Ethiopia, Kenya, Tanzania, Burundi, Senegal, Ivory Coast, Guinea Bissau, Mali and Burkina Faso. Each year around twenty suitably qualified volunteers are needed to undertake various technical jobs related to these projects. Placements are normally for 30 months.

Volunteers should be over 20 years old, in good health both physically and mentally, speak either French, English or Portuguese according to the country of destination and have a driver's licence.

Accommodation within the local community and pocket money are provided.

Write to the General Secretary at the above address for more information on specific projects.

## The Medical Missionary Association
244 Camden Road, London NW1 9HE, UK. Tel: (01) 485 2672

The MMA acts as an agent channelling young doctors, nurses, dentists and paramedical workers to various mission and church organisations in many countries of the world. Apart from its "Oyster Scheme" (see separate entry), it does not have any voluntary work of its own overseas but recruits for most of the Protestant missionary societies of the UK.

As the MMA acts only as a channel, it is prepared to deal with requests from qualified Christian personnel of any nationality. The conditions of service vary, according to the usual practice of the society concerned. A quarterly magazine, *Saving Health,* is published depicting medical mission work in the world, and listing present openings in the various Protestant mission and church hospitals.

Applicants should apply to the secretary at the above address for information on openings.

## Mennonite Central Committee

21 South 12th Street, Akron, Pennsylvania 17501, USA. Tel: (717) 859 1151

The Mennonite Central Committee is a voluntary relief and development agency supported by the Mennonite and Brethren in Christ churches of North America. They work in 50 countries in Asia, Africa, Latin America and North America, usually in conjunction with other agencies to which they often second personnel. About 1,000 volunteers are engaged each year, and special skills, experience and quaifications are required in the main areas of recruitment. These are: agriculture, economic and technical assistance, education, health and social services. Language training is provided for work in non-English speaking areas. A small monthly allowance is paid and all expenses, including round trip transportation, are met in full. Accommodation is also provided.

Applicants must be members of the Christian Church. Positions in North America are usually held for two years, elsewhere three years is the normal period of service. There are no nationality restrictions, although most applications come from within the North American continent.

Enquiries and applications should be sent to the Personnel Office at the address given above.

## Missions to Seamen

St. Michael Paternoster Royal, College Hill, London EC4R 2RL, UK. Tel: (01) 248 5202

Each year some 20 young men are needed to assist port chaplains in their work of looking after seamen of all nations. During their time with the mission, these volunteers visit sailors on board ship and in hospital, welcome visitors to the mission's club, take a share in the daily worship, and help to man the telephone, the shop, and the canteen. Mission Stations exist in the UK, the USA, Asia, Australia, and Europe, and the longer the individual can spare, the greater will be his chance of serving further afield. The length of service ranges between one month and two years, and preference is given to those who are either about to start, or who have just left, university, and are considering joining the ministry.

Applicants must be over 18, with a driving licence, and should be confirmed members of the Anglican communion. Also valuable are a knowledge of foreign languages, and an ability to swim. Travelling expenses are met, and board and lodging and weekly pocket money provided.

Enquiries should be sent to the Assistant General Secretary at the above address.

## Oyster Scheme

The Medical Missionary Association, 244 Camden Road, London NW1 9HE, UK. Tel: (01) 485 2672

The Medical Missionary Association runs a scheme called "Oyster", which is an acronym standing for "One Year's Service To Encourage Recruiting". Arrangements are made for British doctors to be appointed by a missionary society to a mission hospital in Africa or Asia for a period of one year, possibly two. During this working visit the intention is for the Oyster doctor to bring the enthusiasm and encouragment of an outsider to the existing medical staff, as well as to broaden his own horizons and make a keen supporter of missionary work when he returns to his practice in Britain. It is also hoped that following the one year of service, some candidates will choose to continue a career in the mission field.

The scheme is for registered medical practitioners from the United Kingdom and Eire. It is preferable that they have the mobility of the unmarried. The candidate must satisfy the recruiting missionary society in respect of his or her character, doctrine and health. Candidates must be willing to accept the authority of the permanent mission hospital staff as they will always be stationed along with one or two other experienced doctors.

Applications must be made in good time since the decision and fare bookings are made months in advance. Enquiries may be sent to the Secretary at the above address.

### Project Ladywood
112 Whitecroft Road, Sheldon, Birmingham, UK. Tel: (021) 743 3649

Project Ladywood organises water activities for the handicapped based on several boats, provides hostels for the homeless, creates youth clubs, and provides tapes for the blind and housebound. Volunteers are needed in all these fields. Water skills and swimming ability are very useful. Handicapped people are also used as volunteers. Volunteers are usually recruited for one year or less and food and accommodation are provided on the boats. The most important requirement is that volunteers should be Evangelical Christians.

Those interested should apply to the Team Leader at the above address.

### Project Trust
Breacachadh Castle, Isle of Coll, Scotland PA78 6TB, UK. Tel: (08793) 444

Project aims to further the education of school leavers, who have "A" levels or Highers, by sending them to work overseas for a year. The work projects take place in Australia, Brazil, China, Egypt, Honduras, Hong Kong, Indonesia, Jamaica, Japan, Jordan, Namibia, Nigeria, South Africa/ Transkei, Sri Lanka, Zimbabwe. Volunteers are mainly involved in social service, farming, or teaching. Individuals must raise a portion of the total costs. Over 100 volunteers a year take this opportunity. Conditions which must be met by applicants include: being a UK national, being aged between $17\frac{1}{2}$ and $19\frac{1}{2}$, and being in full time education up to the time that they go abroad. Once abroad, they receive free board and lodging, and pocket money.

Those interested should apply to The Director at the above address. Applications normally close 1st January in the year of departure.

**Quaker Peace & Service**
Friends House, Euston Road, London NW1 2BJ, UK. Tel: (01) 387 3601

This organisation is engaged in a variety of activities around the world, all of which are committed to practical peace making. QPS supports long term (i.e. at least two year) projects for trained workers in the fields of health, agricultural and rural development, community development education and refugee counselling. There are QPS workers in Africa, Asia and the Middle East. A small number work in Northern Ireland and at the Quaker UN office in Geneva.

Formal membership of the Society of Friends is not essential, but understanding of and sympathy with Quaker objectives is. Food and accommodation are always provided and pension rights, etc, are safeguarded. All transportation expenses are paid.

Applications and enquiries may be sent to the Service Projects Secretary at the above address.

**Returned Volunteer Action**
1 Amwell Street, London EC1R 1UL. Tel: (01) 278 0804

RVA does not send people to work abroad but does give advice and information to people considering working overseas. It is an independent organisation of individuals who have worked overseas as project workers or volunteers in development projects. It works to ensure that the experience of volunteers is put to good use after their return, both through contacts with British community groups and through feedback to overseas development agencies and sending societies regarding the appropriateness of their programmes and methods.

There is an RVA network of local groups and contacts across the country who organise weekends for recently returned project workers, 'Questioning Development' days for prospective volunteers, and conferences, as well as providing a focus for those who want to participate in relevant activities at a local level.

RVA publishes a number of books on volunteering and development, and urges anyone considering working overseas to write for a copy of their pamphlet "Thinking about Volunteering?" (Send £1+ large SAE) to the above address.

**The Salvation Army Service Corps**
National Headquarters, 101 Queen Victoria Street, London EC4P 4EP, UK. Tel: (01) 236 5222

The Service Corps comprises Salvationists and other Christians who are committed to a fixed period of full-time lay service in Salvation Army centres in Britain and Third World countries. Qualified and experienced persons aged 21+, willing to give three years, are required for hospitals, handicapped centres, schools, and agricultural projects, abroad.

Opportunities in Britain are confined to care assistants, social workers, and general service, for homes for children, elderly, and workpeople, and community centres. Minimum age 18.

Applicants should be in sympathy with the Movement's evangelical programme and willing to accept the salvationist life-style of teetotalism and non-smoking. Remuneration is equivalent to that of a Salvation Army Officer.

Application should be made to the Service Corps Officer at the above address.

### Tear Fund (Evangelical Alliance Relief Fund)
100 Church Road, Teddington, Middlesex TW11 8QE, UK. Tel: (01) 977 9144

Tear Fund is a Christian charity which supports Christian development work in the developing countries. The Fund is also involved in emergency relief programmes following natural disasters. All personnel must be fully qualified in their profession, should hold a driving licence, and will be required to undertake language study at the start of their assignments. About 60 volunteers are recruited annually, usually for assignments of three to four years: all should be committed Christians and resident in the UK, preferably British citizens. No age limits are applied, but a high standard of medical fitness is necessary.

Tear Fund workers are at present operating in about 20 countries, mostly in Africa, Asia and Latin America. Full expenses are paid, and workers receive a regular monthly allowance. Accommodation is also provided.

Enquiries should be sent to Miss Jennifer Loughlin, Overseas Personnel Department, at the address above.

### United Nations Association International Service
3 Whitehall Court, London SW1A 2EL, UK. Tel: (01) 930 0679

UNAIS recruits qualified and experienced people to work for two or three years with organisations in Africa, Latin America and the Middle East. In this way it helps selected organisations which aim to strengthen local groups struggling to improve their situation, and to gain a fairer share of resources.

UNAIS recruit in the three main fields of health, agriculture, and water engineering. The countries in which they work are: Bolivia, Brazil, Paraguay, Mali, Burkina Faso, Cape Verde Islands, the West Bank and Gaza.

Volunteers are paid a monthly allowance calculated in relation to the local cost of living which is very adequate for a single person. Their accommodation is also paid for and there are a variety of grants paid during the period of service. Flights and insurance are also paid.

For further information contact the Recruitment Administrator at the above address.

### United Nations Volunteers Programme (UNV)
Palais des Nations, 1211 Geneva 10, Switzerland. Tel: (022) 98 58 50

The United Nations Volunteers (UNV) programme was created in 1970 in recognition of the need for trained professionals for development activities and of the role volunteer service can play in this field. The purpose of the programme is to channel professionally qualified men and women on a volunteer basis into development assistance calling for middle- and upper-level operational expertise; to promote effective participation of youth in development activities; and to assist and cooperate with domestic development service (DDS) organisations on both national and regional levels. The DDS organisations promote self-reliant economic and social development at the grass-roots level through participatory initiatives.

UN Volunteers are agronomists, doctors, economists, engineers, entomologists, geologists, graphic designers, technicians, librarians, mechanics, midwives, youth workers and representatives of 140 other professions. The UN Volunteers are professionals and technicians who possess the requisite educational qualifications, at least two years of professional experience, and meet the linguistic requirements which include proficiency in one or more of the working languages of the UN. The age range of UN Volunteers varies; a typical UN Volunteer, however, has five to seven years of professional experience, the number of years rises to 20 or more in a number of cases. The UNV assignments are for a minimum period of two years, although an assignment may be extended beyond this length of time. Some 1,300 UN Volunteers are working in nearly 100 developing countries. The volunteers are sent to countries only at the request, and on the approval, of host governments.

Additional information may be obtained from the Executive Co-ordinator, at the above address.

## United States Peace Corps
806 Connecticut Avenue, NW Washington, DC 20526, USA. Tel: (202) 254 5010

The goals of the Peace Corps are to help promote world peace and friendship, to help developing countries meet their needs for skilled personnel and to help promote mutual understanding between people of the United States and those of developing countries. There are over 6,000 volunteers and trainees in 62 nations in Latin America, Africa, Asia and the Pacific. Placements normally last for two years plus three months training time.

Volunteers must be US citizens and at least 18 years old. The volunteers receive a monthly allowance for rent, food, travel and medical costs, transportation to and from training sites and overseas placements and a readjustment allowance of US$200 per month, paid on completion of service.

Those interested should apply to the Director, Public Affairs Office, at the above address.

## Viatores Christi
39 Upper Gardiner Street, Dublin 1, Eire. Tel: Dublin 749346/728027

A lay missionary association founded in Dublin in 1960, Viatores Christi has its headquarters and training programme in Ireland. It recruits, trains and helps place volunteers overseas wherever there is need. Besides offering their own skills in such fields as medicine, teaching, carpentry, mechanics, secretarial work, etc. volunteers, as lay missionaries, should be prepared to participate actively in the work of the local Church.

Volunteers must undertake a part-time training course in Ireland for a minimum period of six months. To be assigned overseas they should be practising Catholics, at least 21, in good health and possess some professional qualification or some skill. All assignments are for a minimum of one year but most stay for at least two years. Contracts normally provide for volunteer terms, i.e. return air fare, insurance, living allowance and accommodation provided by the receiving agent.

Applications should be made to the Secretary at the above address. Since it is necessary to be in Ireland in order to undertake the part-time training course, residents in the UK may prefer to contact the Volunteer Missionary Movement.

## Volunteer Missionary Movement

Shenley Lane, London Colney, Herts AL2 1AR, UK. Tel: (0727) 24853

VMM recruits and sends skilled Christian volunteers to work for a minimum of two years in development projects linked with the local churches in Africa and Papua New Guinea. People with the following skills are needed to pass them on to the local communities: midwives, RGN nurses, tutors, doctors, pharmacists, physiotherapists, qualified teachers for secondary schools, and also lay chaplains, secretaries able and willing to teach, qualified agriculturalists, and diploma holders in mechanics, carpentry, building and other technical skills.

Volunteers must be committed Christians aged between 21 and 65 and can be either married or single. The selection procedure includes an initial interview and five day introduction course, and all volunteers attend a five week residential preparation course before going overseas.

Those interested should contact the Director at the above address.

## VSO

9 Belgrave Square, London SW1X 8PW, UK. Tel: (01) 235 5191

VSO is a registered charity which recruits skilled volunteers to work in the following developing areas: Africa, the Pacific, the Caribbean, and Asia. Around 600 volunteers a year are sent to work for a minimum of two years. About half of this number are placed in schools, teacher training colleges and vocational training centres; the remainder work in crafts, trades, engineering, the health services, agriculture and specialist fields such as librarianship and small business development. Applicants must be British or EEC citizens or domiciled in the UK (to be considered domiciled they must have made their home in the UK for several years, intend to live here in the future and have free right of re-entry into the UK).

Participants should be aged 21 or over, and possess a skill or qualification in one of the following fields: agriculture, education, health, technical, business or social development. VSO provides fares, training, various grants, superannuation and National Insurance payments. The overseas employer provides accommodation and a salary based on the local rate for the job.

Those interested should write to the Enquiries Unit at the above address for further details.

## Volunteers in Mission

The Presbyterian Church (USA), 100 Witherspoon, Louisville, Kentucky 40202, USA

VIM is a programme offering opportunities for people, young and old, who are willing to live at subsistence level while helping to meet social needs around the world. All volunteers must be church members and most are required to have some specialised training such as medicine or teaching. Some assignments are for at least a year but summer camps are also arranged.

Further information can be obtained from the above address.

### Youth With A Mission (YWAM)

13 Highfield Oval, Ambrose Lane, Harpenden, Herts AL5 4BX. Tel: (05827) 65481

YWAM is an international charitable organisation which is interdenominational in character. It undertakes evangelical, training and relief ministries in around 80 countries in the world. All tasks are undertaken by volunteers and most are financially supported by their home church, fellowship, friends or family. Volunteers are needed in whatever field they wish to offer their service. Most volunteers stay for one year.

Volunteers must be committed Christians with their own financial support, and willing to attend a basic training course with YWAM before beginning service.

For more information apply to the Director of Personnel Services at the above address.

### Zone de Developpement Rural au Zaire (ZO.DE.RU)

BP: 213 Kinshasa/Kasa-Vubu, Zaire

ZO.DE.RU is a new organisation which is concerned with the development of rural Zaire. Around six volunteers are needed to help with all aspects of this development; in health, education and agricultural areas and as administrators and mechanics. Placements are normally for one to three years.

Volunteers should preferably have at least two years experience in their field and be able to use French in their work. Good health is necessary and women should be aged 18 to 40 years old, while men should be 17 to 35 years old. ZO.DE.RU will supply a letter of invitation to successful applicants and accommodation is provided.

Further information may be obtained from the President at the above address.

## Other Long Term Opportunities

The following organisations have been included in the various sub-sections of the *Short Term* chapter, but also require a number of volunteers for periods of a year and longer.

*Worldwide*

Action Health 2000
Christian Medical Fellowship
Global Outreach U.K.
Institute of Cultural Affairs
Mission Aviation Fellowship

UNIPAL
Voluntary Workcamps Association
of Sierra Leone
WEC International

*North, Central and South America*
Betterway Inc.
Los Niños

*United Kingdom*
Camphill Rudolph Steiner School
Flysheet Camps Scotland
Middle Wood Trust
Paradise House Association

*Europe*
Aktionsgemeinschaftsdienst fur den
Frieden
Arab World Ministries
France Mission Trust

# Short Term

This Short Term section contains a wider selection of opportunities than the Long Term section, just as there are a greater number of people free to take them up. Many of the schemes can be fitted into a fortnight's summer holiday: there are even some that need only a weekend's commitment. But there are also longer ones that can be fitted into a short leave of absence from work, or into a student's vacation or year off.

Whereas the long term volunteer requires a considerable amount of dedication to the cause for which they are working, this is not necessarily true for all short-term volunteers. For example, someone may use one of the schemes of the British Trust for Conservation Volunteers as an economic way of spending an active fortnight in the country. But other schemes require great commitment, such as that operated by Leprosy Mission International which calls for one or two medical volunteers to spend several months abroad helping victims of the disease.

One of the most popular forms of short term voluntary work, the summer workcamp, requires no such dedication. These tend to be most popular with students and other young people, although many organisations will consider elder applicants. These take many forms and can be found from Cuba to Canterbury.

The motives for taking part in workcamps and other short term projects extend beyond the mere ideal of altruism. Experience—whether of a definite practical nature related to a particular course of training or career or at the more general level of broadening one's horizons figures prominently as a reason for signing up. Also, the workcamp image is tied up with having a good time and meeting new friends from a wide range of backgrounds. Many volunteers on short term assignments—and this applies particularly to students on workcamps, archaeological digs and kibbutzim—see their involvement principally as a working holiday or a means of staying somewhere rather more cheaply than would otherwise be possible. Indeed, in some Eastern European countries short term voluntary work may be the only way of getting more than a tourist's view of the way of life. And, although English is the standard language in most international workcamps, the environment can provide invaluable practice for students of other languages. The hours of work expected of volunteers on a workcamp can be light, perhaps just involving working in the mornings: at least part of the remainder of the time may be filled with organised "educational" activities such as outings, lectures etc., intended to give participants a taste of the local culture.

The financial arrangements for short term volunteers are really too varied for generalisations. In some cases pocket money is paid in addition to travel expenses and free accommodation. In other cases no money changes hands at all, or the volunteer may find himself paying to work. It all depends on the source and the extent of available funds. Officially sponsored organisations, like Community Service Volunteers, usually have the funds to provide at least the bare necessities. As another example, kibbutzim, by their very nature, are expected to provide volunteers with free board and accommodation, but could not reasonably be expected to meet everyone's travel expenses, particularly when applicants literally come from all over the globe. Stays on kibbutzim therefore tend to be marketed as "working holidays", as do many archaeological digs for the very same reason—no funds are available to cover all costs. Indeed, participants in many archaeological digs have to pay for their own board and lodging as well.

Because of the great number of organisations requiring short term volunteers, it has been necessary to sub-divide them geographically. One or two organisations thus fall into more than one classification and will therefore be listed more than once. However, the organisations that are truly international in their recruitment policies and activities have been listed separately under the heading *Worldwide*.

Because of the heavy preponderance of British and European organisations, the sections on the *United Kingdom* and *Europe* have been further sub-divided, the UK by types of work, and Europe by country. These divisions are far from clear cut, especially in the UK chapter. Many of the entries under *Religious Projects,* for instance, cut across several of the other classifications; and there is a great deal of overlap between *Child Care* and *Work with the Sick and Disabled,* as jobs involving sick and disabled children tend to be listed in the former category. The subheadings are therefore to be considered as a rough guide only. Entries are otherwise listed in simple alphabetical order within their respective sections or sub-divisions.

# Worldwide

### Action on Disability and Development
23 Lower Keyford, Frome, Somerset BA11 4AP. Tel: (0373) 73064

Action on Disability and Development supports organisations of people with disabilities in their attempt to control their own lives. It has staff and funds and supports organisations primarily in Central and Southern Africa but also in India and the Caribbean. Around four volunteers are needed each year to undertake the first stages of explanatory work with potential Third World partnership organisations. The work involves contacting and holding discussions with organisations of people with disabilities. As part of their training, British volunteers assist by providing logistic support for visitors and partners. Placements occur at any time of the year and last from one to six months.

Volunteers with a disability are encouraged to apply. Volunteers may be of any nationality but should speak the language of the country to be visited (eg French in French-speaking African countries). An experience of developmental issues and an ability to work harmoniously with others is required. Payment of expenses is negotiable but accommodation is usually provided with people in the country visited.

For further information contact the Assistant Director at the above address.

### Action Health 2000: International Voluntary Health Association
35 Bird Farm Road, Fulbourn, Cambridge CB1 5DP. Tel: (0223) 460 853

Action Health 2000 is an international charitable association concerned with the promotion of appropriate health care in developing countries: current projects operate in India, Bangladesh, Tanzania, Zimbabwe and China. Every year 20-25 qualified medical volunteers are sent abroad to help for periods ranging from three months to two years or more.

Most placements are in rural, semi-rural and deprived urban areas and may involve many areas of primary health care, although some positions may be available in general or specialist hospitals teaching local health staff and passing on specific health skills. Applicants should be fully qualified and registered doctors, midwives, nurses or other health workers. The payment of expenses depends on the length of service: those staying for two years or more have all their expenses covered and receive a small allowance.

A number of medical students are also taken on during their training as electives for periods of from six to eight weeks. They are attached to an existing health team, often following a special programme including clinical work, tutorials and visits to other institutions. An elective fee of £47 covers selection, placement, an orientation course, practical help with travel and support while abroad: a membership fee of £12 and approximately £150 to cover board, lodging and health insurance must also be paid.

Applications will be considered at any time of year, but should be sent at least six, and preferably twelve, months before the desired date of starting work. For further information contact the Director at the above address.

## Archaeology Abroad
31-34 Gordon Square, London WC1H 0PY, UK

This organisation provides three information bulletins annually about opportunities for archaeological fieldwork and excavations abroad. Publications are available by subscription. Enquiries should be sent to the Secretary at the above address enclosing a stamped self-addressed envelope.

## British Executive Service Overseas (BESO)
10 Belgrave Square, London SW1X 8PH, UK. Tel: (01) 235 0991

BESO recruits retired volunteer business executives with professional, technical or specialised management skills for short-term assignments in developing countries. Such countries receive financial aid from various international sources, including the United Kingdom, but remain in urgent need of assistance to overcome their shortage of experts with technical, financial and managerial skills. The duration of an assignment averages two to three months. Executives receive neither fee nor salary. BESO makes the air travel arrangements and meets the full cost for both executive and spouse if accompanying (this includes cost of innoculations, travel and medical insurance and other incidental charges). An initial clothing allowance is normally paid to the executive, as is a small local overseas allowance. The host organisation is required to provide suitable accommodation, subsistence and transport during the term of the assignment. Further information on projects in developing countries is available on request to BESO.

Enquiries should be sent to the Director at the above address.

## Campus Crusade for Christ
Pearl Assurance House, 4 Temple Row, Birmingham B2 5HG. Tel: (021) 233 3677

Campus Crusade for Christ recruits volunteers to provide administrative support to people in evangelistic and discipleship ministries in 150 countries. Only about five volunteers are needed in the United Kingdom each year but countries which frequently request volunteers are France, Greece, Cyprus, Germany, Portugal, Kenya and other African countries. Placements are for one year.

Volunteers must have secretarial, bookkeeping and general clerical skills and experience, be in good health and agree with the aims and activities of the organisation. For overseas placements, the appropriate language is required. Volunteers pay for their own expenses but accommodation may be provided.

Applicants should contact the Personnel Co-ordinator at the above address. Non-United Kingdom nationals will be referred to the Campus Crusade for Christ organisation in their home country.

**Canadian Crossroads International**
31 Madison Avenue, Toronto, Ontario, M5S 2R2, Canada. Tel: 416 967 0801

Canadian Crossroads International is a non-profit organisation of volunteers in Canada and 31 other countries in Africa, Asia, the South Pacific, South and Central America and the Caribbean. Volunteers take part in short term work placements; about 200 Canadians are sent overseas, about 60 Third World volunteers are brought to Canada and over 800 volunteers help run the programmes. Volunteers live and work with host families and agencies. The work undertaken varies but could include community development, health care, education, agriculture, construction, etc. Placements are from four months to one year long.

All volunteers must be at least 19 years old. Volunteers are accepted from all countries in which Canadian Crossroads International operates but to qualify for placements in a Third World country applicants must be Canadian citizens or landed immigrants.

Further information can be obtained from the Administrative Assistant at the above address.


**Christian Medical Fellowship**
157 Waterloo Road, London SE1 8XN. Tel: (01) 928 4694

The Fellowship produces a quarterly journal which guides Christian medical students and doctors to voluntary work opportunities in 20 to 30 countries. Depending on the job, placements may be for two to three months or two to four years. Volunteers should approach individual medical missionary organisations from the 40 to 50 listed, but the Fellowship will provide advice on which may suit a person's particular skills and circumstances best.

For further information contact the General Secretary at the above address.


**Christian Movement for Peace**
Bethnal Green U.R.C., Pott Street, London E2 0EF. Tel: 01-729 7985

The main activity of the CMP is the placement of volunteers on voluntary projects throughout East and West Europe, the USA, Canada and North Africa. They seek short term volunteers for summer projects abroad, usually for 2-6 weeks between 10 and 20 volunteers on each project. There is an enormous variety of work available. In France, for example, it may be conservation work, working on the land or social work in deprived urban areas.

Work may also centre on particular issues: last year, for example, there was a project working with Greenpeace in Belgium, one in London supporting an event campaigning about homelessness and another project concerned with the raising of awareness about Namibia by building a float for Notting Hill Carnival.

CMP also organises a series of seminars on contemporary social issues each year that are held in various European countries. Travel subsidies are available for these seminars.

For further details about any of these activities send an SAE to CMP at the above address.


## Concordia (Youth Service Volunteers) Ltd.

8 Brunswick Place, Hove, East Sussex BN3 1ET, UK. Tel: (0273) 772086

Concordia international workcamps take place in Czechoslovakia, France, Germany, Switzerland, Poland, Portugal, Morocco, Turkey, and other countries. Projects include archaeology, reconstruction, forestry, work in parks and gardens, and building schemes for the mentally handicapped. To take one country as an example: in France, camps take place in the Alps and Pyrenees, the Auvergne, and in small rural communes. They have 15 to 20 participants each. Work includes agricultural projects, development of tourist facilities, restoration of monuments and work on the environment. Besides, in addition, running agricultural workcamps in England, where campers are paid for fruit picking and market gardening, there are also opportunities for grape picking in France.

Volunteers for the international workcamps abroad must be aged between 18 and 30 years. Some camps prefer a little knowledge of the language of the country in which they are held. Pocket money and expenses are not paid, but board and lodging are provided free of charge. No work permit or visa is required except for Poland and Czechoslovakia. A registration fee is payable.

For voluntary camps abroad the British Concordia only accepts British volunteers. For details write to the above address enclosing SAE.


## Coordinating Committee for International Voluntary Service

1 rue Miollis, 75015 Paris, France. Tel: 56 82731/32

The CCIVS was founded in 1948 by the United Nations Educational, Scientific and Cultural Organisation (UNESCO) as a permanent committee to coordinate the workcamps of the then existing voluntary service organisations, which were mainly in Europe and North Africa. It now has 110 affiliated organisations, including national organisations in 52 countries and 24 international and regional organisations with branches in over 100 countries. At least half of the CCIVS affiliates are in Africa, Asia and Latin America.

The CCIVS promotes voluntary service activities by providing information for organisations and individuals, organizing seminars and conferences, and raising funds for projects of affiliated organisations. Among its useful publications are *Workcamps Organisers,* a constantly updated list of all the workcamp organisations with which it has connections, *New Trends in Voluntary Service* and a *Campleader Handbook* for the training of those interested in participating in international workcamps. They also publish a quarterly bulletin about members' activities entitled *News from CCIVS.*

On request to the above address, the CCIVS will send a list of its publications and information on short term voluntary service; please enclose four international reply coupons with your letter.

**Council on International Educational Exchange (C.I.E.E.)**
205 East 42nd Street, New York, NY 10017. Tel: (212) 661 1414

The Council on International Educational Exchange is a non-profit organisation that, in affiliation with cooperative organisations throughout Europe, sponsors voluntary service projects for young people in the USA and abroad. Participants have the chance to explore, in a cross-cultural setting, international perspectives on global issues such as hunger, literacy, development, and unemployment while working closely with 15-20 other volunteers from many countries.

The work, generally lasting for three weeks, involves manual labour or social service and is of great value to the communities in need. There is a wide range of project possibilities in the summer, including forest conservation in Czechoslovakia, archaeological digs in Kentucky and Portugal, care for the elderly in West Germany, and construction of a water trench in Turkey. Participants' costs are minimal: $100 application fee plus transportation. Room and board are provided by the workcamp sponsor.

For information please contact the Co-ordinator, International Workcamps, at the above address. (Please note: C.I.E.E. is involved with placing American citizens only. Other nationalities should contact a major voluntary service organisation in their home country.)

**Crusaders**
2 Romeland Hill, St Albans, Herts, AL3 4ET. Tel: (0727) 55422

Crusaders runs Christian young people's groups and adventure holidays where the emphasis is on evangelism and Bible Teaching. As well as long term voluntary leadership of Christian youth groups, volunteers are needed to help with young people's holidays and expeditions in Britain and abroad.

Around 300 holiday helpers are needed during the summer vacation to help with young people's holidays and houseparties at over 50 sites in Britain. Camps may be for a week or weekend. The children are aged from 8 to 16 years and the group size varies between 15 to 70 children. Helpers supervise and organise all of the group's activities; sports, crafts, Bible studies, etc.

The number of expeditions undertaken changes from year to year. In 1988 there were two expeditions, one to Peru and one to Tanzania. Only two to four leaders are needed on each trip as the group size is usually 10 to 20 young people, aged 16 to 21 years old. Expeditions last for one or two weeks.

All leaders must be aged 18 years or over, speak English, have a Christian commitment and leadership qualities. Skills in specialist sports and outdoor activities are desirable but not necessary. Applicants pay for all expenses.

Applications should be made to the Director at the above address.

**Earthwatch**
680 Mount Auburn Street, Box 403N, Watertown, MA 02272, USA. Tel: 617 926 8200

Earthwatch recruits paying volunteers to help research scientists in fields from archaeology to zoology on short term research projects in 42 countries and 27 states of America, year round. The scholars who request Earthwatch volunteers are based at universities and museums worldwide. Around 2,900 volunteers take part in the projects which last for two or three weeks. Team volunteers may learn to excavate, map, photograph, observe animal behaviour, survey flora and fauna, gather ethnographic data, make collections, conduct oral history interviews, measure astronomical alignments, assist in diving operations, lend mechanical or electrical expertise, record natural sounds, and share all other field chores associated with professional expedition research.

All English speaking volunteers aged 16 and over are welcome although some projects may require special skills such as languages and sporting or practical skills. Some projects may also have health restrictions as they take place in remote areas or at high altitudes, etc. Volunteers pay a share of the project costs, ranging from £260 to £785, which includes accommodation costs.

Those interested should apply to the Director of Public Affairs at the above address.

### Emmaus International
183 bis, rue Vaillant-Couturier, 94140 Alfortville, France
Tel: (1) 48 93 29 50

Started in Paris in 1949, there are now some 300 communities in over 20 countries, mainly in Europe but also in Africa, Asia and North and South America. These communities try to provide a meaning in life for those without one—that meaning being to help others in need. Each community is autonomous and independent of race, sex, religion, politics, age, etc. Living conditions are usually simple and the work hard.

Two communities which accept long term volunteers are: Stichting Emmaus, Nederland, Julianalaan 25, PO Box 175, 3720, GD Bilthoven, Nederland and Emmaus Westervik, SF-10600, Ekenes, Finland.

Other Emmaus communities in Europe organise workcamps for volunteers during the summer. Volunteers must usually speak English or the language of the country being visited, be over 18 years old and able to work at least two weeks. Accommodation and food are provided but volunteers pay all other costs.

Those interested in long term or summer voluntary positions should apply to the Secretary at the above address for more information on individual communities.

### Foundation For Field Research
787 South Grade Road, Alpine, CA 92001, USA. Tel: (619) 445 9264

The Foundation supports researchers in the field by recruiting volunteers willing to donate a share-of-cost and their labour to the projects. Projects all over the world involving research in archaeology, botany, wildlife research, paleontology, folk medicine, primitology, entomology, marine biology, marine archaeology, ornithology and ecology are supported. Around 200 volunteers are required annually on projects lasting from five to 14 days, all year round. Volunteers undertake whatever tasks the researcher feels are necessary to fulfill the goals of that project; on archaeological projects volunteers help with excavations, on wildlife project volunteers make observations and take notes, etc.

Some expeditions may require the volunteers to have special qualifications such as scuba qualifications or to be able to hike distances, etc. Volunteers may be of any nationality. Accommodation is provided but the volunteers pay a share-of-cost to support the project.

Those interested should apply to the Treasurer at the above address.

### Global Outreach UK

108 Sweetbriar Lane, Exeter, Devon EX1 3AR. Tel: (0392) 59673

Global Outreach UK is a Christian evangelical missionary society with representatives in 26 countries. Christian camps, Bible courses, radio broadcasting and in particular establishing churches are all methods used to propagate the Gospel. Opportunities exist for volunteers as career and short term missionaries, members of summer outreach teams and itinerant evangelists. A whole-hearted agreement with Outreach's Statement of Faith is required, and volunteers must be over 18 years old. Volunteers must supply a doctor's certificate of good health and are responsible for raising their own funds.

Career missionaries are placed in churches financially unable to support a full time Pastor, but able to provide accommodation and if possible, part salary, with the balance coming from interested churches and individuals.

A short term missionary programme is designed for young graduates of Bible school, single or married couples, who require 'in service' training. The volunteers are attached to a local church for periods of 12 to 24 months and work with the Pastor in all aspects of the church programme.

Around 40 volunteers are needed for the six week summer programme in which volunteers are attached to churches and share in special outreach and local programmes.

For further details on volunteer requirements, financial information and other facts, contact the General Secretary at the above address.

### HCJB UK

131 Gratten Road, Bradford, West Yorkshire BD1 2HS. Tel: (0274) 721 810

HCJB undertakes media and medical ministries in Ecuador, South America, Italy and the United Kingdom. Around 50 volunteers are needed each year to help with various projects. Audio and broadcasting engineers, announcers, script writers and other communication volunteers are needed for media ministries, nurses and laboratory technicians are required for the medical ministries in Ecuador and youth workers, printers, secretaries, office helpers, etc are needed for each. Placements vary from one to three months or longer, all year round.

All volunteers are welcome but they must be committed Christians and in agreement with this organisation's Statement of Faith. Only medical volunteers must speak Spanish but it is an advantage to speak Italian or Spanish if wishing to serve in Italy or Ecuador. Volunteers must raise their own financial support and accommodation on a rental basis is provided. No visas are required for periods of less than three months.

For more details contact the Personnel Secretary at the above address.

## Horizons: Mission without Bounds
Glanmore Road, Llanelli, Dyfed, Wales SA15 2LU. Tel: (0554) 750005

Horizons organise work teams and expeditions for committed Christians in Britain, France, Italy, the Middle East and Africa which are designed to place Christians in front-line administration, literature production, building and vehicle maintenance, etc. In addition to the 100 full time staff, around 350 short term volunteers are needed annually to work for one week or longer, with the main concentration of teams being from Easter to October. No particular skills are required and the minimum age varies depending on the country to be visited, 16 years being the lowest accepted. Volunteers are responsible for raising their own funds. Accommodation is provided but must be paid for by the volunteer.

Write to the British Team Leader at the above address for more details.

## The Institute of Cultural Affairs
41 Miranda Road, London N19 3RA

The Institute of Cultural Affairs, a registered charity, runs a Volunteer Service Programme to select, train and place volunteers overseas. Opportunities for service are available in a wide variety of settings, in rural and urban areas in both developed and developing countries. 160 volunteers have been trained and have served in 20 countries since the programme was set up in 1980. Interested enquirers are asked to attend an Orientation Weekend which sets out the issues and approaches of volunteering and local development. Prospective volunteers then attend a three-week residential preparation period before final decisions about placement are made.

Volunteers spend a minimum of nine months overseas, and are responsible for raising money to cover all costs including travel, insurance, training, local accommodation and pocket money, usually totalling about £2,000. They become members of a team, living and working with trained local staff. They may become involved in supporting local development activities, assisting in training courses, administration tasks, or research and development of new programmes.

The freshness and energy volunteers bring to their work overseas benefits them on their return due to their new and direct awareness of the cultural perspectives and socio-economic realities of other peoples. People with initiative, maturity and enthusiasm are encouraged to apply. Language ability and experience in health and teaching are advantages. School-leavers are considered if they have some work experience, and have spent extended periods away from home. For further details contact Alan Berresford at the above address.

## International Christian Youth Exchange (ICYE)
International Office of ICYE, Goethe Strasse 85-87, 1000 Berlin (West) 12, Federal Republic of Germany

ICYE is an international organisation composed of autonomous national committees in over 25 countries which offers young people over 16 years old the chance to live overseas for six months or one year. The volunteers are hosted by a family or in an alternative living situation and attend high school and perform voluntary service work in the community in which they are living. (Volunteers aged over 18 years only perform voluntary service work.) This work may include work with children or the aged, involvement in rehabilitation, women's or disabled programmes, teaching, etc. ICYE is present in countries in Africa, Asia, Europe, Latin America, the Pacific and the United States of America. Departure to the host country takes place in July of each year.

Age limits vary between 25 and 30 years old for different countries but no special skills are required. Volunteers should supply a health certificate. There are scholarships available but usually each volunteer pays a participation fee to the sending committee, which covers administration, travel and insurance costs.

Volunteers should apply through the ICYE National Committee in their country. Where ICYE does not have such a committee the nearest committee suffices. Further information can be obtained from the Programme Executive at the above address.

### International Eye Foundation
7801 Norfolk Avenue, Bethesda, Maryland 20814, USA

The International Eye Foundation send certified ophthalmological volunteers to Latin America and Africa. Volunteers must be certified ophthalmologists, ophthalmic nurses, technicians or technologists. Around 26 volunteers are needed annually for periods of two weeks or more, all year round.

Applicants may be of any nationality provided they have the necessary qualifications and are in good health. Accommodation is usually provided but not expenses or pocket money.

Those interested should contact the Assistant to the President at the above address for more details.

### The Leprosy Mission International
50 Portland Place, London W1N 3DG. Tel: (01) 637 2611

The Leprosy Mission International is an interdenominational Christian organisation operating both directly and in co-operation with churches, governments and voluntary groups in over 30 countries. The main aim is to meet the total needs of people affected by leprosy and to work towards the eradication of the disease. One or two medical volunteers (nurses, physicians and physiotherapists) are required each year as the need arises. Placements vary from a few months to a year.

Volunteers must be in good health and younger than 61 years old. In addition to having medical skills, simple bookkeeping and typing skills are useful. Accommodation is provided, expenses paid and a bursary given.

Those interested should contact the Personnel Director at the above address for more information.

### The Lisle Fellowship, Inc
433 West Sterns Road, Temperance, MI 48182, USA. Tel: (313) 847-7126

The Lisle Fellowship is an educational organisation which seeks to improve the quality of human life through human understanding among people of diverse cultures. The foundation of Lisle is aimed at creating an education for "world mindedness." Since the Fellowship's work began in 1936, over 11,000 persons have participated in its programme. Lisle offers programmes of up to six weeks in such places as Alaska, Georgia, Columbia, India, Bali, Houston and the Middle East. Programme emphasise personal development, inter-cultural group living experiences, small group field work assignments in the local community, and group times to integrate learning and usually take place in the spring and summer. Orientation takes place in a "home centre" prior to field visits. Volunteers might find themselves working in an Indian rural village, an Eskimo community, or a Houston soup kitchen. Each programme is primarily designed as a personal learning experience.

Programmes are open to students, teachers, and others over 18 years of age. Lisle looks for people from diverse cultural backgrounds who have an ability to get along with and work with others. Programme fees are offered at the lowest possible cost, in order to provide for people of all economic resources. Limited financial aid is available to participants who demonstrate a need for assistance. Participants in the Fellowship's programme may be eligible for college credits.

The programme fee, which covers board and lodging and travel related to the programme ranged from $420 to $2,295 in 1988. Applications should be made to The Lisle Fellowship at the above address.

### Mobility International USA (MIUSA)

PO Box 3551, Eugene, Oregon 97403, USA. Tel: 503 343 1284

MIUSA is a non-profit making organisation that exists to increase the opportunities for educational exchange and travel for people with disabilities. MIUSA's programmes include organising international educational exchange programmes which include disabled and non-disabled people working together in the USA and overseas. MIUSA programmes have been with Italy, England, Germany, Costa Rica, China, and the USSR. Themes of the exchanges vary, but the goals are to increase international understanding through contact between people, and to improve the lives of disabled people around the world by sharing information and strategies for independent living. The exchange experiences last three to four weeks, and usually include a community service component and a stay with a family in the host country.

Persons with disabilities and able-bodied persons are encouraged to apply. Applicants must have an interest in independent living and an international understanding. Fees and specific requirements vary depending on the programme. For further information regarding MIUSA contact the Director at the above address. Enclose an International Reply coupon and a self-addressed envelope.

### Nothelfergemeinschaft der Freunde e.V.

Auf der Körnerwiese 5, D-6000 Frankfurt 1, Germany. Tel: (069) 599557

This organisation recruits about 800 volunteers each year to work on workcamps in Germany, Turkey, Israel, Ghana, Togo, Kenya, India and the Philippines. Activities include: cooperation in non-profit institutions, construction works, path construction, painting etc, domestic and social work. Food, accomodation and insurance are provided, but volunteers must be prepared to finance their own transportation and incidental expenses. The camps, which are either for the age group 16-17 years or for those 18 years and over, are of about a month's duration. But volunteers may attend two or three camps consecutively. The camps generally run from the end of June to the end of October although occasionally there are camps in March/April. Applications for work outside Germany are open to Germans only.

Although applicants need have no special qualifications, manual skills are very useful. A knowledge of the English or French language is necessary.

Enquiries may be sent to the Secretary General, at the above address.

### Project Hope
Health Sciences Education Center, Millwood, VA 22646, USA. Tel: 1 800 544 4673

Project Hope provides assistance in establishing or upgrading existing health personnel training programmes in developing countries. Around 300 volunteers are needed each year to act as educators in this project. Placements are for two months or longer all year round as academic years differ from country to country.

Volunteers must be permanent residents of the United States of America with teaching experience within a health care profession, the ability to train other trainers and a professional licence in the United States. Travel expenses, accommodation and meals are provided.

Those interested should apply to the Recruitment Assistant for further information.

### Project Phoenix Trust
68 Rochfords, Coffee Hall, Milton Keynes MK6 5DJ. Tel: (0908) 678038

Project Phoenix Trust run group study-tour and interest holidays to Europe and Africa for severely physically disabled adults. At present a minimum of two tours, lasting from seven to 14 days, are organised each year—usually around Easter, September or December. Around 20 helpers are needed for each tour as the ratio of helpers to holiday-makers is at least $1\frac{1}{2}$:1. Helpers are full members of the tour group and provide all the personal care needed by the holiday-makers, from pushing wheelchairs to lifting and personal hygiene.

Volunteers must have a good command of English and should be fit, caring and between 19 and 50 years old. Applicants who are visually or hearing impaired or have obvious health problems will not be accepted. Nursing qualifications are needed for two of the helpers in each group and a knowledge of the language of the country being visited is useful. It is not essential to have experience of caring for disabled people as training will be given.

Volunteers are expected to contribute around £170 towards their own costs, with the Trust providing the balance. Accommodation, normally in a room with a disabled person, is provided but helpers must pay for incidentals. All excursions are included.

Inquiries should be made to the Secretary at the above address.

## Service Civil International/International Voluntary Service

162 Upper New Walk, Leicester, LE1 7QA. Tel: (0533) 549430

International Voluntary Service is the British branch of Service Civil International (SCI), an international voluntary movement which was begun in 1920 by Pierre Ceresole, a Swiss pacifist, with the aim of furthering reconciliation between participants in the Great War. Its objectives are to promote peace, international co-operation and friendship through the means of voluntary work. The "Service Civil" in its name describes its role as an alternative to military service; for example during the Second World War International Voluntary Service, the British branch of the organisation, was able to provide alternative service for conscientious objectors. There are now SCI branches in 25 countries and partner organisations in 20 more, which organise annually about 350 short term projects (two or three weeks) in Asia, Europe and the USA, involving up to 6,500 volunteers.

The national programme in each country is autonomous and develops its programme according to its special needs and possibilities. All volunteers accepted must appreciated the aims and objectives of SCI, and be prepared to work as a team in basic conditions.

An international workcamp consists of a group of between 10 and 20 people from many different countries who live and work together for two to four weeks on a community project. Volunteers not only participate in the work, but also take part in discussions and the team life of the group. The projects undertaken vary from manual work with rural communities to helping with a playscheme for children in an inner-city area, or work and study on such subjects as ecology, conscientious objection, or solidarity with oppressed groups.

Service Civil International stress that a workcamp is not just a cheap holiday; volunteers are normally expected to work an unpaid 40 hour week. Meals and basic accommodation are provided, but participants cover all other expenses themselves (including travel). Volunteers should be at least 18 years old. Applications are welcomed from people of all racial, cultural and social backgrounds and from people with physical disabilities.

For further information about Service Civil International projects British applicants should contact International Voluntary Service at the above address. Others should contact the address in their country listed below: where there is no address contact the International Secretariat at 783, 10th Main, Block 4, Jayanagar, Bangalore 560 011, India.

| | |
|---|---|
| Austria | SCI, Schottengasse 3a/1/4/59, 1010 Vienna |
| Belgium | SCI, Rue Van Elewyck 35, B 1050, Brussels |
| Belgium | VIA, Venusstraat 28, 2000, Antwerp |
| F.R. Germany | SCI, Blucherstrasse 14, 5300 Bonn 1 |
| Finland | KVT Rauhanasema, Veturitori, 00520 Helsinki 52 |
| France | SCI, 129 Rue du Faubourg Poissonniere, 75009 Paris |
| Greece | SCI Kallistratoy 69, 15771, Zografoy, Athens |
| Rep. of Ireland | VSI, 37 North Great Georges Street, Dublin |
| Italy | SCI, Via dei Laterani 28, 00184 Rome |
| Netherlands | VIA/ Bethaniestraat 20, 1012 CA Amsterdam |
| Northern Ireland | IVS 122 Gt. Victoria Street, Belfast |

| Norway | ID Rozenkranzgt 18 N 0160 Oslo 1 |
|---|---|
| Spain | SCCT Rambla de Catalunya, 5 pral. 2.a 08007 Barcelona |
| Sweden | IAL Barnangsgatan 23, 11641 Stockholm |
| Switzerland | SCI, Postfach 228, CH-3000 Bern 9 |
| USA | SCI, Innisfree Village Rte 2, Box 506, Crozet Virginia 22932 |

*Other organisations co-operating with Service Civil International*

| Bulgaria | NCVB 11 Stamboliski, Sofia 1000 |
|---|---|
| Czechoslovakia | CKM Zitna ulice 12, 12105 Prague |
| Denmark | MS Borgergade 10 - 14, 1300 Copenhagen |
| Hungary | MIOT P.O. Box 72, 1388, Budapest |
| Netherlands | SIW Willemstraat 7, Utrecht |
| Poland | OHP Nowy Swiat 18/20, 00-920 Warsaw |
| Portugal | FAOJ Av Duque d'avila, 137 - 1097 Lisbon |
| Turkey | Genctur Cad 15-3 Sultenahmed Yerabatan Istanbul |
| Yugoslavia | RK-ZSMSS Dalmatinova 4, Dom Sindikatov, 6100 Ljubljana |
| USA | Volunteers For Peace, Tiffany Road, Belmont Vermont 05370 |

In Britain IVS also organise a "Development Education and Exchange Scheme" (D.E.E.P.) that involves a short term exchange of two to three months with countries in Asia, West and Southern Africa, involving workcamps and sometimes other activities. Before people apply for this they must take part in a programme of "Questioning Development" weekends: they will also be expected to become involved in IVS Development Education work on their return to Britain. The selection process takes place in February. For further information on this contact IVS-D.E.E.P., 28-30 Mosley Street, Newcastle-on-Tyne NE1 1DF, enclosing a stamped addressed envelope.

**Quaker International Social Projects (Q.I.S.P.)**
Friends House, Euston Road, London NW1 2BJ. Tel: (01) 387 3601

Q.I.S.P. recruits British applicants for its own community service projects in the UK and for those run by similar agencies overseas: mainly Eastern and Western Europe, Scandinavia, Turkey, North America and North Africa. People sent abroad would be expected to have previous experience of voluntary work in Britain. The UK projects organised by Q.I.S.P. are one to three weeks in length, residential, and composed of volunteer groups seven to 20 people in size. Most take place in the summer although there are a few at Christmas and Easter. The projects aim to aid local communities and activities may be manually (decorating and construction etc.) or socially (with children, or people with a disability) based. All projects have a study element of some kind and there is usually at least one project each year studying a specific international issue: development, East-West relations or disarmament, for instance. Every year about 250 volunteers are involved, about half of whom come from countries other than the UK.

Essential qualities for applicants is that they speak good English and are able to work hard and get on with other people. A knowledge of foreign languages, first aid, craft skills or the ability to drive may also be useful on various projects. Volunteers should be over 16 years old (18 years for some projects). Volunteers with a disability are welcome to apply. Food and accommodation are free, but volunteers must pay their own travel expenses and provide their own pocket money. There is a registration fee that varies according to income. UK applicants should write to the address above. Those from abroad should apply through an organisation in their own country. A free newsletter is published three times yearly.

### Samaritans
5666 La Jolla Blvd., La Jolla, CA 92037, USA. Tel: (619) 456 2216

Samaritans organise workcamps, study tours and other mission programmes to enable youths and adults to serve others during vacation periods. As well as conducting programmes within the United States of America, Samaritans offer workcamps, usually on building projects, in over 20 other countries for periods of one or two weeks. Volunteers must be Christians and at least 16 years old.

Those interested should contact the Executive Director at the above address for more information.

### TECNICA
2727 College Avenue, Berkley, CA 94705, USA. Tel: (415) 848 0292

TECNICA currently sends volunteers to Nicaragua (and hopes to soon include southern African countries) to train local people in their area of expertise. Around 500 volunteers are sent annually, at all times of the year. Volunteers are matched with projects in a wide variety of fields including banking, computing, engineering, manufacturing, etc. Most placements are for two weeks with some longer assignments lasting for up to one year.

Volunteers of all nationalities are accepted provided they are able to obtain the appropriate visas. Only those in good health should apply and volunteers must be experts or proficient in their field. Spanish speaking applicants are preferred for Nicaragua but interpreters can be provided. Volunteers pay for all travel costs and accommodation.

Applications can be made to the Program Co-ordinator at the above address.

### United Nations Association (Wales) International Youth Service
Welsh Centre for International Affairs, Temple of Peace, Cathays Park, Cardiff, CF1 3AP, South Wales, UK. Tel: (0222) 223088

The UNA (Wales) International Youth Service offers facilities for people from Great Britain to attend International Volunteer Projects within Wales, and most countries in Eastern and Western Europe, the United States, Canada, India and certain African countries. These projects normally last between two and four weeks during the summer and involve work on a variety of schemes including hospital work, social work, playschemes, and environmental work. The aim of these projects is the encouragement of international understanding, and development of community projects. The projects normally consist of between 10 and 15 volunteers aged over 18.

Volunteers are required to meet their own travelling expenses to the projects, but once there they are provided with free board and accommodation. On acceptance, volunteers have to pay a registration fee, which is £17 for projects in Wales, and £22 for projects abroad. The registration fee includes membership of UNA (Wales) for one year.

Those interested should write to the IYS Officer at the above address, enclosing a SAE, for further details.

## United Society for the Propagation of the Gospel
15 Tufton Street, London SW1, UK. Tel: (01) 222 4222

The Experience Exchange Programme is a scheme run by the USPG to give committed Christians an opportunity to share in the way of life, work and worship of a Christian community in another country for 6-12 months. Placements may be in parishes, education institutions or other local centres. There is a very limited number of placements for school leavers of 18 years. Newly qualified or older mature people are more easily placed. Participants need to be in good health and adaptable, and are usually expected to raise a good part of their expenses.

Root Groups, another scheme, is an opportunity for Christians aged 18 to 30 to live in a small community, while giving their time and talents to a local church in Britain. Each Root Group has between two and five members and is commissioned to a church in Britain which is usually Anglican but sometimes ecumenical. Work varies greatly according to the location, and in some parishes the members will be expected to use their initiative in finding ways in which to become involved—through youth work, visiting housebound people, children's activities, work with unemployed people and disabled people, and help with church services. Community life within each group is also important. This may involve pooling money, collective worship and mutual support. Volunteers must have a Christian commitment or deep interest in the Christian faith. A sense of humour, openness and perseverance are also necessary. Musical abilities, a driving licence and experience of working with children, although not essential, would be useful.

Overseas visitors are accepted if they are eligible to work in the UK and able to pay their own fares. Physically disabled volunteers and others from disadvantaged groups are particularly welcome. Volunteers are expected to stay for at least one year, starting in September, and work flexible hours six days a week. There is one month's annual holiday with occasional long weekends.

Those interested should contact the Mission Personnel Team at the above address.

## WEC International
Bulstorde, Gerrards Cross, Bucks SL9 8SZ. Tel: (0753) 884631

WEC International seeks to evangelise the remaining unevangelised areas of the world in the shortest possible time. As well as spreading The Gospel, WEC volunteers also give practical help with community development projects. Small numbers of volunteers are needed to help full-time WEC volunteers in over 20 countries of the world. Unskilled volunteers or students can give service during summers to help with building work, looking after children and other practical work. For those with skills or training, (secretaries, teachers, mechanics, nurses, doctors, builders, etc), there are more opportunities and placements are for one to two years.

All volunteers must be evangelical Christians. Some knowledge of French and a driver's licence are useful. Volunteers are responsible for their fares to and from the field but while in the field, they receive a small monthly allowance.

Those interested should contact the Candidates' Secretary at the above address.

## WWOOF (Working Weekends on Organic Farms)

WWOOF exists to give people the opportunity of gaining first hand experience of organic farming and gardening in return for spending a weekend or longer working on a farm. Since WWOOF began in England in 1917, similar schemes have developed in other countries around the world. Each of the groups listed below is an independent group with its own aims, system, fees and rules. They are all similar in that they offer volunteers the chance to learn in a practical way the growing methods of their host. Each group will supply a worklist booklet to members from which volunteers can choose a farm.

WWOOF Schemes:

APOG, Jordvett, Herman Fossgate 9, N5000, Bergen, Norway.

INTEGRAL, c/o Co-ordinator De Agriculture Ecologica, Apdo 2580, 08080 Barcelona, Spain.

MAWOOF, Jeanne Nye, 1601 Lakeside Ave 607, Richmond, VA 23228, USA.

NATUR ET PROGRES Liste des stages, 53 Rue Vaugirord, 75006 Paris, France.

NEWOOF, New England Small Farms Institute, PO Box 937, Belchertown, MA 01007, USA.

SATIVA, Route 2 Box 242-W, Viola, Wisconsin 54664, USA.

VHH, c/o Inna Busck-Petersen, Garsdalsveg 30, 8800 Vigorb, Denmark.

WEEBIO, Dellisee Adolphe, Chaupreheld 64, B-4081 Cherron, Belgium.

WWOOF (UK), Don Pynches, 19 Bradford Road, Lewes, BN17 1RB, Sussex.

WWOOF (Aus), Lionel Pollard, Mt Murrindal Co-op, Buchan, Vic 3885.

WWOOF (Germany), Stettiner Str 3, D-6301 Pohlheim, West Germany.

WWOOF (NZ), Tony West, 188 Collingwood Street, Nelson.

WWOOF (Eire), Annia Sampson, Ballymalone, Tuamgraney, Co Clare.

WWOOF (California), 13201 Harding, Slymar, CA 91342, USA.

WWOOF (Nth West), Neal Bittner, 3231 Hillside Road, Deming, WA 98244.

WWOOF (Maritimes), John Vanden Heuvel, RR5, Bridgetown, Nova Scotia, Canada BOS 1CO

When writing to an overseas group, enclose the appropriate number of International Reply Coupons. British volunteers wanting more information should contact Don Pynches at the United Kingdom address given above.

**World Council of Churches - Youth Sub-Unit**
150 route de Ferney, PO Box 66, 1211 Geneva 20, Switzerland. Tel: (022) 916 065

The Youth Sub-Unit has a programme called Ecumenical Youth Action which sponsors workcamps in Africa, Asia, Latin America and the Middle East. Volunteers from all nationalities and faiths share in work and live in a local community. Theological discussions and manual work such as agricultural, construction and renovation projects form an important part of the programme. Workcamps are held between April and September with the length being from one to three weeks.

Volunteers should be aged 18 to 30 years. They must arrange and pay for their own travel and insurance. Around £3 per day is expected to be contributed towards the camp's expenses.

Those interested should write to the above address for a workcamp programme but should then apply directly to the individual camps.

**Youthshare, Church of Scotland**
121 George Street, Edinburgh EH2 4YN, UK. Tel: (031) 225 5722

Youthshare runs a scheme in which young people with some specific practical experience or professional qualification work with the church overseas. The countries in which the scheme operates include India, Pakistan, Israel and various countries in Africa. Teachers, accountants, administrators, medical personnel and agriculturalists as well as general workers are all needed. In addition, all applicants should have a firm Christian commitment and be willing to serve others. Volunteers are normally recruited for a period of 9-12 months.

Applicants must pay for their own travel to their placement, but once there they receive board, lodging and out of pocket expenses. Those taking part should normally be aged between 18 and 30, but older people may be accepted. Applicants should also be Scottish and/or a member of the Church of Scotland.

Those interested should write to the Youthshare Secretary at the above address.

# United Kingdom

## Agencies and Sources of Information

### Community Service Volunteers
237 Pentonville Road, London N1 9NJ. Tel: (01) 278 6601

CSV is a national volunteer agency which matches young volunteers with full-time community service projects throughout the UK. Placements are from four to twelve months. The range of projects includes work with physically and mentally handicapped, the elderly, the young, in hospitals, in homes, with the homeless and with young offenders, with ex-offenders, in Social Services Departments and all kinds of community settings. Nearly 2,000 CSVs find placements every year.

Volunteers from the UK are aged between 16 and 35. Everyone is welcome. No qualifications or experience are necessary. All volunteers receive travelling expenses within the UK, full board and lodging (if working away from home), pocket money and out-of-pocket expenses.

Those interested should write to the above address for information and an application form.

### The Royal Association for Disability and Rehabilitation (RADAR)
25 Mortimer Street, London W1N 8AB. Tel: (01) 637 5400

Every year RADAR publishes a list of holiday centres for the disabled which require help from volunteers for a few weeks. These centres are run by several agencies and organisations including Social Services Departments, MENCAP, BREAK, The Shaftesbury Society, The Winged Fellowship Trust, and PHAB. The list published by RADAR specifies the type of help needed. In some cases the volunteer must be fit, or have medical training, while in others the job may be suitable for an active pensioner. The list also mentions whether food, travel expenses and accommodation are provided.

Those interested should write to the Holidays Office at the above address.

## Archaeology

### Archaeology Unit
Northamptonshire County Council, 2 Bolden House, Wootton Hall Park, Northampton NN4 9BE. Tel: (0604) 700493

This Unit undertakes archaeological excavations at various sites in Northamptonshire. Volunteers assist with the excavations and recording of finds. Around 20 volunteers are needed between May and September for periods of up to 13 weeks. United Kingdom residents are preferred but other applicants will be considered. Volunteers must be aged over 16 years, literate in English, numerate and capable of physical work outdoors in all weather.

Accommodation in hostels and subsistence expenses of up to £40 per week are provided.

Apply to the County Archaeologist at the above address.

## Canterbury Archaeological Trust Limited
92a Broad Street, Canterbury, Kent CT1 2LU. Tel: (0227) 462062

The Trust undertakes excavations, often at short notice, of multi-period sites in Canterbury and the nearby district. Most work is undertaken during the summer season but volunteers are sometimes needed during the winter. The minimum placement is for two weeks. Volunteers undertake digging and finds processing at various Iron Age, Roman, Saxon and Medieval sites. The number of volunteers required depends on the number of sites open but is usually around 100 volunteers per season.

Volunteers must be over 18 years old, reasonably fit and with a working knowledge of English. Experience is useful but not necessary. Subsistence payments are sometimes made to volunteers who stay for more than two weeks. Campsite places are provided or hostel accommodation for a minimal cost can be arranged.

Contact the Director at the above address for more details.

## Council for British Archaeology
112 Kennington Road, London SE11 6RE. Tel: (01) 582 0494

The Council publishes *British Archaeological News* which carries advertisements for volunteer help on archaeological sites in Britain. This publication commences in February each year and comes out every two months thereafter. The annual subscription for 1989 will be £7.50 for the UK: £8.50 for Europe: £8.50 for surface mail outside Europe: £11.50 for airmail outside Europe. US$ payments also acceptable: send International Postal Reply Coupon for details.

## Dorset Natural History and Archaeological Society
Dorset County Museum, Dorchester. Tel: (0305) 62735

The Archaeological Society acts as a co-ordinating body for digs in the County of Dorset putting those interested in participating in excavations in touch with the Directors of particular projects. The number of volunteers needed each year depends on the number of excavations taking place, the needs being determined by the organisers of individual digs. The length of time for which volunteers are recruited will also be decided by the Directors.

Volunteers should be able-bodied and at least 18 years of age. No special qualifications are essential, but they are always useful. Applicants may be of any nationality.

Volunteers can obtain a list of excavations for a particular year from the Secretary of the Society at the above address, and then should apply to the Directors of individual projects.

## Grosvenor Museum Excavation Section
Chester City Council, 27 Grosvenor Street, Chester CH1 2DD. Tel: (0244) 21616

The Museum conducts archaeological excavations on sites from the Roman to post-medieval periods in Chester and the surrounding area. A number of volunteers are required to assist with the cleaning, sorting, and marking of finds from the excavations away from the sites of the excavations.

Volunteers should be aged at least 16, and preference is given to those with, or hoping to obtain, experience in archaeology, ancient history or museum studies. The work takes place around the year and volunteers are needed for periods of at least 2 weeks; subsistence money is payable for a maximum of three months in one financial year. Expenses are paid at the following rates for these living away from home; on working days (Monday-Friday) £4.00 for inexperienced volunteers, or £6.10 if experienced, per day, plus a maximum of £10 per week lodging allowance and £15.90 maximum towards travelling expenses. No accommodation is provided, but advice on local guest houses or the YWCA can be provided on request. For further details contact the Finds Assistant at the above address.

### Oxford Archaeological Unit
46 Hythe Bridge Street, Oxford OX1 2EP. Tel: (0865) 243888

The Unit excavates archaeological sites in the Oxford area before they arc destroyed. Around 50 volunteers a year are taken on to provide practical help with these excavations; most are needed between July and September but some are needed around the year. No previous archaeological experience is necessary but applicants should be aged over 16, physically fit and willing to work long hours out of doors. Those taking part are advised to have anti-tetanus injections. Some help may be given with expenses, and although no accommodation is provided a camp site is normally available for those with their own camping equipment.

Applications should be sent to the Director at the above address.

### Wharram Percy Village Excavation
Wharram, Malton, North Yorkshire

Volunteers are required to assist with the archaeological excavation of a church, parsonage, water mill, and farm houses dating back to medieval and earlier periods. Approximately 60 volunteers take part annually assisting with digging, trowelling, cooking, clerical work and drawing, washing and sorting finds. The minimum age is 18 and volunteers should be physically fit but there are no special skills required. Volunteers usually take part for three weeks and the excavation work is carried out in July only. There is a free camping site and free dormitory accommodation. Food must be paid for in the first week but is free for the next two.

Applications should be made to Francesca Croft, 5 South Street, Wiveliscombe, Somerset TA4 2LZ.

# Child Care

### Association For All Speech Impaired Children
347 Central Markets, Smithfield, London EC1. Tel: (01) 236 3632

Each year AFASIC organises outdoor Activity Weeks in the summer at various outdoor pursuit centres, hostels and guest houses in Britain. Each child is attached to a "young person helper" (Link), a volunteer who acts as a friend and support for the week.

Volunteers should be over 18 years and in good health. No experience is required and training is given. Board and lodging is provided. Volunteers must provide their own travel expenses though every effort is made to cut this cost by linking helpers to share transport or to use Association vehicles which are being taken for use on Weeks.

Those interested should apply to: Mr J. L. Richards, 21 Rhos Avenue, Middleton, Manchester M24 1EG. Tel: (061) 643-1960 (after 6 pm or at weekends).

### Basecamp
Marthrown of Mabie, Mabie Forest, Dumfries DG2 8HB. Tel: (0387) 68493

Basecamp organises residential programmes for young people aged 15 to 19 years who are experiencing behavioural and emotional difficulties. Referred by Juvenile Courts, Children's Panels, Social Service Departments and social workers, groups of five to eight children attend Basecamp, a remote residential centre, for either three months during spring or autumn, or for one to three weeks during the summer months.

Around five volunteers are needed for a minimum of 12 months to act as Project Assistants on these programmes. Volunteers should be in good health, over 23 years old, licensed drivers and have experience in outdoor activities, expeditions, or youth social work. Board, lodging or food allowance, training allowance and pocket money are provided.

During summer around 16 volunteers are needed to assist in conservation work and site work at the residential centre. Workcamp volunteers should be over 16 years old, in good health and interested in the countryside and conservation work. Board and lodging for the one to three week long camps are provided.

Applications to the Director at the above address.

### Birmingham Phab Camps
474 Kingsbury Road, Erdington, Birmingham

This organisation runs holiday camps each summer in England for equal numbers of physically handicapped and able bodied children with the aim of helping the physically handicapped children to integrate with their able bodied contemporaries. There are five camps a year, three of which cater for different age groups; Junior (7-10), Senior (11-13), Teenage (14-16), and 16 plus. The first two camps take 40 children, the third 20, and the fourth 12-15. The fourth camp is run for severely multiple-handicapped children of various ages. This is a particularly demanding holiday and preference will be given to volunteers who have had experience of this type of work before. 20 volunteers are needed for this holiday. Many children who are physically handicapped have little opportunity to mix with and form friendships in their peer group, and the camps are designed to remedy this isolation and overcome prejudice. There is a wide range of activities from swimming and discos to seaside and camping trips, in which all the children take part. The camps are run entirely by unpaid volunteers, of whom 80 are needed each year. The volunteer will work at a camp for up to 10 days with a team including an experienced leader, two cooks, and a qualified nurse. The Junior Camp is normally held in a boarding school, while the Army provides the Senior Camp with a site.

Volunteers should be aged between 17 and 30, and speak recognizable English which children will understand. Obviously the ability to communicate with children is important. Special skills in sports, crafts, and art plus previous experience and a driving licence are an asset, but not essential. Dependability, initiative, resilience and a capacity for hard work are of much more importance. There are a limited number of places for disabled volunteers. Training days are held before each camp, where medical staff from special schools give advice on special problems, and the team plans the camp programme. Accommodation is provided, but expenses and pocket money are not. Transport from Birmingham to the camp and back is paid.

Volunteers should apply to the Volunteer Recruitment Officer at the above address.

## Birmingham Youth Volunteers
24 Albert Street, Birmingham B4 7UD. Tel: (021) 643 8297

This organisation needs volunteers to help on its activity holidays for underprivileged children during the school summer holidays. Each volunteer would help for one week only. Four Adventure Camps are run in Pembroke, South Wales during July and August for children aged 10 to 15. Four residential holidays for children aged 5 to 10 are run in the Midlands during August.

Volunteers look after children on trips, take part in group activities, swimming, games, craft sessions etc. It is hard work being with children 24 hours a day but, despite the stamina and patience required, it is very rewarding. BYV also need mini-bus drivers with clean licenses, and people prepared to cook for groups of up to 60.

Travel expenses to and from Birmingham may be paid, but personal expenses on the holiday are not. Accommodation and food are provided.

Applications are accepted from young people aged 17 and over and resident in the UK. They should be sent to the Co-ordinator at the above address.

## BREAK
20 Hooks Hill Road, Sheringham, Norfolk NR26 8NL
Tel: (0263) 823170/ 823025

Around 40 volunteers a year are needed to help provide holiday, emergency, and short term care for handicapped and deprived children and mentally handicapped adults in three residential centres in Norfolk. Applicants are accepted for anything between one and 12 months. The work itself involves a certain amount of routine housekeeping, but most of it is with guests, with games, outings, and so on. It can be very demanding, and so good health is essential.

Anyone over 17 with a good command of English can apply, but expenses are only paid for travel within the British Isles. Food, accommodation, and pocket money of around £14.50 per week are provided.

Those interested should contact the Director at the above address.

## Caldecott Community
Mersham-le-Hatch, Ashford, Kent. Tel: (0233) 23941

The community is a residential treatment centre and special school for about 80 children between the ages of 5 and 18. The children are taken into care, which is provided around the year, after suffering complete breakdowns due to stresses at home. Contact is maintained with home as much as possible especially during the holidays. There is a primary school within the community which prepares the younger children for entry into secondary schools in the area. A few volunteers are taken on to assist the 40 adults in the community, living with family-type groups of 10 children.

There are no special skills required, but the volunteers should enjoy being with children and some ability in sports, music, arts and crafts or possession of a driving licence would be an asset. Volunteers are usually taken on for between three months and a year. Board, lodging, travelling expenses and £15 per week are provided.

Those interested should apply to Liz Fisher at the above address.

## Camphill Rudolf Steiner School
Murtle Estate, Bieldside, Aberdeen AB1 9EP. Tel: (0224) 867 935

This is a residential school for children and adolescents in need of special care. Volunteers are needed to live-in and help care for the young people in a home and teach in the school setting. A full time commitment is required with volunteers expected to join in the community life as fully as possible, and emphasis is placed on Christian ideals, social responsibility and the development of the individual. Duties include caring for the young people both physically and emotionally in houses, teaching in classrooms, general domestic tasks, arranging sports and craft activities and working on the land. Around 80 volunteers of any nationality are needed all year round. Placements are usually for at least a year, but in some cases may only be for six months.

Applicants must be willing to live with and fully involve themselves in the community activities with the young people, physically fit, mentally stable, aged over 19 years and have respect for Christian ideals. Exceptions are made for people with certain medical conditions but otherwise no-one with drug habits is accepted. Board, lodging and weekly pocket money are provided. Volunteers who stay for the entire agreed period have their return fare home paid.

Apply to the Staff Committee at the above address.

## Children's Community Holidays Ltd.
34 Mount Charles, Belfast BT 1NZ. Tel: (0232) 245650

Children's Community Holidays is a non-profit making organisation involved primarily with cross community work in Northern Ireland. The winter programme comprises of running youth clubs and playgroups in various cities and organising some residential weekend camps for children. During July to August about 800 children aged 8 to 16 are taken on 10 day residential holidays. The children are divided into two or three year age groups but are mixed in terms of religious, geographic and economic backgrounds. Around 300 volunteers are needed for the 16 to 24 holidays run per summer. Positions offered include minibus drivers, caterers, domestics, matrons, clerical staff, supervisors and directors of holidays. Recruitment is for 10 day periods but volunteers may work for three consecutive periods. While the majority of positions are available during summer, some volunteers are needed in the winter.

All applicants are required to agree to the DHSS pre-employment vetting scheme which includes a scrutiny of police and statutory agency disciplinary records. Volunteers must have a basic understanding of English and applicants for supervisors positions must have experience with working with children. Those wishing to work as domestics must be older than $16\frac{1}{2}$ years, while supervisory staff must be older than $17\frac{1}{2}$ years, on July 1. Pocket money paid depends on the position held but is between £25 and £86 per 10 day period.

Apply to the Deputy Director at the above address.

### Children's Country Holidays Fund (Inc.)

1 York Street, Baker Street, London W1H 1PZ. Tel: (01) 935 8371

Every year the Fund provides holidays in the country, at the seaside, in private homes or established camps, for almost 3,500 disadvantaged London children. The arrangements for the children's holidays are undertaken by voluntary workers, under the umbrella of a small administrative staff in Head Office. Volunteers are also needed to act as train marshals supervising the children's travel to and from London.

There are no special requirements for camp supervisors, beyond a minimum age of 18, good health, and the ability to supervise children aged between nine and thirteen. The holiday periods vary between ten to fourteen days, and holidays always take place during the six weeks of the school summer holidays.

Those interested should write to the Director at the above address to find out how they can help.

### CLAN

40 Warren Road, Stirchley, Birmingham B30 2NY. Tel: (021) 459 3723

This organisation provides short holiday breaks for children aged from 7 to 13 who would not normally be able to visit the country. The camps may be up to a week long and are held during the summer vacation at attractive sites in the West Midlands.

Around 10 volunteers a year are needed to help look after the children and organise leisure activities. No special requirements are expected of volunteers other than that they be mobile and aged over 16. Board, lodging and up to £10 to cover travelling expenses are provided.

Applicants should contact the Treasurer at the above address.

**Community Action Projects (C.A.P.)**
Goodricke College, University of York, Heslington, York. YO1 5DD. Tel: (0904) 412328

CAP runs three types of holiday for a total of 300 children who would not normally get a holiday; most have special needs because they come from low income, broken or unsettled family backgrounds. Easter and summer camps for 7 to 13 year olds consist of site-based drama, craft, sport activities and day trips. Venture Weeks in August for 14 and 15 year olds are more adventurous outdoor pursuit holidays, including hill walking and abseiling.

Around 100 volunteers are needed to help with the general running of the camps as well as participating in and initiating activities. Anyone over 18 years with enthusiasm would be welcomed, but people with specific skills including first-aid, driving and walking experience are also required. Accommodation is provided. For further information contact the Community Action Officer at the above address.

**Dorset Children's Holiday Scheme**
c/o Area Youth Office, 33 Trinity Street, Dorchester. Tel: (0305) 251000, ext. 4577

The Scheme provides holidays for around 100 children from Dorset each year who have been selected by social workers as being in need of a break for varying reasons. This might be because they come from a family which is at risk of breaking down during the holiday period, because a parent may be handicapped by physical or mental illness, or simply because parents are unable to provide holidays for their large families. The sites of the holidays vary from year to year, but they normally take place in youth centres and other similar buildings. All staff on the sites are volunteers. Besides keeping an eye on the day to day running of the camp, staff also supervises sailing, swimming, riding, canoeing, theatre trips, and beach activities, which all help to create the atmosphere of a real family holiday. Holidays take place between late July and early September.

The volunteers who participate in the scheme each year are expected to cover all their own expenses as nothing is provided except board and lodging. No special abilities are necessary, apart from the patience and firmness necessary to work with children aged between 8 and 14.

Applicants should contact Mr R. White, South Winds I.T. Centre, 11 Cranford Avenue, Weymouth, Dorset or Mr D. Jenkins, Child and Family Guidance Clinic, Damers Road, Dorchester, Dorset. References are required and applications should be submitted before the end of March.

**Flysheet Camps Scotland**
Finniegill Children's Farm, Lockerbie, Dumfriesshire. Tel: (05766) 211

Since 1980 Finniegill has been developed as a children's farm and wilderness centre by Flysheet Camps Scotland, a registered charity. It aims to provide a place for children to stay and gain some experience of living at close quarters with nature for any period from a day to a week. The camp is run by both long and medium term volunteers, who tend to be young and without a regular job, with the help of around 150 volunteers a year who stay on the camp for a period of 1 or 2 weeks. The work to be done consists of all the activities necessary to make the camp as self sufficient as possible, from cutting peat or building huts to making yoghurt or bread, as well as looking after the children. The living conditions are very primitive; the farm has no electricity, and is very isolated. Accommodation consists of mattresses on the floor of an old farmhouse. A contribution of under £2 a day towards the cost of food is normally expected. No particular skills or qualifications are expected of volunteers, but it is prefered that volunteers stay for a few days to get the feel of the place before they commit themselves to staying for a longer period.

Those interested should send a stamped addressed envelope to the Resident Organiscr at the above address for further details.

### Leicester Childrens Holiday Home

Quebec Road, Mablethorpe, Lincs LN12 1QX. Tel: (0521) 72444

This Home provides summer holidays for groups of 40 girls and 40 boys from socially deprived backgrounds in the Leicester area. The two week-long camps are held from May through to the end of August each year. Around 15 volunteers are needed for the entire season to help care for the children, to cook and undertake other duties including taking sports or musical activities.

Volunteers may be of any nationality provided they are 18 to 30 years old, fit, energetic and enjoy outdoor activities. Volunteers with musical or sporting skills are preferred. Board, accommodation and £30 per week are provided.

Applicants should contact the Matron at the above address.

### Liverpool Children's Holiday Organisation (LCHO)

Room L8, Wellington Road School, Wellington Road, Dingle, Liverpool L8 4TX. Tel: (051) 727 7330

LCHO provides week-long residential holidays in supervised rural settings in Britain for local children who would not normally have a summer holiday away from home. 20 to 30 volunteers are needed to act as supervisors and matrons for groups of school age children. Volunteers are responsible for their group of children for 24 hours a day.

Applicants must be 18 to 65 years old and fit, but only volunteers who have completed a residential training course with LCHO or a similar organisation will be accepted as supervisors, and applicants for matron positions must have First Aid and nursing qualifications. Recruitment usually occurs from January to March for that year's summer holiday period. Accommodation is provided and expenses paid.

Applicants should contact the Fieldworker at the above address.

### London Children's Camp

33 Farren Road, Forest Hill, London SE23 2DZ

This organisation needs some 40 volunteers to help run three 11 day camps on a site at Lowestoft in Suffolk each summer during the school holidays. The camps are for boys and girls from London, who would not otherwise get a holiday away from home. The age-group catered for is 9-14 year olds, and about 80 children attend each camp. An Organiser and Deputy with a small catering staff and 16-20 volunteer "leaders" run the camps. The children, in groups of six or eight, sleep in tents and a leader is assigned to each group to see that the most is made of the holiday. He of she is involved in running the widest variety of activities. Outings and competitions are organised for larger groups and each leader takes a turn at the various duties: dining room, preparing supper, issuing sports equipment, etc. A converted farmhouse incorporates the cooking and dining facilities. The leaders sleep in tents but there are locker-rooms for storing possessions, and a wood cabin on the main field for relaxing and coffee. The site of the camp is 35 acres of grass and trees stretching to cliffs, foreshore and beach. Outbuildings house washing and toilet facilities, hot showers and drying rooms. There is usually some time during a hectic but rewarding stay for a quiet drink off site during moments of calm!

Applicants must be at least 18 years of age and in good health. An ability to get on with children (sometimes difficult ones) is essential. All nationalities are welcome, as long as English is spoken. The minimum length of stay is two weeks, the maximum seven. Free board and lodging are provided, and pocket money of £10 a week is paid.

More detailed information sheets will be supplied on the application of volunteers to the Secretary at the above address.

### The National Autistic Society
276 Willesden Lane, London NW2 5RB. Tel: (01) 451 3844

There are limited opportunities for volunteers to work with autistic children on special projects lasting a week or fortnight during the school vacations or on a longer term basis. Most of this work is in autistic schools themselves, but some help is needed in the homes of the children. If the volunteer visits the child at home the National Society only makes the initial connection, after which arrangements are made between the parent, child and the volunteer.

The basic requirements are good health, a large supply of energy and clear speech. A driving licence would be useful as well as any qualification applicable to working with handicapped children. Travel expenses and weekly pocket money would probably be paid; however accommodation can seldom be furnished.

Applicants who send their enquiries to the National Society office in London will be sent a list of the special schools and units around the country.

### Tadworth Court Children's Hospital Holiday Project
Tadworth Court, Tadworth, Surrey, KT20 5RU. Tel: (0737) 357171

Between July and September every year the Holiday Project provides holidays for mentally and physically handicapped children, thus providing a break for their families. At any one time there are up to 16 children on the unit aged between 4 and 16. Help is needed from between 16 and 20 volunteers a year to provide care: feeding, bathing and changing the children, organising play and activities and generally befriending them. Volunteers also act as escorts for children on outings to the seaside, etc., on a one to one basis. Trained staff are available to assist at all times.

Participants must be at least 18 years old and should preferably have some experience with children: they are required for periods of at least one month. Accommodation and a meal allowance of £4 per day are provided, as are travelling expenses within the mainland UK.

For further details contact the Team Leader, Holiday Unit at the above address.

# Conservation and the Environment

### British Trust for Conservation Volunteers
36 St. Mary's Street, Wallingford, Oxfordshire OX10 0EU. Tel: (0491) 39766

The British Trust for Conservation Volunteers undertakes practical conservation work in parks, forests, nature reserves and other open spaces throughout the UK. There are also over 500 local groups and every year 55,000 people are active in the various projects. Over 550 conservation working holidays are run all year round, and last for 1-2 weeks; there are also weekend conservation projects based in London.

Anyone aged between 16 and 70 with an interest in conservation is welcome; foreign volunteers should be aged over 18 and speak reasonable English. Accommodation and food are provided, although volunteers are asked to bring sleeping bags.

For details send a 32p stamp and an A4 envelope to the above address.

### Cathedral Camps
Manor House, High Birstwith, Harrogate, North Yorkshire HG3 2LG. Tel: (0423) 770385

Cathedral Camps undertake the conservation and restoration of Cathedrals and their environments, including tasks that have hitherto been postponed because of a lack of resources. Between the end of July and the first week in September around 400 volunteers take part in 7 day camps, each consisting of between 13 and 30 people. The minimum age is 16; many of the participants come from schools and 6th form colleges, or are involved in the Duke of Edinburgh Award Scheme, but volunteers are also recruited from abroad through various organisations.

For further information contact the Cathedral Camps Chairman at the above address.

### Conservation Volunteers - Northern Ireland
The Pavilion, Cherryvale Playing Fields, Ravenhill Road, Belfast BT6 0BZ Tel: (0232) 645169

Conservation Volunteers involve people in all types of practical conservation work throughout Northern Ireland. Tasks include dry-stone walling, erosion control, tree planting, creating nature areas, etc. Projects continue all year round and volunteers are needed on a day-to-day or project basis, but working holidays lasting for one week are offered only during the summer months.

Volunteers must have reasonable English skills and for the working holidays, be aged at least 16 years old. On-site training is given for those with no experience. Food and accommodation is provided for volunteers on the working holidays but travel and lunch expenses are paid for local volunteers only.

Those interested should contact the Publicity Officer at the above address.

### Derbyshire County Council
Community and Tertiary Section, County Offices, Matlock, Derbyshire. Tel: (0629) 580000 extn. 6487

The Derbyshire International Work Camp is organised annually and is held at Shipley Country Park and Elvaston Castle Country Park. Recent projects have included the construction of woodland walks, dry stone walling, the construction of foot bridges, fishing pond platforms and a trim track. Accommodation is provided in a Residential School, and a varied and extensive leisure programme is arranged.

Volunteers should be over 16 and under 21. The Work Camp takes place between mid July and mid August and the cost is approximately £25 per week; this covers food and accommodation. There are 20 free places available annually for young people from Derbyshire. The Work Camp also qualifies under the Duke of Edinburgh's Award Scheme. Application should be completed and forwarded to the above address by 1 May.

### Festiniog Railway Company
Porthmadog, Gwynedd, North Wales. Tel: Porthmadog (0766) 2340

Hundreds of volunteers are needed throughout the year to help in the operation and maintenance of the narrow gauge railway between Porthmadog and Blaenau Ffestiniog. Railway enthusiasts and non-enthusiasts of any nationality may apply provided they speak good English. The minimum age is 16 years.

Further information may be obtained from the Volunteer Officer, Festiniog Railway Company.

### Forest School Conservation Camps
Bourne Cottage, Park Lane, Heytesbury, Warminster, Wiltshire BA12 0HE
Tel: (0985) 40377

Forest School Conservation Camps, a national organisation for young people, aims to encourage the idea that socially necessary work should be undertaken by volunteers on behalf of the general community. It carries out small practical conservation jobs throughout Great Britain, in particular assisting the John Simonds Trust at Bradfield in Berkshire to establish a children's Country Centre on an old manor farm complex where there is a wide variety of work to be done. Similar camps can be found in Dorset, Essex and Cambridgeshire, providing plenty of scope for the conservationist.

There are no special requirements to be met, beyond a minimum age of 17 years (18 for those from abroad). Each camp lasts for one or two weeks, but weekend activities are also included. Volunteers are asked to bring their own (lightweight) tents if possible but they can be borrowed when necessary.

No travel expenses or wages can be paid, and contributions towards food and expenses depend on the arrangements made with the sponsors of the work to be done. Efforts are made to keep expenses down.

Those interested should contact the Work Camps Secretary at the above address for further details.

### Garry Gualach Outdoor Centre
Invergarry, Invernesshire, Scotland. Tel: (08092) 230

Located in an isolated part of the West Highlands, the centre aims to provide active outdoor holidays for paying guests as well as conserving and protecting the environment. A number of volunteers are needed to help construct this centre by doing tasks such as building, making roads and paths, planting trees and other agricultural and horticultural work.

Volunteers are needed for periods of two weeks to two months at any time around the year. Board and lodging is provided.

For further details contact the Director at the above address.

### Middle Wood Trust
Backsbottom Farm, Roeburndale West, Lancaster LA2 8QX

The Trust exists to advance educational research in the fields of ecology, farming, forestry, horticulture, wildlife and countryside management, crafts and low energy technology. Short and long term volunteers are needed to help with building, farm work, organic vegetable growing; forestry and educational work. Volunteers are taken on initially for a test period of a few days or longer if necessary. The work is available around the year; conditions can be hard from November to March. Applicants must speak English, be practical and enthusiastic. No pocket money or expenses are paid, but meals and basic accommodation can usually be provided.

For further details contact the Information Officer at the above address.

### The Monkey Sanctuary
Murrayton, Nr. Looe, Cornwall PL13 1NZ. Tel: (05036) 2532

The Monkey Sanctuary was established in 1964 near Looe in Cornwall. As the first place where the Woolly Monkey survived and bred outside of its natural habitat in the South American rain forests, it serves as a conservation centre and is open to the public at Easter and during the summer months. Most of the several dozen volunteers are needed during these periods to help with various duties including preparing food for the monkeys, maintaining and cleaning the monkey enclosures, domestic tasks and attending to the public. During winter volunteers are still needed mainly for maintenance work. Volunteers can choose to stay for periods of two to several weeks but only volunteers staying for long periods, or making repeated visits may be asked to take on more responsible tasks with the monkeys.

Applicants must be fluent in English, in good health and over 18 years old. Board and lodging is provided and depending on the individual's need, pocket money or expenses may be paid.

For further information contact the Head Keeper at the above address.

**The National Trust Volunteer Unit**
PO Box 12, Westbury, Wiltshire, BA13 4NA

The National Trust organises Acorn Camps for outdoor conservation work projects throughout England and Wales from March to late October. Camps vary in size from 12 to 20 volunteers, and last for a minimum of one week. However the volunteer may join two or more camps.

The minimum age for participants is 17 years, for overseas visitors 18 years. Volunteers pay £17 minimum a week to help cover the cost of board and lodging, and must pay their own travel expenses. Accommodation is provided but volunteers must bring their own bedding or sleeping bags.

Application forms and further details can be obtained from Beryl Sims at the above address. All requests should be accompanied by postage (or an International Reply Coupon, if applicable). Early application is advisable.

**Royal Society for the Protection of Birds (RSPB)**
The Lodge, Sandy, Bedfordshire SG19 2DL. Tel: Sandy (0767) 80551

Volunteers are needed to take part in the RSPB's Voluntary Wardening Scheme which operates on 25 of their nature reserves throughout England, Scotland and Wales. Duties vary but may include basic management such as building paths or digging ditches, dealing with visitors, as well as bird monitoring.

The Scheme operates throughout the year, and volunteers aged 16 years or over and in good general health are welcome to take part. There are some openings for slightly handicapped volunteers. An interest in natural history is desirable. Accommodation is provided free but volunteers are responsible for their own travelling expenses and food during their stay. The minimum stay is one week, though many volunteers work for a fortnight or more.

Further information and application forms may be obtained from the Reserves Management Department at the above address.

**The Scottish Conservation Projects Trust**
Balallan House, 24 Allan Park, Stirling FK8 2QG. Tel: (0786) 79697

The Scottish Conservation Projects Trust was founded specifically to support and promote practical outdoor conservation in Scotland. Conservation tasks include the management of nature reserves and other places of wildlife interest, the improvement of public amenities and access to the countryside, the environmental renewal of Scottish towns and cities and educating the public to appreciate Scotland's natural heritage. Around 5,500 volunteers are needed annually to help with all aspects of practical outdoor conservation work on residential and non-residential projects, fund-raising and publicity. Trust management and training courses. Training in tree-planting, dry-stone dyking, fencing and habitat management is given. Long term volunteers are recruited for several months while residential projects normally run for 10 days. Most volunteers are needed between March and October but some projects are undertaken during winter.

Volunteers are given training but a working knowledge of English is desirable. The minimum age of volunteers accepted is 16 years and volunteers must be aware that some tasks are physically demanding. Accommodation and food are provided at a cost of £2.50 per night.

Those interested should apply to the Appeal Director at the above address.

## Waterway Recovery Group

Millbrook Grange School, Parkfield Drive, Kenilworth, Warks. Tel: (0926) 511634

The Waterway Recovery Group is the national co-ordinator for voluntary work on the UK's derelict canals. Canal Camps are challenging outdoor restoration projects lasting about a week; the work includes lock chamber clearance, building work, demolition, vegetation control and environmental conservation. Basic accommodation in village halls is provided at a cost of £18 per week. There are week long camps all summer until the end of October and then occasionally throughout the winter. All camps take place on a wide variety of canals and archaeological sites in England and Wales. Volunteers must be over 16 and speak good English.

A free information pack is available from Neil Edwards, Canal Camps, 17 Reynolds Gate, South Woodham Ferrers, Essex, CM3 5FA.

## West Wales Trust for Nature Conservation

7 Market Street, Haverfordwest, Dyfed SA61 1NF. Tel: (0437) 5462

The Trust is responsible for two island reserves (Skomer and Skokholm) and various other woodland, river and marshland nature reserves within Dyfed. Between 75 and 100 volunteers are needed to help with scientific research, patrolling reserves, advising visitors and repairing and maintaining buildings, hides and footpaths. Most volunteers are recruited from April to September but on some sites volunteers are needed all year round.

Volunteers may be of any nationality provided they are at least 17 years old. Accommodation and free transport are provided on the island reserves but volunteers must supply their own food.

Contact the Administrative Officer at the above address for further information.

# Religious Projects

## Careforce

c/o Scripture Union, 130 City Road, London EC1V 2NJ. Tel: (01) 250 1966

Careforce is a scheme set up by four Evangelical Christian bodies in which young Christians are placed in churches and institutions caring for the disabled and disadvantaged in British cities. Around 55 volunteers are needed to undertake practical work to assist in the church ministry and other institutions, and when suitable assume varying degrees of responsibility and leadership in spiritual work. Placements begin in September and last for eight to 12 months.

Volunteers must be committed Christians with an above average degree of maturity, aged 18 to 23 years old and in good health. For practical reasons it may be difficult to place people from other nationalities. Board, lodging and an allowance of £15 per week are provided.

Those interested should apply to the Organising Secretary at the above address.

### Carnoch Outdoor Centre

Carnoch House, Glencoe, Argyll, Scotland PA39 4HS. Tel: (08552) 350

Carnoch is a Christian residential holiday and outdoor centre based at Glencoe in the West Highlands of Scotland. Courses in skiing and hillwalking are offered between January and April, while in summer canoeing, sailing, windsurfing and walking are offered. Positions for about four volunteers as domestic helpers in Carnoch House are available for two to six months at a time. Occasionally maintenance workers and extra instructors in various seasonal activities are needed.

Volunteers may be of any nationality provided they speak fluent English and are 18 to 40 years old. All volunteers should be reasonably fit and if applying for an instructor's post, qualified or experienced in the particular activity. A driver's licence is useful but not essential. Board, lodging and pocket money are provided.

Apply to the Warden at the above address.

### The Church Army

Independents Road, Blackheath, London SE3 9LF. Tel: (01) 318 1226

The Church Army is a Society of the Anglican Church which has existed for over 100 years. During the summer months many evangelistic campaigns are mounted by volunteers at the seaside, and other 'holiday' centres. There is also a 'Christian Service Scheme' for those prepared to serve with the Society for a year following a short training period. Adequate renumeration and accommodation are provided.

Applicants are generally school or university leavers; but all volunteers over the age of 18 are welcome. Apply to the Church Army Headquarters at the above address.

### The Corrymeela Community

Ballycastle, Co. Antrim, BT54 6QU, N. Ireland. Tel: (02657) 62626

Corrymeela is an ecumenical Christian community working for reconciliation in Northern Ireland and the world at large. It runs an administrative centre in Belfast and a residential centre at Ballycastle on the North Antrim coast where people from all backgrounds can come together and meet in an easy, relaxed atmosphere. Opportunities exist at the Ballycastle centre for volunteer helpers on both a long and short term basis. The commitment of the long term volunteers is generally for 12 months commencing in September of each year, and the volunteers receive their room and board plus a small weekly allowance. During the months of July and August, a number of additional volunteers are welcomed for periods of one to three weeks, to assist with family groups and projects or as summer staff helpers, assisting with recreation, arts and crafts, cooking, laundry etc. The lower age limit for all volunteers is 18 years.

Those interested in long term volunteer work should contact the Volunteer Co-ordinator at the above address. A leaflet, *Summer Opportunities,* which details all possible involvement during July and August is published in March of each year and those interested should apply to the above address. In England, further information about Corrymeela is available from the Corrymeela Link, P.O. Box 118, Reading.


## The Grail
125 Maxwell Lane, Pinner, Middlesex HA5 3ER. Tel: (01) 866 2195/0505

The Grail is a Christian lay community which runs a conference centre and is involved in work with family and youth groups, fundraising and counselling. Volunteers assist with all these tasks, domestic work and the maintenance of the garden, as well as having the opportunity to participate in courses held in the conference centre. Around 10 volunteers a year are needed but there is a maximum of three at any one time. Placements are for three months to one year except during summer when volunteers are accepted for a minimum stay of one month.

Any practical skills are useful but not essential. Volunteers may be of any nationality provided they are in good health and over 18 years old. Board, lodging and weekly pocket money are provided.

Applications should be made to the President at the above address.


## Hothorpe Hall
Theddingworth, Lutterworth, Leicestershire LE17 6QX. Tel: Market Harborough (0858) 880 257

A Christian conference and retreat centre which needs volunteers each year to look after the guests as well as maintain the facilities. Although summer is the busiest season for camps and conferences, volunteers are needed throughout the year. The wide range of jobs includes kitchen work, housekeeping, maintenance, and gardening. Volunteers with special skills in such areas as art, music and plant-tending will be able to make valuable and interesting contributions.

Volunteers should have a firmly rooted commitment to the Christian faith, although participants are accepted from many different denominational backgrounds. Participation in community worship, devotions and discussions will be expected. Applicants must be over 18 years and in good health. The centre endeavours to create an international mixture among its staff, although all must conform to British immigration regulations.

Applications and information may be obtained by writing to the Secretary at the above address.


## London City Mission
175 Tower Bridge Road, London SE1 2AH. Tel: (01) 407 7585

The London City Mission has a varied programme of voluntary work within the Greater London and inner city areas which includes Christian community work, open-air meetings, door-to-door visits, working with homeless people, running youth camps and children's clubs and providing a support system for the 35 Mission centres in London. One year voluntary evangelism schemes run from September to September, summer projects are held in July and August (two weeks minimum) and a one-week scheme operates all year round. Approximately 200 volunteers are taken on each year.

All volunteers must be committed Christians with membership of a church which is in sympathy with the evangelical tradition and speak English. Volunteers should also be 18 to 30 years old, in good health and willing to undertake a variety of projects requiring hard work and commitment. The ability to drive or speak other languages would be useful. Volunteers are asked to contribute towards the board and accommodation that they receive and the one-year volunteers are also allocated a small amount of pocket money.

Those interested should apply to the Youth Secretary at the above address.

### Tell A Tourist
PO Box 718, Hailsham, East Sussex BN27 3QY. Tel: (0323) 847790

Tell A Tourist is a joint venture involving a number of missions and evangelical societies in which teams of Christian volunteers share their faith on the streets with tourists. Volunteers use singing, preaching, street theatre and personal conversation to share their faith. Over 200 committed Christians are needed for two week campaigns during Easter, July and August of each year. Nearly all campaigns take place in Britain but Tell A Tourist is extending to other European cities.

Volunteers must be at least 18 years old. Accommodation is provided.

Those interested should apply to the Administrator at the above address.

### Time for God
2 Chester House, Pages Lane, London W10 1PR. Tel: (01) 883 1504

This is a scheme which provides an opportunity for the applicant to serve for between six months and one year in a church-based placement. The scheme is sponsored by the Methodist, Anglican, Baptist, and United Reformed Churches and the National Council of YMCAs. Every year some 60 volunteers are needed to care for children, the elderly, the homeless or the handicapped in caring organisations such as the National Children's Home, YMCA, or to help with work of all kinds in local churches or community centres. Full board and lodging is provided by the placement. Volunteers receive £15.25 (Jan 88 figure) per week pocket money, and travel expenses are paid for the journey to the placement for an exploratory visit and on start of service. Volunteers are entitled to a week's holiday, with pocket money and fares home, for each four months of service (volunteers from overseas should be given fares for a reasonable journey in Britain).

Christian applicants of any nationality or denomination are welcomed, provided that they speak fluent English and are between 17 and 25 (or between 18 and 25 for overseas applicants). Those interested should write to the Organiser at the above address for an Applicant Booklet and a leaflet entitled *Questions about the 'Time for God' Scheme*.

# Social and Community Schemes

### Bondway Night Shelter
35-40 Bondway, P.O. Box 374, London SW8 1SJ

Bondway provides emergency accommodation for 120 homeless men and operates a soup run for these forced to sleep out. 14 full time volunteers assist a salaried staff group with practical work, administration and supervision of the shelter. Volunteers work throughout the week with shifts covering the full 24 hours. They must be prepared to stay for between six months. In exchange they receive accommodation, travel expenses to the project and an allowance of £35 per week.

Applicants need to be available for interview and aged between 18 to 30. For more information contact the volunteer co-ordinator at the above address.

### The Carr-Gomm Society Ltd
38 Gomm Road, Rotherhithe, London SE16 2TX. Tel: (01) 231 9284

The Carr-Gomm Society is a charitable housing association which provides small permanent homes for single lonely people. Residents can be men or women, of all ages and from a wide variety of backgrounds. In each Carr-Gomm house, residents have their own room and share meals and communal areas; in most houses there is a residential housekeeper who looks after the day-to-day needs of the residents. The Society aims to create the type of family-like environment where lonely people can begin to overcome feelings of isolation.

Founded in 1965, the Society currently manages 60 houses in 13 London boroughs; houses around the rest of the country are managed by autonomous local Carr-Gomm groups.

The Society needs full-time volunteers in London, the average length of stay being six months. Volunteers are normally based at the Society's Head Offices; besides helping there, volunteers assist with the day-to-day running of the houses, and help befriend lonely residents.

Volunteers should apply directly to the Head Office of the Society, at the above address.

### Cecil Houses (Inc)
2 Priory Road, Kew, Richmond, Surrey, TW9 3DG. Tel: (01) 940 9829/9

Cecil Houses was founded in 1926 and consists of two hostels for homeless women and three residential homes for the elderly of both sexes. Volunteers are required to assist either in the care of the elderly or the homeless women, or with domestic work etc.

The minimum age is 18 years, the period of engagement six to 12 months. Volunteers work a 39 hour week over a seven day shift, with two days off a week. They receive £15.25 per week in payment, and free board and shared accommodation is provided. All nationalities are welcome although they must be able to read and understand English. Applications should be made in English to the Placements Officer, Mrs M. Francis at the above address.

## Edinburgh Cyrenian Trust

20 Broughton Place, Edinburgh EH1 3RX. Tel: (031) 538 4871

The Edinburgh Cyrenian Trust runs two communities for single, homeless men and women aged 18 to 30 years old; one in Edinburgh and another on a smallholding outside Edinburgh. Around 22 volunteers are needed each year to live with the residents and befriend them. Other tasks include performing various housekeeping and book-keeping tasks. Placements are for six months at a time.

Volunteers must be fluent in English, 18 to 30 years old, energetic and have initiative. Applicants with a full driving licence are preferred. Travel expenses to attend an interview are paid. Successful applicants receive one-way travel to the project, accommodation, pocket money and holiday and termination grants.

Applicants should apply to the Administrator at the above address.

## Great Georges Community Cultural Project

Great Georges Street, Liverpool 1. Tel: (051) 709 5109

The Project is a centre for experimental work in the arts, sports, games and education housed in the centre of Liverpool. At any one time there are both full time and short term volunteers on the staff who spend up to 12 months on the Project. Ideally one month is seen as the minimum period, although there are exceptions, e.g. some volunteers join the Project specifically to work on a playscheme which lasts for two weeks. The general work of the scheme is shared as equally as possible, with everyone being prepared to do some administration, cook, sweep the floor, play with kids, talk to visitors as well as supervise the activities. The centre, or the 'Blackie' as it has become known, has gained an important position in the life of the city, as it provides opportunities for local people which would otherwise simply not exist. Among these are work shops for photography, cooking, dance, music, film, pool, reading, writing, drawing and typing. In addition entertainments are arranged there, which have recently included original poetry, performance art, contemporary music, modern dance and the showing of films.

A bed and food are provided for those who are staying for more than a month and are unable to pay for their own; anyone able to pay for themselves or staying less than a month is asked for £15 a week towards food and accommodation, unless some arrangement is made in advance. Although skills in arts and crafts are useful, more important are stamina and a sense of humour.

Requests for further information should be made to the Duty Officer at the above address.

## Holiday Care Service

2 Old Bank Chambers, Station Road, Horley, Surrey RH6 9HW. Tel: (0293) 774 535

Holiday Care Service is a national charity, providing free information and advice on holidays for those with special needs. Volunteers are taken on for the 'Holiday Helpers' project, which aims to find carers or companions to enable individual disabled or elderly people to take an independent holiday in Britain or abroad. Work ranges from guiding a blind person to the total care of a disabled person. A register of volunteers is maintained and volunteers are notified when a suitable holiday opportunity arises. Over 300 volunteers have registered but more are needed. Holidays are generally one to three weeks in duration and may be taken throughout the year.

Ideally volunteers should have previous experience of caring for elderly or disabled people, however training can be arranged for those without experience. All volunteers must be physically fit and aged at least 18 years. A driving licence and experience of pushing wheelchairs are other skills which may be required.

The holiday maker meets all the costs of the volunteer's accommodation and travel, but volunteers must provide their own spending money.

Further information can be obtained from the Co-ordinator at the above address.

## Homes for Homeless People
TPW Recruitment, 4th Floor, Smithfield House, Digbeth, Birmingham, B5 6BS

Homes for Homeless People, (formerly National Cyrenians) is a national federation of local housing groups running projects for single homeless people throughout the UK. Most projects are long or short-term houses but there are some emergency accommodation centres and day centres as well. The aim of the organisation is to treat the homeless as individuals with individual problems.

The local groups are legally and financially autonomous. They run over 70 projects staffed by approximately 65 temporary project workers (volunteers) and 40 permanent salaried workers.

These groups are constantly needing new workers to help in the running and day-to-day life of their projects. No experience or qualifications are needed. The work is demanding (both physically and emotionally), and involves the ability to get on with people in residential situations and often take responsibility. It is particularly relevant and rewarding to those who wish to gain experience for social or community work courses or future work.

Workers receive board and lodging, plus pocket money. There is usually a minimum six months commitment but shorter periods can sometimes be arranged. If interested contact TPW Recruitment at the above address.

## Iona Community
Iona Abbey, Iona, Argyll, Scotland. Tel: (068 17) 404

The Iona Community receives groups of people, mainly from areas of social deprivation, during a season from March to October. Approximately 70 volunteers aged 18 years upwards, are required each year to assist with catering, housekeeping, driving, guiding, gardening, crafts, programme leadership, music, coffee house staffing and maintenance. Volunteers stay for between six and eight weeks. The only requirements are a driving licence and a minimum age of 23 years for the person doing the driving job and some kind of practical experience for those doing the maintenance, craft, music and programme work.

Travel expenses within Britain are paid plus a weekly allowance. Board and lodging are provided.

Those interested should apply to the Administrator at the above address.

## The MRC Common Cold Unit

Harvard Hospital, Combe Road, Salisbury, Wilts. SP2 8BW. Tel: (0722) 22485

The unit is engaged on research into cold and flu virus, conducted with the help of around 500 volunteers per year who are willing to catch a cold or flu. Only a mild form of infection is given, and only one in three volunteers actually develop symptoms of illness. Accommodation is provided in 2 or 3 bedroomed flats: a vital part of the experiment involves keeping volunteers isolated from everybody except their flatmates and the medical staff. Volunteers must be able to look after their own entertainment: colour TV & radio, game facilities, library books and newspapers are provided. They can take walks in the surrounding countryside but must remain 30 feet from anyone they meet.

Applicants must be aged between 18 and 50 and of good health. Volunteers are needed for periods of ten days, from Monday to Thursday week, around the year. Food, accommodation, pocket money of £1.75 per day and return rail travel to the Centre from anywhere in England, Wales or Scotland south of Glasgow are provided.

For further information contact the Administration Officer at the above address. Regrettably, the Unit may be closing down in 1990, and so applications should only be sent for 1989.

## National Federation of City Farms

The Old Vicarage, 66 Fraser Street, Windmill Hill, Bedminster, Bristol BS3 4LY. Tel: (0272) 660663

This Federation is concerned with obtaining land and buildings in cities and involving the community in establishing their own independent city farms, i.e. establishing gardening projects, housing animals such as goats, chickens, sheep and pigs, arranging farm visits, educational programmes and training and organising therapeutic activities for disabled people. Volunteers are required for periods of two weeks or longer to help with building, gardening, animal care, teaching crafts, community development work, etc. All nationalities are welcome provided that they speak good English and get on well with people of all ages. Maturity is an advantage. Accommodation is rarely provided.

Anyone interested can obtain further information from the Federation Co-ordinator at the above address.

## The Ockenden Venture

"Ockenden", Guildford Road, Woking, Surrey, GU22 7UU. Tel: (04862) 72012/3

Volunteers are needed to look after refugees in the UK. Many of these refugees, although not all Vietnamese, are whole families that are housed in various reception centres. Unaccompanied refugee minors are cared for in two childrens homes at Haslemere and Oxford, while physically handicapped young refugees stay in a home in Camberley, Surrey. At present they recruit approximately 15 volunteers each year. They are required to stay for six months and preferably longer. The minimum age of acceptance is 18 years. They receive £20 per week, plus free board and accommodation.

The work involved is partly domestic but can include driving, property maintenance and gardening. It does include a full involvement with the refugees, assisting the older ones to become adjusted to life in the UK and the younger ones to assist in their development by encouragement and assistance in their studies for example.

Further details are available from the Personnel Officer at the above address.

### The Outward Bound Trust: City Challenge

Chestnut Field, Regent Place, Rugby CV21 2PJ. Tel: (0788) 60423

City Challenge is the urban equivalent of Outward Bound's outdoor activity schemes. Whereas Outward Bound courses involve activities such as canoeing, sailing, rock climbing etc., a typical City Challenge course might involve community service, work with playgroups or work in psychiatric or geriatric hospitals, hostels for the homeless or in a hospital for the mentally handicapped.

The participants in these courses are young people aged between 17 and 25 from a range of industrial, commercial and educational backgrounds who are normally funded on the courses either by their employers or by a charitable institution who wish to help them to broaden their experience of the world and develop a sense of responsibility. There are around 40 participants on each course who live together in a residential centre, with full board, transport and all equipment provided.

For full details contact the Director at the above address.

### Petrus Community Trust

82 Holt Road, Liverpool 7 2PR. Tel: (051) 263 4543

Petrus provides a variety of accommodation and support for homeless single people in Liverpool. Current projects are three residential projects, two long-stay hostels and a 'dry house' for homeless alcoholics. Around 24 volunteers are needed year round to undertake a mixture of domestic, welfare and administrative tasks. Placements are for six to nine months.

Volunteers need no special skills but should be fluent in English and 18 to 25 years old. Travel expenses to attend an interview are not paid. Successful applicants receive travel expenses on arrival, board, accommodation, weekly pocket money of £35 and holiday and termination payments.

Those interested should contact the Director at the above address.

### Sidmouth International Festival of Folk Arts

The Knowle, Sidmorton, Devon GX10 8HL. Tel: (03955) 5134

This Festival encourages international friendship and understanding via the promotion of folk music, dance and song. The Festival is usually held in late July and lasts for seven to ten days. Around 200 volunteers are needed for the duration of the festival to act as stewards at events, guides and interpreters for overseas performers, etc.

Volunteers of all nationalities are accepted provided they speak English. Interpreters must have a working knowledge of another language but otherwise volunteers need no special skills.

For further details contact the Festival Director at the above address.

### The Simon Community

St. Joseph's House, 129 Malden Road, London NW5. Tel: (01) 485 6639

The Community offers residential care to the homeless and rootless in four houses: their headquarters, at 129 Malden Road, London; 32 Pancras Road; at Simonwell Farm, on Sole Street, Petham, near Canterbury and at 10 Anton Street, London NW1. Around 40 volunteers a year are needed to help with both the running of these houses and the tea runs from which the homeless people are found. Volunteers are needed on either a full or part time basis; full time is no understatement, as residential volunteers must be prepared to work a 16 hour day and sleep on the floor if necessary. The work is demanding and volunteers should be prepared to experience situations which will test their initiative, stamina and patience.

Full time volunteers, who should be over 18 and speak good English, are given food and lodging in the house to which they are assigned. After a probationary period of four weeks they must be prepared to commit themselves for a further period of three, six, nine or twelve months. During this time they will receive pocket money of £10 per week, plus a tobacco allowance. A driving licence would be useful, and part time workers with transport are also very welcome.

Applicants should contact the Community Leader at the above address.

### Tipton Congregational Church

The Malthouse Stables, Hurst Lane, Tipton, West Midlands DY4 9AB. Tel: (021) 520 7861

Over the five days and nights of Christmas, this church provides food, clothing and accommodation for homeless people. This programme, 'Open Christmas', catered for about 800 homeless people in 1987. Over 100 volunteers of all ages are needed to care for these people. Food and accommodation are provided.

Contact Rev Tom Hodgson at the above address for more information.

# Work with the Sick and Disabled

### Association of Camphill Communities

Camphill Rudolf Steiner Schools, Murtle House, Bielside, Aberdeen AB1 9EP

This Association was set up in 1978 to bring together the many different interests and concerns of the 30 or so Camphill communities in the British Isles. These communities for handicapped children and adults or those with special needs are all based on anthroposophy as founded by Rudolf Steiner. Opportunities for living and working as volunteers within a Camphill community exist for longer and shorter periods. In general, one able bodied volunteer is needed for every two community members.

The Association can supply more information on individual member communities but applications to work as volunteers should be sent to the individual centres. The addresses of current member communities are given below.

Bolton Village, Danby, Whitby, North Yorks YO21 2NJ. Tel: (0287) 60871

Cherry Orchards Camphill Community, Canford Lane, Westbury-on-Trym, Bristol BS9 3PF. Tel: (0272) 503 183

The Croft, Highfield Road, Old Malton, North Yorks YO17 0EY. Tel: (0425) 474 291

Camphill Devon Community, Hapstead Village, Buckfastleigh, South Devon TQ11 0JN. Tel: (0364) 42631

Delrow College and Rehabilitation Centre, Hilfield Lane, Aldenham, Watford, Herts. WD2 8DJ. Tel: (09276) 6006

Grange-Oaklands, Newnham-on-Severn, Glouc. GL14 1HJ. Tel: (0594) 516246

Larchfield Community, Hemlington, Middlesborough, Cleveland TS8 9DY. Tel: (0642) 593688

Camphill Milton Keynes Community, 7 Sterling Close, Pennyland, Milton Keynes MK15 8AN. Tel: (0908) 674856

Mount School Community, Wadhurst, East Sussex TN5 6PT. Tel: (089288) 2025

Pennine Camphill Community, Boyne Hill House, Chapelthorpe, Wakefield WF4 3JF. Tel: (0924) 255281

Shelling Community, Horton Road, Ashley, Ringwood, Hants. BH24 2EB. Tel: (0425) 477488

Camphill Houses, Heathfield Cottage, 32 Heath Street, Stourbridge, W. Midlands DY8 1SB. Tel: (0384) 372575

William Morris Camphill Community, William Morris House, Eastington, Stonehouse, Gloucestershire GL10 3SH. Tel: (045382) 4025

Coleg Elidyr, Nangwyn, Rhandirmwyn, Llandovery, Dyfed SA20 0NL. Tel: (05506) 272

Clanabogan Camphill Community, Omagh, Co. Tyrone, BT78 1TL. Tel: Omagh 41627

Glencraig Community, Craigavad, Holywood, Co. Down BT18 0DB. Tel: (02317) 3396

Mourne Grange Village Community, Newry Road, Kilkeel, Co. Down BT34 4EX. Tel: (06937) 62229

Balltytobin Community, Callan, Co. Kilkenny. Tel: (056) 25114

Dunshane House, Brannockstown, Co. Kildare. Tel: (045) 83628

Duffcarrig House, Gorey, Co. Wexford. Tel: (055) 25116

Beannachar, Banchory-Devenick, Aberdeen AB1 5YL. Tel: (0224) 868605

Camphill Blair, Drummond, Blair Drummond House, By Stirling FK9 4UT. Tel: (0786) 841341
Corbenic College, Drumour Lodge, Torchry, Nr. Dunkeld, Perthshire PH8 0BY. Tel: (03503) 206
Loch Arthur Village Community, Beeswing, Dumfries DG2 9JQ. Tel: (038776) 224
Newton Dee Village, Bielside, Aberdeen AB1 9DX. Tel: (0224) 868701
Ochil Tower, Auchterarde, Perthshire PH3 1AD. Tel: (07646) 2363
Camphill Rudolf Steiner Schools, Nurtle, Bielside, Aberdeen AB1 9EP. Tel: (0224) 867935
Simeon Care Communities, Cairnlee Estate, Bieldside, Aberdeen AB1 9BN
Templehill Community, Glenfarquhar Lodge, Auchiblae, Kincardine AB3 1UJ. Tel: (05612) 230

### Association for Spina Bifida and Hydrocephalus
22 Upper Woburn Place, London WC1H 0EP. Tel: (01) 388 1382

The Association needs volunteers each year to help run independence training courses for young people with spina bifida and hydrocephalus. The courses are designed to help the young people, who are physically handicapped, to look after themselves, learn basic skills such as cooking, shopping, etc., and gain social independence. Each volunteer is matched with a young person to work on a programme with advice from ASBAH's professional staff. The courses last for one week and are held at the Association's residential centre in Ilkley, West Yorkshire, between March and November.

All nationalities are accepted but volunteers must have sufficient knowledge of English to communicate with the young people. The minimum age is 18. Accommodation, meals and the cost of travel within the UK are provided.

Applications should be made to the DLA Department.

### Bermondsey and Brook Lane Medical Mission
5 Oaklands Road, Bromley, Kent. Tel: (01) 464 8629

The Mission takes on about six volunteers each year to carry out auxiliary work in its homes for the elderly and physically handicapped in Bermondsey, Bromley and Bognor. They are usually taken on for six months at a time and the only requirements are that they should have a good command of the English language and be strong enough to lift patients. Accommodation and pocket money are provided.

Those interested should write to the above address.

### CARE for Mentally Handicapped People
9a Weir Road, Kibworth, Leicester LE8 0LQ. Tel: (053) 753 3225

CARE establishes rural village communities with residential and workshop facilities for mentally handicapped adults. There are around 60 villagers per community who undertake a variety of activities in workshops including printing, market gardening and horticulture, woodwork and making soft toys. 20 to 30 volunteers aged 19 years and over are needed year round to help with caring and social activities for villagers in communities in Devon, Leicestershire, Kent, Sussex, Lancashire and Northumberland. Placements may be from one to six months.

Only British volunteers with good English pronunciation and comprehension are accepted. Board, lodging and £25 pocket money per week are provided.

Those interested should apply to the Community Director at the above address.

### Churchtown Farm Field Studies Centre
Lanlivery, Nr. Bodmin, Cornwall. Tel: (0208) 872148

This Centre offers educational courses in environmental studies with field trips to the sea, moor, ponds and woods; as well as outdoor pursuits which include sailing, rock-climbing and canoeing. All these activities are specifically for both physically and mentally handicapped people of all ages.

Approximately 20 voluntary assistants are taken each year to help the handicapped. There are no special qualifications required but they should be between 18-24 and in good health. Qualifications, in the science related subjects and or experience in outdoor activities would be an advantage. They are recruited for three months at a time, but occasionally for up to a year. Return rail fares, accommodation and pocket money of £13 per week are provided.

Those interested should apply to the Administrator at the above address.

### Help the Handicapped Holiday Fund
147a Camden Road, Tunbridge Wells, Kent TN1 2RA

This Fund arranges about five group holidays for handicapped people each year. Recent holidays have been to Majorca, Swanage, Isle of Sheppey and Cliftonville. All holidays last for one week and take place between May and September. Each year around 100 volunteers are required to care for the disabled participants on these trips. Volunteers may apply to assist with one or more holidays.

Volunteers may be of any nationality provided they are strong and healthy and are between 18 and 60 years old. Experience in helping disabled people is an advantage. Full board, accommodation and travel from Tunbridge Wells are provided but no other expenses are paid.

Those interested should apply to the Holiday Organiser at the above address.

### Horticultural Therapy: Land Use Volunteers
Goulds Ground, Vallis Way, Frome, Somerset BA11 3DW. Tel: (0373) 64782

Horticultural Therapy is a charity that helps people with handicaps or disabilities to enjoy and benefit from gardening, horticulture and agriculture. Its volunteer service, Land Use Volunteers, posts people who have training or experience in horticulture or agriculture at hospitals, residential homes and daycentres to set up projects based on these two fields of activity. They thus provide training, work and recreation for people who are physically and mentally handicapped. Volunteers must be over 18 years old and must have experience or training in horticulture and agriculture. The minimum length of posting is six months. Free accommodation and meals are provided together with an allowance of £20 per week (1988).

Land Use Volunteers can only consider people for interview if they are already resident in or visiting the UK. No registration fee is charged. Costs of travelling to the UK cannot be paid.

For an application form, contact Co-ordinator L.U.V. at the above address. Enclose SAE or International Reply Coupon.

**The Ladypool Project**
112 Whitecroft Road, Sheldon, Birmingham B26 3RG. Tel: (021) 743 3649

This project is a registered Christian charity which provides canal and sailing holidays for disabled children and adults, school groups and elderly people. The project operates all year round in the West Midlands but a sailing camp is also held at Dartmouth in June which only caters for disabled children. Volunteers are needed to help with all aspects of the project; cleaning boats, cooking, helping the guests, sailing, etc. The more volunteers the better as some boats are under-used due to lack of help. Apart from the camp which only lasts for a month, volunteers specify how long they can help, but the work does require a 24 hour commitment.

Volunteers should be over 17 years old and able to speak English and swim. Food and accommodation in bunks or on the decks of boats is provided, but everyone helps with chores. Most volunteers are Christians but this is not a requirement.

For further information write to Rev Tom Hodgson at the above address.

**Leonard Cheshire Foundation**
26-29 Maunsel Street, London SW1P 2QN. Tel: (01) 828 1822

The Leonard Cheshire Foundation is a registered charitable trust running homes throughout the UK for severely handicapped people, mainly physically disabled adults. Voluntary workers are needed in many homes to assist with the general care of residents who require help with washing, dressing and feeding as well as with hobbies and other recreational activities.

Volunteers should be aged 18 to 30 (the latter age is flexible). Preference is generally given to those planning to take up medical or social work as a career. Volunteers work up to a 39 hour, five day week, with one week's paid holiday for every four month's service. The minimum period is one month, but most jobs are for between three and 12 months.

Full board, lodging and pocket money of £20 per week is provided, this rate being reviewed each April. Volunteers must pay their own travel costs to the home. Overseas applicants must be able to speak good English. Applications should be sent to the Secretary to Personal Advisor at the above address.

**MENCAP — The Royal Society for Mentally Handicapped Children and Adults**
MENCAP Holiday Services Office, 119 Drake Street, Rochdale OL16 1PZ
Tel: (0706) 54111

Each year the MENCAP Holiday Services Office arranges a programme of holidays for mentally handicapped people of all ages, based in borrowed premises of many kinds — schools, farmhouses, adventure centres and guest houses — and covers the country from the Lake District to Cornwall. Some children are severely and multiply handicapped and will need almost constant attention. Others who are less handicapped can enjoy adventure or guest house holidays where the accent is placed upon enjoying outdoor activities or the 'traditional' type of seaside holiday. The success of these holidays depends upon volunteers who spend a week or two with them each year, receiving assistance towards their travelling costs with MENCAP providing for their board and lodgings.

Prospective volunteers should be over 18 years old, enjoy using their initiative and have strong arms, stamina and a sense of fun. Flexibility is essential due to the wide range of jobs to be done. Those interested should contact the Holidays Officer at the above address. Those interested in working in the north of England should apply directly to: Mencap North Division, 43 East Parade, Harrogate, North Yorks HG1 5LQ.

**Medical Research Council Dunn Clinical Nutrition Centre**
100 Tennis Court Road, Cambridge CB2 1QL. Tel: (0223) 312 334

The Unit is concerned with the effect of diet on health. As part of the studies accommodation is provided to volunteers in return for eating a specially prepared diet and, depending on the study, giving various samples. Diets vary but usually consist of subsets of normal food groups (eg high fibre versus low fibre). Volunteers are allowed free access to recreational facilities and may be permitted to have other employment but must only eat food specified by the diet. Up to six volunteers can be accommodated for studies ranging from a few days to several months.

A medical examination is compulsory prior to acceptance as certain medications and conditions may influence the outcome of the study. Volunteers must be literate and at least 20 and preferably 25 years old. Travel expenses are paid, pocket money of £2.85 per day is provided and an additional payment of £10 to £20 per study period is usually given.

Enquiries should be addressed to the Receptionist at the above address.

**Paradise House Association**
Paradise House, Painswick, Stroud, Glos. GL6 6TN. Tel: (0452) 813276

Paradise House is a long-term home for 30 adolescents and adults suffering from a wide range of mental handicaps who are in need of special care. Its activities are based on the work of Rudolf Steiner. The residents time is divided into training, work, adult education and recreation. Between 12 and 15 volunteers work as full members of staff for periods of at least a year helping to organise the activities, which include teaching the basics of housekeeping, gardening, farming, craft work etc.

Although specific skills in crafts, cooking, gardening or farming would be useful, it is more important that the volunteers should be enthusiastic and genuinely interested in this demanding work. There are no strict age limits, but applicants aged over 20 are preferred. Volunteers are provided with free board and lodging and pocket money of around £12.50 per week, and are also given £330 a year to pay for holidays.

Applications should be made to the Principal at the above address.

### Queen Elizabeth's Foundation for the Disabled
Leatherhead, Surrey KT22 0BN. Tel: (037 284) 2204

Approximately 300 helpers a year are needed in the Foundation's four units for the disabled in the south of England. The different units have different functions: Queen Elizabeth's Training College in Leatherhead provides vocational training and hostels for 192 disabled people; Dorincourt, off Oaklawn Road, Leatherhead, is a hostel and workshop for 55 severely disabled employees; Banstead Place, off Park Road, Banstead, Surrey is a residential centre for the assessment and further education of severely handicapped school leavers; and Lulworth Court on Chalkwell Esplanade, Westcliff-on-Sea, Essex, is a holiday and convalescent home for severely paralysed men and women. The voluntary work undertaken can vary from assisting with all kinds of fund-raising to helping the staff to look after and entertain those on holiday at Lulworth Court. Some 150 resident volunteers give their services in this way every summer.

Anyone over 18 is welcome to help: every possible qualification and skill are needed, but the only necessities are cheerfulness and a will to help. Travel expenses are refunded in part for those who have to travel long distances, and in full for those who live locally. Bed, board, and out of pocket expenses are paid to residential volunteers.

Applicants should contact the Director at the above address.

### Richard Cave Multiple Sclerosis Home
Servite Convent, Leuchie, North Berwick, East Lothian EH39 5NT. Tel: (0620) 2864

The Home is run by the Order of Servite Sisters as a holiday home for sufferers of multiple sclerosis of all ages. Around 25 volunteers a year are taken on to assist with health care, take patients for walks, write postcards for them and accompany them on special outings. Placements are for a minimum of two weeks from March until December or January and although it is possible to stay for as long as 12 months, most stays are for around eight weeks.

Driving licences, nursing qualifications and any other skills are useful but not essential. Applicants should be between 17 and 25 years old and English speaking. Board, lodging and £20 pocket money per week are provided.

Apply to the Matron at the above address.

### The Shaftesbury Society
2A Amity Grove, Raynes Park, London SW20 0LH. Tel: (01) 946 6635

The Society runs a holiday centre for the physically handicapped and elderly in Essex, which operates between April and October. 200 volunteers are needed each year, for a maximum of two weeks, to help the handicapped get about, dress, etc., to perform domestic duties, and help with the general running of the centre.

At any one time the Society likes to have someone who can drive, and someone with nursing experience at the centre. However volunteers with no special qualifications are welcome to apply. The minimum age for helpers is 17 years and the maximum age for new helpers is 70 years. Applicants should be sympathetic to the Christian aims and principles of the Society. Travel expenses are paid (from UK only) and food and lodging provided.

Applications should be sent to the Holidays Department at the above address.

### Stallcombe House
Sanctuary Lane, Woodbury, Nr. Exeter EX5 1EX. Tel: (0395) 32373

Stallcombe House is a residential farm community in East Devon for mentally disabled adults. Residents of the three households are involved in all aspects of the community, 55 acre farm and small organic horticultural area. Two volunteers are needed annually to help care for the residents: cooking, cleaning and assisting the residents with their daily activities including personal hygiene, hobbies and outings. Placements are for six to 12 months. Other volunteers are needed seasonally to help with farm and garden work, and local volunteers who can work daily or less frequently on an on-going basis will be welcomed.

Residential care volunteers must want to work with people in a caring environment. All volunteers need a working knowledge of English and should be in good mental and physical health. Residential care workers receive accommodation and pocket money of £15 per week but assistance with travel expenses depends on the individual volunteer's circumstances.

Applicants should apply to the Principal at the above address.

### Sue Ryder Foundation
Sue Ryder Home, Cavendish, Suffolk. Tel: (0787) 280252

An international foundation, running a number of homes for the sick and disabled of all age groups. Homes in Britain are for those suffering from cancer and Huntingtons Chorea, the elderly, the physically handicapped, and those who have been mentally ill. In addition, this care is combined with the renovation of historic houses to become new Sue Ryder Homes.

Volunteers are recruited for a minimum of eight weeks service; accommodation is provided, and pocket money of £10 may be paid, depending on the individual's circumstances. Helpers of any nationality or religion are welcome, provided that they are over 16. No special skills are required, although some knowledge of building or nursing would be much appreciated.

Applicants should apply to the above address.

### Winged Fellowship Trust
Angel House, Pentonville Road, London N1 9XD. Tel: (01) 833 2594

Every year some 2,000 helpers are needed in three holiday centres for the physically disabled, located in Surrey, Essex and Nottinghamshire. The purpose of the Trust is not only to provide holidays for severely physically disabled people, but also to enable the families who normally care for them at home to take perhaps their first worry-free holiday in years. Volunteers live in the centres and are given free board and lodging, during which time they not only take care of the physical needs of the guests and help with the domestic chores, but also provide companionship for them.

All that is required of volunteers is that they be over 17 years. Those with nursing qualifications would be particularly welcome. The centres are in operation for nine months of the year, so although travel expenses are not normally paid, there are certain times of the year when help is in short supply, and requests for assistance will be considered, especially if those who are volunteering are unemployed.

Those interested should apply to Leah Card at the above address.

## Woodlarks Camp Site Trust

Woodlarks Camp Site, Tilford Road, Farnham, Surrey GU10 3RN. Tel: (0252) 716279

Over the summer the camp site offers the opportunity for physically handicapped children and adults to have a camping holiday on a wooded camp site. Facilities include a heated outdoor swimming pool, a trampoline, and archery. The camp site is run entirely by voluntary help; every summer around 500 volunteers assist some 500 handicapped people.

Volunteers are normally taken on for the duration of one camp, lasting one week, but some stay for more than one camp.

Accommodation is provided in tents; a small fee is usually paid by helpers to cover the cost of food.

Those interested should contact the Honorary Secretary at the above address.

## Young Disabled on Holiday

c/o Miss Rosemary Girdlestone, 6 Yewland Drive, Boothsmere, Knutsford, Cheshire WA16 8AP. Tel: (0565) 4973

Some 80-100 volunteers are recruited annually to help with holidays for the young disabled. Young Disabled on Holiday began in 1970 with a group of young helpers who were involved in the parent organisation — Holidays for the Disabled — which provides a large scale annual holiday for all ages of physically handicapped. Noticing that the needs of the young were not adequately catered for on this type of holiday, they decided to organise a holiday purely for the young with an age limit for both disabled and helpers, of between 18 and 30. The organisation runs a wide range of interesting holidays in the UK and abroad. In addition to holidays at fixed locations there are boating and camping trips. Activities on the holidays include discotheques, swimming, horse riding, wheelchair sports, barbecues and banquets.

No special qualifications are needed and all nationalities are recruited. The age range is 18-30 years, and the length of time for which helpers are needed is usually one week. Helpers are asked to pay a contribution towards the cost: 40% of the total cost of holidays abroad and 25% on holidays in the UK.

Those interested should apply to the organisation at the above address.

# Youth Activities

### Brathay Exploration Group
Brathay Hall, Ambleside, Cumbria LA22 0HP. Tel: (05394) 33942

The Group organises expeditions and leader training courses in the British Isles and overseas. Expedition members are aged from 15 to 25 years old. Both projects combine adventure with scientific study and volunteers are needed to lead expeditions or to participate as assistant leaders. Volunteers should have experience of working with young people and have mountain, desert, forest, water, cave or scientific skills. Some help with office and support work is also needed.

Around 60 physically fit and enthusiastic volunteers are needed for periods of one week to three months between April and September. Expedition leaders and assistant leaders must be 17 to 65 years old and have attended a leader training course. Volunteers pay for all travel expenses but accommodation, food and insurance are provided.

Apply to the Expeditions Development Officer at the above address for an application form.

### The Down and Connor Youth Council
511 Ormeau Road, Belfast BT7 3GS, Northern Ireland. Tel: (0232) 644 688

The Council is the central body of a Church-based youth organisation that aims to encourage young people to become involved with their community by joining local youth groups in the Diocese of Down and Connor. Around 20 volunteers help the Council itself with its activities and a further 400 work in local clubs and units as youth leaders. In addition to various sports, recreational and social activities these clubs also offer educational training courses. Volunteers do not need any special skills or qualifications, but must be able to work within the beliefs, values and standards of the Catholic Church. The length of service is by arrangement. Accommodation is provided; pocket money may be granted, depending upon the individual placement and the resources available.

For further details contact the Director at the above address.

### Fellowship of Reconciliation
40-46 Harleyford Road, Vauxhall, London SE11 5AY. Tel: (01) 582 9054

The Fellowship organises two playschemes in Northern Ireland for Catholic and Protestant children aged five to 16 years. The sites chosen are usually deprived and segregated areas as the playschemes are an attempt at reconciliation. Volunteers act as play leaders and should be older than 18 years and able to cope with tense situations.

About 30 volunteers are needed for three weeks during the summer. Volunteers receive board and lodging but must pay their own travel expenses.

Apply to the Fieldworker, 67 Woodvale Road, Belfast BT13 3EZ.

### HF Holidays Ltd
142-144 Great North Way, London NW4 IE6. Tel: (01) 203 3381

HF Holidays was established in 1913 as a non profit-making society intended to further the open air leisure movement. In addition to its head office in Hendon it has 22 regional centres around the United Kingdom from which walking excursions, lasting five days each, are organised. It also organises walking holidays abroad from hotels in Austria, France, Italy, Norway, Spain, Switzerland and Yugoslavia.

Around 500 volunteers a year are needed to assist as walking and social leaders on these excursions. Volunteers are needed around the year for periods of up to six weeks. Accommodation, food and expense, in the form of a clothing allowance, are provided, and travel is paid for. Those interested should contact the Chief Executive at the above address.

### Ocean Youth Club
c/o The Bus Station, South Street, Gosport, Hants. PO12 1EP. Tel: (0705) 52841/2

The Ocean Youth Club needs volunteers to act as First and Second Mates on its expeditions and cruises from March to October. There are expeditions to Norway and the Outer Hebrides and cruises to Spain, Northern Europe, the Baltic and the Shetland Islands. The aim of the Club is to provide young people aged 12-24 with the opportunity to take part in adventurous offshore sailing, and so to develop their sense of awareness and responsibility and their ability to work in a team. It has bases throughout the UK. Volunteers work for weekends, weeks and occasionally, on the cruises, from two to three weeks.

All First Mates must have a Yachtmaster Certificate or Professional Sea Qualification, and must have been assessed as suitable by the Club. They should ideally be under 55. Second Mates must have been on an assessment cruise. All volunteers must be fit and able to swim. Accommodation is provided, as are safety and foul weather equipment. First Mates are asked to make a contribution towards their upkeep, and second mates pay £6.00 a day towards the cost of food.

Applications should be made to the Director at the above address.

### Pax Christi
9 Henry Road, London N4 2LH. Tel: (01) 800 4612

Pax Christi is the international peace movement of the Catholic Church. In July and August it recruits a total of 130 volunteers to help run 4 childrens playschemes in Northern Ireland and temporary youth hostels in school buildings in London and Oxford. Playscheme volunteers work for a minimum of three weeks while those in youth hostels work for either two or four weeks. They are given free board and lodging. No special skills or experience are expected of volunteers but they must be aged over 18. One of the main objectives of these schemes is to further the cause of international understanding, and volunteers taking part may be of different religions and nationalities.

Those interested should contact the Workcamps Organiser at the above address for further details.

**YMCA National Centre**

Fairthorne Manor, Curdridge, Southampton SO3 2GH. Tel: (04892) 5228

The YMCA conducts summer camps for young people at various centres in the United Kingdom. 25-30 volunteers are needed to act as domestic and catering staff, to instruct in various outdoor activities such as canoeing, climbing and archery and to conduct various social programmes such as games and campfire activities. Placements are from three to six months long.

Volunteers must speak fairly fluent English, be in good health and aged at least 18 years old. Preference will be given to applicants with a driving licence, first aid certificate or those skilled in counselling or outdoor pursuits. Volunteers will be reimbursed for second class rail travel from the point of entry to the United Kingdom and a small amount of pocket money will be paid. Accommodation is provided.

Those interested should apply to the Staff Tutor for Personnel at the above address.

**Youth Hostels Association Adventure Holidays**

8 St. Stephens Hill, St. Albans, Herts. AL1 2DY. Tel: (0727) 55215

Instructors and leaders are required in a variety of disciplines for the Association's Activity Holiday Programme: leaders for walking tours in England and Wales and sailing/watersports instructors in the Peak District and North Wales. The Association provides full board and accommodation plus £35 per week. Those who are available for two weeks or longer between March-September apply to Lesley Dreyfuss at the above address.

# Other Short Term Residential Opportunities

The following organisations have been included in the *Non Residential* chapter, but under certain circumstances or on specialised projects some residential volunteers are also needed.

British Paraplegic Sports Society
CHANGE
Erdington YMCA
Future Studies Centre
Green Deserts Ltd
International Flat
Jewish Blind Society

Meldreth Manor School
National Association of Probation
and Bail Hostels
North Norfolk Railway
Saturday Venture Association
Tools for Self Reliance

# Europe

## Multi-national

### The Across Trust
Crown House, Morden, Surrey SM4 5EW, UK. Tel: (01) 540 3897

The Trust is a registered charity that arranges weekly pilgrimages to Lourdes and holidays for the sick and disabled from Easter to November each year. These last about 10 days; places visited on the holidays include Austria, West Germany, Berlin, Switzerland, Assisi, Rome, and Holland. Transport is in "Jumbulances" and each group that goes consists of two or three nurses, a doctor (if deemed necessary), a chaplain, male and female helpers, all of whom volunteer their time and expenses to care for the eight or ten sick and handicapped in their "family". Across gives priority to patients in terminal illness, with progressive diseases, those confined to bed or wheelchair, and people with illnesses that make other forms of travel impossible and unsuitable. The group, with a maximum of 24 or 44 persons, live together as a "family" throughout their holiday, with everyone devoting themselves to the needs of their group, 24 hours a day. The work of caring for the sick and handicapped in each group is shared among the nurses and helpers. It is varied and includes dressing, washing, feeding, taking the handicapped to the baths, the grotto, processions, on excursions, shopping sprees, etc.

Volunteers need to be in good health and to be dedicated. Nurses and helpers pay the same as the rest of the "family" for the pilgrimage or holiday, that is about £300. Accommodation is provided in Lourdes at the Trust's purpose-built homes. Once volunteers apply, they will be offered the available dates.

Enquiries for the appropriate application form (e.g. doctor, nurse, chaplain or lay helper) should be sent to the Trust at the above address.

### Bouworde
Tiensesteenweg 145, 3200 Kessel-Lo, Belgium. Tel: 016/25 91 44

Bouworde needs around 800 volunteers to do manual work helping to improve unhealthy and unmodernised housing. These projects take place around the year in Flanders and also in France, Germany, Austria, Italy, Spain, Hungary, Yugoslavia and Poland in the summer.

The minimum period of work is three weeks. Free board, accommodation and insurance are provided, but volunteers must pay for their own travel costs. Participants must be aged at least 18. Applications to the above address.

### Ecumenical Youth Council in Europe
Youth Unit, British Council of Churches, Inter-Church House, 35-41 Lower Marsh, London SE1 7RL. Tel: (01) 620 4444

EYCE organises work camps for study, manual labour and social development in most countries all over Europe. The camps last two to three weeks throughout the summer and provide places for about 30 volunteers each. Both the activities and the studies have topical objectives, and aim to promote Christian understanding and faith. Participants contribute to their expenses and food costs, but accommodation is provided. Volunteers must be over 18 years of age and able to adapt to communal life in a Christian environment.

Applications may be sent to the Field Officer, Youth Unit, at the above address if from British citizens; the international headquarters of EYCE is at Budapest 62, PF.282, 1392 Hungary.

### Internationale Begegnung in Gemeinschaftsdiensten (IBG)
Schlosserstrasse 28, D-7000 Stuttgart-1, Germany

IBG was founded in 1965 by the boy scouts' association. International workcamps lasting three weeks are organised in close conjunction with the local villages. Chosen projects are designed to benefit the whole community, such as the construction of children's playgrounds, hiking paths, public gardens, afforestation, etc. Besides undertaking many projects in Germany, IBG organises camps in Switzerland. In exchange for 30 hours of work per week, volunteers receive food and lodging, insurance and some spare-time excursions.

Applicants between 18 and 30 from all over the world are welcome. Volunteers are advised to bring a sleeping bag and heavy footwear, as well as musical instruments, games and records from their own countries. The registration fee is 90DM (about £30) which should be submitted with the application form.

Enquirers to the above address will be sent a brochure containing dates and locations of the various workcamps.

### Internationale Bouworde
St. Annastraat 172 6524 GT Nijmegen, The Netherlands. Tel: (080) 226074

Internationale Bouworde (or International Building Companions) gives volunteers the opportunity to assist in socially useful building projects in about 35 countries throughout the world. Some 700-800 volunteers are recruited annually in Holland from early June to mid-September to participate in workcamps lasting from two to five weeks. British campers will be integrated in mainly Dutch groups. In Europe workcamps take place in Belgium, Holland, Germany, France, Switzerland, Denmark, Austria, Italy, Spain, Portugal, Greece and Turkey. The actual construction work provides the most important element of the camps, and volunteers are expected to treat it as such. It acts as a focus for the other aspects such as the encounter with fellow-participants and with the local population.

Volunteers should be at least 18 years old and be able to meet the physical demands of the camps (eight hours a day of labouring work). They must be willing to adapt to foreign attitudes and life-styles. The volunteer himself has to pay travel costs to Holland, pocket money, and a contribution to the general costs of the organisation, ranging from £15 for Belgium and Holland to £95 for Greece and Turkey (the average contribution is about £40).

Internationale Bouworde pays travel costs from a central point in Holland to the camp abroad, insurance, and provides board and lodging. All nationalities are welcome.

British and Dutch applications should be made to the Director at the above address. Other nationalities should apply to the relevant address from the list below:

Osterreichischer Bauorden, Hornesgasse 4, A-1031 Wien, Austria
Bouworde, Tiensesteenweg 145, B-3200 Kessel-lo, Belgium
Les Compagnons Batisseurs, Rue des Immeubles Industriels 5, F-75 011 Paris, France
Les Compagnons Batisseurs, Rue Notre-Dame de Graces 63, B-5400 March-en-Famenne, Belgium
Internationaler Bauorden, Liebigstrasse 23, D-6520 Worms-Horchheim, Germany
Internationale Bouworde, St Annastraat 172, NL-6524 GT Nijmegen, Holland
I.B.O. Soci Costruttori, Via C. Battisti 3, I-20 071 Casalpusterlengo (MI) Italy
Companheiros Construtores, Rua Pedro Monteiro 3-1, P-3000, Coimbra, Portugal

## TOC H

1 Forest Close, Wendover, Aylesbury, Bucks, UK. Tel: (0296) 623911

About 600 volunteers over the age of 17 are needed annually to participate in about 60 projects including playschemes, camps, discovery holidays, work with the handicapped and elderly and community work at home and abroad. Most of the camps are conducted in Britain, although there are also a few vacancies in Germany. The principle is to build a friendly and caring relationship during the one week camps.

All nationalities are welcome to apply and the only requirements are a friendly compassionate nature and willingness to work hard, often in emotionally or physically demanding situations. A driving licence could be useful. Board and accommodation are provided. The minimum age is 17.

Enquiries should be sent to the Publicity Officer at the above address enclosing a stamped self-addressed envelope.

## Tutmonda Esperantista Junulara Organizo—TEJO (World Organisation of Young Esperantists)

Nieuwe Binnenweg 176, NL-3015 BJ Rotterdam, Netherlands. Tel: (010) 361539

Besides arranging Esperanto courses for workcamps of other organisations, TEJO also organises its own summer camps in several countries, mostly in Europe. The projects include working on archaeological sites and enhancing the environment. Volunteers are recruited for two to five weeks and accommodation is usually provided.

No prior experience is needed, although a few camps are limited to Esperanto speakers, some camps include Esperanto lessons for beginners. The camps are usually composed of people aged 16-30.

Enquiries should be sent to the Commission of External Relations at the above address.

### Universities and Colleges Christian Fellowship (UCCF)

38 De Montfort Street, Leicester LE1 7GP. Tel: (0533) 551700

All of the Fellowship's activities have Christian teachings and evangelical aims as their basis. Around 300 volunteers are needed to take part in evangelical teams, help with camps, community activities and church-based work in Britain, Ireland and Europe. These activities may last from one week to one month during the summer vacation.

Volunteers may be of any nationality but must be committed Christians. Languages may be required for some evangelical teams in Europe. Most activities require a contribution for board and food although some activities may pay expenses. The volunteer meets all travel expenses.

UCCF also publish Vac Pac, a directory of summer volunteer activities for Christian students. It is available each February at no cost.

Those interested in UCCF's activities or Vac Pac should apply to the Assistant to Head of Student Ministries at the above address.

# Belgium and Holland

### Annee Diaconale Belge

Service Protestant de la Jeunesse, Rue de Champ de Mars, 5, 1050 Bruxelles, Belgium. Tel: (02) 513 24 01

Part of the Service Protestant de la Jeunesse, or Protestant Youth Office, arranges for volunteers to spend between 9 and 12 months in Christian or other institutions in Belgium. Around 10 volunteers a year are placed in childrens homes, old peoples homes, etc. Volunteers receive free food, accommodation and laundry, their travelling expenses and pocket money of around £65 per month. Placements begin in September.

Participants should be aged between 18 and 26 and have a basic knowledge of French. Whatever their background all candidates' applications will be welcome. Possession of a driving licence and/or a teaching certificate would be advantageous.

Contact the Secretary at the above address for further details.

### Archeolo-J

Avenue Paul Terlinden 23, 1330 Rixensart, Belgium. Tel: (02) 653 8268

Archeolo-J organises international workcamps at archaeological excavations in Belgium. Volunteers assist with all aspects of the excavations; digging, drawing finds and surveying the sites. Around 100 volunteers aged 12 years and older are needed to work for periods of three weeks in July. Accommodation in tents is provided.

Write to the President at the above address for more information.

**Belgian Evangelical Mission**
60 Main Street, Lubenham, Market Harborough, Leicester LE16 9TF. Tel: (0858) 34627

The Belgian Evangelical Mission conducts summer evangelical campaigns in a number of towns and villages in both French and Dutch speaking Belgium. Around 30 volunteers from Britain are needed to join the international campaign teams which last from two to six weeks. Another six to ten volunteers are needed to join church-planting teams, also in Belgium. These teams last from one to two years, from September to July each year.

Volunteers may be of any nationality provided they are Christians and can provide a home church recommendation. Applicants for the church-planting teams must speak either French or Dutch and pay around £205 per month. Summer evangelical team members pay £24 per week and a £5 deposit. All volunteers must pay for their own travel but accommodation is provided.

Those interested should apply to the Administrator at the above address.

**Entraide et Amitie ASBL**
9 rue du Boulet, 1000 Bruxelles. Tel: (02) 512 36 32

This organisation recruits and places volunteers in hospitals and institutions for the elderly in Belgium. The emphasis is on humanitarian work; speaking with patients, helping them with their meals and generally assisting the patients with their daily routine. Around 450 volunteers are needed annually, all year round. Normally volunteers help for blocks of 12 days, working four or more hours a day.

Volunteers must speak French and be prepared to attend a one day preparation session. Accommodation is not provided but travelling expenses may be paid.

For further information contact the Psychologist at the above address.

**SIW, Internationale Vrijwilligersprojekten**
Willemstraat 7, Utrecht, Netherlands. Tel: (030) 317721

SIW organises international workcamps in the Netherlands during the months of July and August for young people from East and West Europe. The work may involve working in houses for battered women, social work in institutes for the handicapped or playschemes for children. Camps last two or three weeks but volunteers may plan to attend two in succession. As a rule, the working week will consist of 30-35 hours in five days. Leisure time is free; however some group expeditions may be arranged free of charge for the 15 to 25 volunteers. Each camp has its own cultural programme and some camps devote time to discussions and excursions around a central topic.

Volunteers must be between 18 and 30 years of age. There are no restrictions on nationality and so there are usually between seven and ten nationalities represented in each camp. Housing and sanitary facilities are always provided in schools, farms, huts and tents, though they may be primitive. There is a registration fee of DFL65 but in special circumstances this may be reduced.

Enquiries from outside Holland should be sent to the workcamps organisation in the applicant's own country. In Britain this is the Quaker Workcamps.

## Universala Esperanto-Asocio

Nieuwe Binneweg 176, 3015 BJ Rotterdam, Netherlands. Tel: (010) 4361539

Esperanto is the international language invented by Zamenhof, a Polish oculist, in 1887. It now has more than a million speakers throughout the world. The Universala Esperanto-Asocio is the world organisation for the advancement of Esperanto. Its Head Office is situated in Rotterdam, where a staff of ten to twelve workers from various parts of the world, both paid and voluntary, are involved in day-to-day administration, accounts, mail-order services, congress organisation, editing and production of books and magazines, and maintaining a library. The Association has another office in New York to deal with contacts with the UN. Thus the Association needs one or two volunteers from time to time to help with its work. The minimum period of service for volunteers is nine months, the maximum one year.

Volunteers must speak Esperanto fluently as this is the working language of the organisation. Other qualifications may be necessary depending on the specific vacancy. Applicants must be between 18 and 29 years of age. Free accommodation is provided, and insurance and a small living allowance is paid. Residents of EEC countries do not need a visa or work permit. Volunteers from other countries will need both. A period of six to twelve months should be allowed for the acquisition of these permits.

Applications should be made to the Director at the above address.


# Eire

## An Oige: the Youth Irish Hostel Association

39 Mountjoy Square, Dublin 1, Eire. Tel: (01) 363111

The 55 youth hostels around Ireland operated by An Oige are run almost entirely by volunteers, 150 of whom are taken on each year. The jobs to be done include maintaining the hostels, doing office work, fund raising, taking part in conservation work in the countryside and arranging and leading groups. A number of volunters are specifically needed to work as Assistant Hostel Wardens over the summer season, from June to September. Volunteers receive free overnight accommodation and, in some cases, pocket money and travel expenses. Those interested should contact the Officer in charge of Hostel Wardens at the above address.

## An Taisce - The National Trust for Ireland

The Tailors' Hall, Back Lane, Dublin 8, Eire. Tel: (01) 541786

An Taisce is concerned with the conservation of all aspects of the physical environment, natural or man-made. It has over 5,000 members and organises national and local projects in Ireland to focus attention on environmental issues. Projects take place all year round. Membership is open to all and an on-going commitment from members is desirable.

Enquiries should be addressed to the Central Office Secretary at the above address.

### Comhchairdeas: Irish Workcamp Movement
7 Lower Ormand Quay, Dublin 1, Eire. Tel: (01) 729681

This Organisation promotes the organisation of workcamps in Ireland and places 12-20 volunteers on each camp. Camps involve working with disabled people, building adventure playgrounds, organising playschemes, renovating and/or decorating work. Food and accommodation of a basic nature are provided. Applicants must be over 18 years of age. Depending on the type of project, there are frequently positions for handicapped volunteers.

In England enquiries should be sent to Quaker Workcamps.

### Glencree Centre for Reconciliation
Glencree, Bray, Co. Wicklow, Eire. Tel: Glencree 860963/2

Every year the Centre require six long-term volunteers who spend nine months to one year living and working in the Centre. Four short-term volunteers are taken on for three months from June to August.

Volunteers are responsible for the day to day maintenance of the centre and also work in such areas as the farm, garden, reception, office, bedrooms, laundry, and catering. Volunteers assist in the running of various programmes including farm education for young people, youth encounter programmes, workcamps and environmental programmes.

Community living is an important aspect of the work and prior experience or an avid interest in community living is a valuable asset. In general, volunteers need to be self-initiating, motivated and interested in peace related work.

Board and accommodation are provided and a weekly stipend of £20. Minimum age 20 years.

If interested write to the Centre, c/o the Centre Co-ordinator. Long term volunteers' term commences in March of each year.

### Glen River YMCA National Centre
143 Central Promenade, Newcastle, Co. Down BT33 0HN, Northern Ireland. Tel: (03967) 24488

The Centre is an outdoor education centre which needs volunteers to act as domestic staff, cooks, instructors in outdoor pursuits such as canoeing, hill walking, archery, etc. and tutors in personal development. Around 14 volunteers are required for eight or nine weeks during summer and in winter two or three volunteers are needed for weekend activities.

Volunteers should be physically and mentally fit, aged 17 years or older and fluent in English. Volunteers for instructor positions should be skilled in the relevant activity and for volunteers older than 25, a driver's licence is useful. Board, lodging and pocket money of £18 per week are provided.

Applications should be made to the Centre Director at the above address.

### Groundwork (Ireland)
43 Bayview Drive, Killiney, Co. Dublin, Eire. Tel: (01) 822563

Groundwork organises workcamps of varying duration in order to conserve areas of natural wealth currently under threat in Ireland. Projects include conserving the oakwoods of the west coast of Ireland and the raised bogs of the midlands. Volunteers are needed for various tasks including removing rhododendrons from native woodlands and filling in drains in threatened raised bogs. The work is usually quite strenuous. Workcamps are usually conducted in summer and autumn; those on the oakwoods last for one week while one day or weekend camps are used to care for the bogs.

Volunteers must be in good health and aged between 16 and 65 years. Accommodation is provided.

Those interested should contact the Secretary at the above address for a brochure and application form around March of each year.

## Irish Georgian Society
Leixlip Castle, Leixlip, Co. Kildare, Eire. Tel: (01) 244211

This society aims to preserve the architectural heritage of Ireland by carrying out rescue and repair work on buildings. Under supervision, volunteers help with the restoration of old buildings. Work includes stripping and reglazing windows, painting, clearing gardens, etc. and sightseeing trips are organised on the weekends. Around 50 volunteers are needed annually, from May through to the end of August, usually for two week periods.

No special skills are required and volunteers may be of any nationality. Accommodation is provided but volunteers pay around £15 per week towards food costs.

Those interested should contact the Executive Director at the above address.

## Irish Wildlife Conservancy
Ruttledge House, 8 Longford Place, Monkstown, Co. Dublin, Eire

The Irish Wildlife Conservancy undertakes reserve management, species protection and environmental surveys and research in the Republic of Ireland. Around ten volunteers a year are needed to assist with this work as voluntary wardens for periods of one week to three months. Volunteers should be over 16 years old and in good health. Previous ornithological experience is an advantage. Accommodation in caravans or camp sites is usually provided.

Those interested should write to the Reserves Division at the above address for further information and an application form, enclosing a SAE.

## The Simon Community
P.O. Box 1022, Lower Sherriff Street, Dublin 1, Eire. Tel: (01) 711606

The Simon Community is a voluntary organisation which provides accommodation, food and companionship for homeless and rootless people. Full and part-time volunteers run night shelters, community houses, soup runs and other services for the homeless in Cork, Dublin, Dundalk and Galway. All nationalities are welcome and no formal or special qualifications are required. Personal qualities such as compassion, sensitivity, and adaptability are most important. Fluency in English and the ability to communicate are essential.

Accommodation and a weekly pocket money allowance are provided. Volunteers are expected to stay for a minimum of three months and two weeks holiday with an allowance are given every three months.      Further information can be obtained from the National Director.

# France

### Arab World Ministries
2 Radmoor Road, Loughborough, Leics., LE11 3BS. Tel: (0509) 239525

There are opportunities to help with routine clerical and secretarial work at a media centre in Marseille. Social activities are run in conjunction with evangelistic work among North African immigrants in France. Accommodation is provided but participants are expected to provide for their own financial needs at a level which is set annually by the mission. Volunteers are recruited for a minimum period of one month, with the maximum being two years. All nationalities are welcome. The work begins with an orientation period in which volunteers can become acquainted with the customs and beliefs of North Africans.

A driving licence and a knowledge of French are useful but not essential. Participants should be at least 18 years of age. All enquiries should be sent to the above address.

### Association pour le Developpement de l'Archeologie Urbaine a Chartres
12 rue du Cardinal Pie, 28000 Chartres, France. Tel: 37 21 35 65

This association undertakes urban rescue excavation work at sites in the town of Chartres, France. The project is a long term research project on the archaeological and historical development of Chartres, covering its economic, cultural and social evolution from Roman and medieval times. Volunteers are needed to dig and also work in the laboratory, washing, classifying, repairing and drawing finds. Work takes place five days a week. Recruitment is for a minimum of three weeks during the months of April to October.

No special skills are needed but volunteers must be at least 18 years old, or if 16 or 17 have parental consent. Food and accommodation is provided but volunteers must pay a £5 registration fee.

Apply to the Secretary at the above address.

### Association le Mat
Le Viel Audon, 07120 Balazuc, France. Tel: 75 37 73 80

This Association undertakes restoration, reconstruction, farm and agricultural activities at the village of Audon in the Ardeche region of France. Around 300 volunteers are needed each summer to assist with this work, although only groups of 80 people can be catered for at any one time. Volunteers can choose their daily task from those offered as long as they work at least five hours per day.

Volunteers should be 17 to 25 years old. Camping areas are provided and some beds are available but volunteers must pay for food (about £4 daily), £1 for insurance and a joining fee of around £5.

Those interested should contact the Co-ordinator at the above address for more information.

## Association des Paralysés de France
17 Boulevard Blanqui, Paris 13. Tel: 580 82 40

The Association needs some 1,500 volunteers each year to help in its work with people suffering from paralysis. Much of the work is a matter of helping the handicapped get around, i.e. pushing wheelchairs etc. and assisting the handicapped when they go on holiday usually in specially organised groups.

Volunteers may be of any nationality, but must be at least 18 years old and enjoy good health. Boys who can speak at least a little French are especially needed. Expenses and pocket money are paid. The length of time volunteers work for is a month on the holidays. No special qualifications are needed.

Applications should be made to the Holiday Officer at the above address.

## Chantiers d'Etudes Médiévales
4 rue du Tonnelet Rouge, 67000 Strasbourg. Tel: 88 37 17 20

These workcamps lasting between 10 and 15 days undertake to restore and maintain mediaeval buildings and sites. The projects include old houses near the Cathedral in Strasbourg, two fortified chateaux at Ottrott near Strasbourg and a site along the Rhone River in Ardèche. These sites become cultural and recreational centres. Food and basic accommodation (in tents or huts) is provided for the volunteers on the payment of fees. These vary between £30 and £50 per session. Apart from preserving historically important buildings and converting them into places which will benefit the community, the Chantiers d'Etudes Médiévales also aims to provide the participants with cultural enrichment and physical exercise.

Applicants of all nationalities will be accepted for the 250 places available each year. The minimum age limit is 16 years, although applicants under the age of 18 required parental permission.

Enquiries should be sent to the Secretary at the above address.

## Club du Vieux Manoir
10 rue de la Cossonnerie, 75001 Paris. Tel: (1) 45 08 80 40

This non profit making association is dedicated to the rescue and restoration of endangered monuments and historical sites. Each year 4,000 volunteers contribute to the preservation of France's heritage and at the same time acquire manual and technical skills as well as some knowledge of archaeology and history. Apart from working on a site, club members may take part in research, publication or committee work. There are three permanent sites: at Guise in the province of Aisne, at Argy in Indre and at Pontjoint in Oise. Volunteers are invited to arrive at any time provided they come equipped with sleeping bag and camp cooking utensils. Special arrangements can be made for groups of scouts, factory employees and children from holiday camps. There are several summer vacation sites throughout the country at which the minimum length of stay is 15 days. Participants must pay 48 francs per day for their board and lodging, which may entail accommodation in the monument itself.

All volunteers must be very fit. Initial membership in the Club du Vieux Manoir costs 50 francs. The minimum age is 13; however, for the centre for specialised courses in restoration at the Château d'Argy, the minimum age is 17. All nationalities may participate.

Further details may be obtained by sending a stamped self-addressed envelope to Thérèse Beckelnyck, Animatrice Permante, at the above address.

## Collège Cévénol (International Workcamp)
Chambon-sur-Lignon 43400, Haute Loire. Tel: 71 59 72 52

This workcamp takes place during July each year for three weeks at the Collège Cévénol International in the Massif Central. The surrounding country is wooded and mountainous and provides an invigorating setting for the camp activities. The present school at Chambon-sur-Lignon has been partly built by workcamps held at the site, and in fact it is this construction work, landscaping and maintenance which forms the work done in the summer. The camps also offer language classes for foreigners run by the campers themselves. In the evenings discussion groups meet or those who wish to can use the time for relaxation. There are sometimes excursions to the summer festival at Avignon. It will suit those who like a bracing experience, and mixing with young people of all nationalities.

Volunteers should be aged between 16 and 30 years, and in good health. Accommodation is provided at the school itself, food is provided, and all other facilities. The participation fee is about 600 F, some scholarships being available. Campers are expected to join in all group activities. All nationalities are welcome.

Application forms can be obtained from Monsieur le Directeur du Collège Cévénol, Camp International de Travail, at the above address.

## Cotravaux
11 rue de Clichy, 75009 Paris. Tel: 48 74 79 20

Cotravaux is a co-ordinating body for voluntary work organisations in France. It aims to develop the services provided by workcamps, and to find new workcamp opportunities. The kind of work done by the individual organisations covers a wide range including projects in cities, villages, the countryside and wooded areas, help for the homeless, tourism and youth, and intervention when natural disasters occur. Most workcamps take place during the summer vacations, from the end of June to September. A few workcamps of shorter duration are open during the Easter and Christmas vacations. Most workcamps last three to four weeks. During the summer, teams can succeed each other at the same work site. Organisations with which Cotravaux has links include Concordia, Moulin des Apprentis, Neige et Merveilles, Service Civil International, Jeunesse et Reconstruction, Alpes de Lumieres, Compagnons Bâtisseurs, Etudes et Chantiers, Union R.E.M.P.ART., Solidarités Jeunesses M.C.P. and Chantiers Rencontres Internationales. For information on the individual organisations volunteers should apply to each one directly.

Conditions for participation, type of accommodation provided, and expenses paid, obviously vary from organisation to organisation. As stated above, volunteers should apply to the individual organisations for information: their addresses can be obtained from Cotravaux.

## The Department of Archaeology and Prehistory

Sheffield University, Sheffield S10 2TN. Tel: (0742) 78555

The Department is conducting archaeological excavations and fieldwork mainly in the Auvergne in France around Clemont Ferrand. The objective is to learn more about the origin and development of urbanisation in the area in the 2nd and 1st centuries B.C. and its impact on rural settlement, and the interaction between man, settlement and environment in post glacial times.

A small number of volunteers are needed to help the Department's own students with excavation, processing of finds and surveying. The excavations normally take place from July to September, and participants should be prepared to stay for at least three to four weeks. Accommodation is provided on a camp site, and meals are taken at the camp base, a late medieval house, at a cost of 30 F a day.

Those interested should write to Dr J. R. Collis, Reader, at the above address.

## Département d'Histoire Université

57 rue P. Taittinger, 51 100 Reims. Tel: 08-27-48

About 20 volunteers are required for three weeks in July or August to assist in the archaeological excavation of a 10th-12th century motte and bailey castle of the Counts of Champagne at Charot-Epernay. Volunteers of all nationalities are welcome but they should be able to speak French or English, be in good health and at least 18 years old.

Accommodation is provided, and those who have archaeological experience receive free meals. Others must pay for the evening meal.

Applications should be sent to Annie Renoux at the above address.

## France Mission Trust

The Old Chapel, Chapel Lane, Minchinhampton, Gloucester GL6 9DL. Tel: (0453) 884454

This Trust offers volunteer opportunities in France to evangelical Christians. Volunteers may join evangelical teams during Easter and summer vacations, undertake building and decorating of church properties or perform bi-lingual secretarial work. Around 20 volunteers are recruited annually; team members usually serve a minimum of two weeks while other volunteers work for a maximum of two years.

Volunteers must be at least 18 years old and of normal health. Evangelical team members must speak conversational French and pay for their travel, insurance and board, although accommodation is provided. Other volunteers need to be skilled and experienced in the appropriate field and must pay for their travel and insurance but receive free board and lodging.

British residents should apply to the Honorary Secretary at the above address while other volunteers should apply to the Trust offices in their own countries.

### Groupe Archeologique du Mesmontois
Mairie de Macain, 21410 Pont de Pany, France. Tel: 80 30 05 20

The organisation undertakes archaeological digs and restoration work near Dijon, France. About 40 volunteers are needed to help with tasks which include sketching and photographing the finds, model making and restoration. The digs last from one to eight weeks and are held during July and August.

Volunteers skilled in any of the above areas are especially welcome but no qualifications or skills are obligatory. The minimum age of volunteers accepted is 17 years. Volunteers pay about £5 per week towards the board and lodging provided.

Those interested should apply to M. Roussel at the above address.

### Labo Anthropologie: Equipe de Recherche no. 27 du C.N.R.S.
Campus de Beaulieu, 35042 Rennes Cedex, France. Tel: 99 28 61 09

This project is concerned with archaeological digs in Brittany, France. Around 60 volunteers are needed to take part in the digs held during summer each year.

Volunteers should be at least 18 years old, physically capable of undertaking outdoor work and interested in archaeology. Camping and board are provided.

Those interested should apply to Dr J. L. Monnier at the above address.

### Laboratoire d'Ethnologie Prehistorique
31 rue du Proffesseur Calmette, 92190 Meudon, France. Tel: 1 45 34 39 13

This organisation undertakes an archaeological excavation at Verberie in France. The aim of the project is to reconstruct the everyday life and economy of the reindeer hunters who inhabited the area by excavating the open air site consisting of hut structures and hearths. Around ten volunteers are needed each summer to assist with the diggings and to be trained in fine excavation techniques. Volunteers are normally recruited for three week periods.

Volunteers with archaeological experience are preferred. No particular qualifications are required but the minimum age limit is 18 years. Board, lodging and insurance are provided.

Those interested should apply to Dr F. Audouze at the above address.

### Muséum National d'Histoire Naturelle
Institut de Paleontologie Humaine, 1 rue Rene Panhard, 75013 Paris

The Professor at this museum organises archaeological excavations in France each year from April to August. Volunteers are required to assist with these excavations and they should be prepared to stay for the duration of the camp which is between two weeks and one month. There is a camping site but volunteers must provide their own tents, etc. They must also pay their own travelling expenses although expenses will be paid while at the camp. Further information can be obtained from Henry de Lumley at the above address.

### Ministère de la Culture

Direction de l'Archeologie, 4 rue d'Aboukir, 75002 Paris, France. Tel: 40 15 80 00

The Ministry compiles an annual list of archaeological excavations requiring volunteers in France. The list is drawn up during spring for that summer season. Around 10,000 volunteers are needed in total, as assistants in all aspects of archaeological excavations for periods of two weeks to one month. The minimum age of volunteers accepted is usually 18 years. No special skills are needed for most teams but some leaders may require experienced volunteers. Accommodation in houses or at campsites is provided.

Write to the Information Scientist of Excavations to receive a list.

### Ministère de la Culture et de la Communication

Direction Regionale des Affaires Culturelles, Circonscription des Antiquites Historiques et Prehistoriques, 6 rue du Chapitre, 35044 Rennes Cedex, France. Tel: 99 79 21 32

This Ministry organises archaeological excavations in Brittany. About 200 volunteers are needed to assist with all aspects of the excavations. The excavations occur mainly from April to September for periods of two to four weeks and cover from prehistoric times to the Middle Ages.

Volunteers must be at least 18 years old, need a basic knowledge of French and those with practical archaeological or related experience are welcome. Good health and an anti-tetanus injection are essential. Accommodation is provided.

Write to the Director at the above address for detailed information on the sites, enclosing an International Reply Coupon.

### Pax Christi

44 Rue de la Sante, 75014 Paris, France

The French branch of Pax Christi, the international peace movement of the Catholic Church, runs temporary youth hostels over the summer in Avignon, Lourdes, Vezelay, Trébeurden, Le Gue du Loir and La Madone de Fenestre. Each of these hostels, or 'Centres de Rencontres Internationales' is run by an international team of about 10 volunteers.

Volunteers should be aged over 18 and be prepared to live together as a close Christian Community sharing the work, leisure time, etc.

For further information contact Fr. Ronan Le Henaff at the above address.

### Pierre Seche de Vaucluse

La Cornette, 84800 Salimane, France. Tel: 90 20 71 82

This organisation studies and conserves the dry-stone heritage of the plateau of Vaucluse. During the summer workcamps are held for volunteers of all nationalities. Around 50 volunteers are needed to help with dry-stone walling preservation but no special skills are required. Workcamps are only for those aged at least 16 years and last for around 15 days.

Write to the Treasurer at the above address for more information.

### La Riobe

c/o J. P. Burin, President, 4 Rue Jobbe Duval, F 75015 Paris, France. Tel: (01) 48 28 87 05

In August La Riobe organises an archaeological dig lasting for two weeks on a Gallo-Roman site 72 km to the east of Paris; for the rest of the year work is consducted over the weekends. The work to be done includes digging, cleaning and restoring the finds and organising a collection of finds. Around 20 volunteers help in the summer workcamp, and between 60 and 70 in all take part in the weekend camps. Participants should be aged 18 or over and speak enough French to make themselves understood. They should also possess proof that they have had an anti-tetanus injection. They must also pay around 15 francs for insurance and 35 francs a day towards their food.

For further details contact Mr J. P. Burin, President, at the above address.

### Service Archeologique du Musee de la Chartreuse

191 rue St-Albin, 59500 Douai, France. Tel: 27 87 26 63

This organisation conducts archaeological excavations in the medieval town of Douai. Volunteers are needed to assist with the excavations and drawing maps. Workcamps generally consist of 150 volunteers for a minimum of 15 days during the months of July and August. All volunteers are welcome provided that they speak English or French and are at least 18 years old. No special skills are necessary but volunteers with experience may be able to obtain a staff position. Innoculation against tetanus is advisable.

Accommodation is provided and staff receive expenses and pocket money. A registration fee of £10 to cover insurance costs must be submitted with the application form.

Contact the Director at the above address for more details.

### La Sabranenque

Saint Victor la Coste, 30290 Laudun, France. Tel: (33) 66 50 05 05

La Sabranenque is a non-profit-making organisation working for the preservation of the rural habitat by restoring abandoned rural sites for present day use. Saint Victor la Coste serves as the headquarters for the organisation as work projects are mainly in southern France, although there are three sites in Italy. Around 150 volunteers are needed for work which includes restoration of roofs, terraces, walls and paths, planting local tree species, and the reconstruction of small houses. Techniques are learned on-the-job. Workcamps last a minimum of two or three weeks during the summer, and occasionally stays of two months or more are possible. Spring and autumn workcamps are for volunteers who speak French as a second language.

Volunteers must be at least 18 years old and in good health. No language skills or previous experience are required for summer workcamps, but non-EEC volunteers must obtain a French visa for their period of stay. Board and lodging are provided at a cost of about £200 per two-week project.

Applications to the Programme Co-ordinator at the above address.

## Service de l'Urbanisme Archeologie
Hotel de Ville, BP 667 59033, Lille, Cedex, France. Tel: 20 49 50 00

Every year this organisation takes on between 25 and 30 volunteers to assist with archaeological excavations in Lille, France. The excavations take place during the summer with workcamps lasting from one to three weeks. Volunteers of all nationalities are welcome to help with all activities although some knowledge of French is preferred, and the minimum age is 17 years. Board and lodging are provided.

Volunteers should apply to the Town Archaeologist at the above address.

## Union REMP.ART (pour la Réhabilitation et L'Entretien des Monuments et du Patrimonie Artistique)
1 rue des Guillémites, 75004 Paris. Tel: (1) 42 71 96 55

Over 150 workcamps are operated in every part of France. About 4,000 volunteers are employed to restore and maintain chateaux, churches, villages and the old quarters of cities which are of unique historical or cultural value. REMP.ART strives to revivify rather than merely preserve ancient buildings and sites. Another of their aims is to remain sensitive to the temperament and requirements of the local community. Volunteers are accepted for weekend workcamps and for spring and summer vacation projects, although the usual minimum length of stay is 15 days. Participants must pay 30 or 40 francs per day for food and accommodation in cabins or tents. For people whose tastes, studies or professional aspirations have prompted an interest in archaeology, architecture or the history of art and ecology, the association organises courses which provide an opportunity to learn the practical techniques of restoration.

Volunteers of all nationalities are welcome, although knowledge of some French language would be an asset. The minimum age is 16 years in some cases and 18 for more difficult jobs.

Applications and enquiries should be sent to the above address.

## Unité de Recherche Archeologique No 12
Centre National de la Recherche Scientifique, 3 rue Michelet, 75006 Paris, France

This Unit is a Paris-based team of professional archaeologists, running a long term fieldwork project in the river Aisne valley (about 140 km north-east of Paris). The archaeology of this valley is being destroyed by gravel excavation and this project aims to combine rescue excavation of the threatened sites with studies of the region. About 20 volunteers of all nationalities are needed as diggers during summer excavation programmes from July to late September.

Volunteers should be aged 18 to 40 years and of reasonable fitness as eight hour days are worked. Some knowledge of spoken French is desirable as is an interest in archaeology. The minimum stay is for two weeks. Accommodation in farm buildings or camp sites, food and daily hot showers are provided.

Write to the Director at the above address for more details, leaving enough time to apply by early June.

# Germany, Switzerland and Austria

## Aktionsgmeinschaftsdienst für den Frieden (AGDF) (Action Committee Service for Peace)
Blücherstrasse 14, D-5300 Bonn, Germany. Tel: 02 28/2291 92

This is an umbrella committee for 20 Christian, peace development and social service organisations within Germany, many of which recruit from around the world. The function of AGDF is primarily a coordinating one, acting as liaison between its member organisations, willing volunteers, the government and the Federation of Protestant Churches. Altogether approximately 5,000 persons per year participate in workcamps, work with conscientious objectors and other services supported by the members. The type of work and length of employment varies according to the country of service and the type of volunteer service. There are both short term projects of under three months and longer terms of up to two or three years in development services.

Applications which are sent to the above address will be forwarded to the appropriate organisation. These include Aktionsgemeinschaft Friedenswoche Minden: Aktion Suhnezeichen Friedendienste; Eirene, International Christian Service for Peace; Christlicher Friedensdienst (CFD); Versöhnungsbund; Welfriedensdient; and Oekumenisches Begegnungszentrum.

## Arbeitskreis Freiwillige Soziale Dienste
Stafflenbergstr. 76, 7000 Stuttgart, Germany. Tel: (0711) 2159 420 417

This organisation, which is somewhat similar to CSV in the UK, organises volunteer work for one year in the Evangelical church of the Federal Republic of Germany and West Berlin. Volunteers work mostly with people who are in difficulty and in need of a helping hand, for example, with ill, handicapped or old people, but work also to a certain extent in kindergartens or homes for children and young people.

Throughout the one year's programme there are seminars and discussions led by trained group leaders. Getting in contact with other people during the practical work and the seminars, implies the chance for each volunteer to increase his personal growth and learning through new experiences.

Volunteers need a good knowledge of the German language, an ability to speak it being most important. They should be 18 and 25 years of age. Accommodation is provided and social security and pocket money is paid. Volunteers must pay their own travel expenses to and from Germany.

Applications should be sent to the above address, where they will be forwarded to the regional centre. Those interested need to apply one year ahead.

## Aufbauwerk der Jugend in Deutschland e.V
Bahnhofstr. 26, 3550 Marburg/Lahn, Germany. Tel: (06421) 65277

Aufbauwerk der Jugend organises international workcamps lasting for 2-3 weeks around Germany every July and August. Around 350 volunteers a year are involved in these projects, which have objectives such as renovating parks, footpaths and playgrounds, restoring community buildings and work in playschemes and with the handicapped. Each camp normally involves between 12 and 15 people. In exchange for between 30 and 35 hours work a week volunteers receive free board and lodging.

Volunteers must be aged between 16 and 25 and speak German or French or English. They must also be able to provide a medical certificate of health at the camp.

Applications can be made to the above address, or to Concordia in Britain.

## Christlicher Friedensdienst Deutscher Zweig e.V.

Rendeler Strasse 9-11, 6000 Frankfurt-Bornheim 60, Germany. Tel: (069) 459071

This organisation conducts work camps on ecological and peace projects in West Germany for international volunteers. Volunteers work in childrens' centres, on conservation projects, etc. which require light manual work and occasionally campaigning activities. Ample time is provided for the discussion of questions which arise from the work and for leisure activities. Work camps are from two to three weeks long, are conducted from June to September and cater for around 150 volunteers.

No special skills are required but a knowledge of English would be beneficial. Volunteers should be at least 18 years old. Board and lodging are provided but volunteers pay their own travel expenses.

Interested volunteers from Britain and Ireland should apply to the Christian Movement for Peace, Pott Street, Bethnal Green URC, London E2 0EF.

## I.J.G.D. (Internationale Jugendgemeinschaftsdienste Bundesverein e.V — Gesellschaft fur Internationale und Politische Bildnung)

Kaiserstr. 43, D-5300, Bonn 1, Germany. Tel: (0228) 22 10 01

I.J.G.D. organises a number of international work camps and workshops in West Germany and West Berlin that last for between two and four weeks. The projects include renovating educational centres, assisting with city fringe recreational activities and conservation work. They take place around Easter and from June to the end of September.

Around 1,800 volunteers take part in these schemes every year. Participants should be aged between 16 and 25, and able to do physical work. Food, accommodation and insurance are provided but participants must cover their own travel expenses.

Those interested should contact the Secretary General at the above address.

## International Arbeitsgemeinschaft fur Wander, Ski, Radund Rettungswesen (AWSR)

9000 St. Gallen, Rosengartenstr. 17, Switzerland. Tel: (071) 256 444

This organisation is concerned with environmental issues in Switzerland; the preservation of soil, air, water and forests, problems caused by the consumer society and the benefits of living alternatively. Workcamps to tackle environmental tasks are held during July and August for periods of eight to

22 days. Around 70 volunteers are needed each year to clean forests, build foot and mountain paths and undertake other tasks.

Volunteers must be able to communicate in German and should be aged between 17 and 27 years old. Accommodation, food, transport from the camps to the work site and pocket money are provided but volunteers must pay for their own travel to the camps. A registration fee of around £18 must be paid and insurance cover must be taken.

Volunteers should apply to the above address.

## Osterreichischer Bauorden
Postfach 186, Hornesgasse 3, A-1031 Wien, Austria
Tel: (0222) 73-81-18/ 73-52-54

Every June, July and August Osterreichischer Bauorden organises around 30 projects in Austria with aims such as building homes and community centres for the handicapped, the poor, the young and the old, or constructing sports fields, etc. About 500 volunteers a year take part in the projects, which last for between three and four weeks each.

Female applicants should be aged 18 to 30 and male applicants should be aged 17 to 30. They should have a basic knowledge of German and be willing to do manual work: previous experience of building work would be useful. Participants are given free board and lodging and insurance is arranged.

Those interested should contact the secretary at the above address for an application form.

# Scandinavia

## APØG
c/o Lokkegt. 23, N-2600, Lillehammer, Norway. Tel: 62 59974

APØG supplies contacts for volunteers who wish to work on ecological farms in Norway. Volunteers must be prepared to undertake the farm work for a minimum of four weeks but in order to stay for more than three months volunteers must obtain a work permit. Farm work is available all year round.

No special skills or experience are required. Board and lodging are provided but payment of pocket money varies from farm to farm.

Applications should be made to Torbjorn Dahl at the above address.

## Kansainvalinen Vapaaehtoinen Tyoleirijarjesto Oy (International Voluntary Workcamp Organisation)
Rauhanasema, Veturitori, 00520 Helsinki, Finland. Tel: 358 0 144 408/144 418

The aims of KVT are, through the co-operation of young people, to contribute to international peace and friendship and to make people aware of their social responsibilities and act to abolish social injustice. To put these aims into practice KVT arranges voluntary workcamps for young people of different nationalities, runs meetings, seminars, and discussion groups and keeps in touch with organisations with similar aims in Finland and other countries.

It co-operates with CCIVS (Co-ordinating Committee of International Voluntary Service) and has been the Finnish branch of SCI (Service Civil International) since 1981. About 300 volunteers are recruited annually by the organisation, of whom two thirds are Finns. To date, workcamps have taken place in all but six European countries. Camps last from two to four weeks.

The minimum age for most camps is 18 years, although some do have a lower age limit of 16 years. A basic knowledge of English is necessary and some camps may need special qualifications. All nationalities are recruited and visas or work permits are not needed. Board and lodging are always provided by KVT or the organisation the work is done for, as is insurance. Travel expenses and pocket money are not paid.

Non-Finnish volunteers should apply to the International Voluntary Service in their own country. For the UK the address is IVS, 162 Upper New Walk, Leicester LE1 7QA.

### Mellemfolkeligt Samvirke (MS)

Department for International Youth Exchange, Borgergade 14, 1300 Copenhagen K., Denmark

Besides arranging for the participation of about 900 Danes in workcamps abroad every year, MS also organises international workcamps in Denmark, Greenland and the Faroe Islands open to foreign volunteers. The main objective of these workcamps is to bring participants into contact with the social problems found in every society. The camps also provide an opportunity for young people, from all over the world, to live and work together with the local inhabitants. Camps in Denmark consist of an extensive range of projects such as construction of a playground, nature conservation, work/study camps, etc. Many camps in Denmark are open to disabled persons. In Greenland, the camps are organised in small settlements where the participants renovate buildings, build new sheep pens, etc. In the Faroe Islands the projects comprise construction of playgrounds and community centres.

The minimum age limit for participation is 17 and the volunteers must be willing to spend two to three weeks in a camp during July and August. Food, accommodation and insurance is provided but the volunteers must pay their own travelling expenses.

Applications from British applicants should be made through IVS, 162 Upper New Walk, Leicester LE1 7QA.

### The Swallows in Denmark

Osterbrogade 49, 2100 Copenhagen O, Denmark. Tel: 01261747

The Swallows provide financial support for organisations in India and Bangladesh by collecting old furniture and clothes and selling the goods in flea markets. During the summer, The Swallows conduct workcamps for international volunteers to assist with these tasks. Around 15 volunteers are needed each year to stay one, two or three weeks.

Volunteers must be either at least 16 years old or accompanied by an adult.

English speaking volunteers are preferred. Board and accommodation are provided but volunteers must pay for their own travel expenses.

Applicants should apply to the Co-ordinator at the above address.


### Valamo Monastery
SF-79850, Uusi-Valamo, Finland. Tel: 72 619 11

Every year the brotherhood organises international workcamps for between 250 and 300 volunteers who help with their work both outside in their garden, the fields and forests, and with their domestic work in the kitchen, etc. A number of volunteers are also needed around the year. Most volunteers stay between two weeks and one month and even longer if necessary.

Those interested should contact Brother Chariton at the above address.


### Nansen International Childrens Centre
Barnegarden, Breivold, Nesset, 1400 Ski, Norway. Tel: 02/94 67 15

Breivold is a long term relief centre for teenagers with very special needs. It is situated on a renovated farm 25 km from Oslo. Help is needed in all aspects of the centre. Applicants with skills of a practical nature and with initiative to tackle and follow through ideas with the minimum of supervision are needed. Domestic work is also included in the rota and all volunteers take turns with cooking, cleaning etc. There are many possibilities for sports, hobbies etc. and the leaders are expected to activate the youths in all areas of life. The most important aspect of the work is to motivate the participation of the youths and to encourage care about the future.

Volunteers at Breivold must be prepared to work very hard, the hours being long and very tiring. Volunteers should preferably be over 22, a driver and with some experience of working with young people. Volunteers receive full board and lodging and 300 NKR per week. Send an International Reply Coupon for all correspondence. Apply to the Director at the above address.


### The Norwegian Youth Council (LNU)
Rolfe Hofmos Gate 18, Oslo 6, Norway. Tel: (02) 670043

LNU is a committee for international and youth work, recruiting about 500 young people each year to work in Norway. Volunteers stay with Norwegian families, and although much of the work is agricultural, volunteers will also be involved with the day to day running of the household and helping with the children. The programme is quite energetic and there are opportunities for travel to Northern Norway. The minimum stay is four weeks, the maximum three months.

Volunteers do not require any special skills, but farm experience is an advantage. If Norwegian is not spoken, the recruit should consider the possible problems of isolation and communication this may cause. The volunteer should be aged between 18 and 30, and will require a medical certificate and references. Board and lodging are provided, and pocket money is a minimum of Kr 300 a week.

Further details and application forms may be obtained from the Secretary, Working Guest Programme, at the above address.

# Spain, Portugal, Italy and Cyprus

### ATEJ (Associacao de Turismo Estudantil e Juvenil)
Rua Miguel Bombarda 425, 4000 Porto, Portugal. Tel: 69 81 49

ATEJ organises international workcamps in Portugal for young people during the summer months. Projects undertaken include working five to six hours per day on farms and in hospitals, reconstructing monuments, etc. for periods of six to eight weeks.

Applicants must be aged between 18 and 25 years and have a knowledge of Portuguese, Spanish, French or English. Board and lodging are provided but volunteers must pay their own travel expenses. A registration fee of £1.50 is also required.

Write to the Director at the above address for further details.

### Agape Centro Ecumenico
1 — 10060 Prali, Torino, Italy. Tel: (0121) 80 75 14

Agape is an ecumenical conference centre in the Italian Alps for national and international meetings. It was built by an international group of volunteers between 1947 and 1951 as an act of reconciliation after the war, and is sponsored by the World Council of Churches. Each year 12 volunteers help the permanent staff to run the centre which is especially active over the summer. The jobs to be done include working in the kitchen and laundry, cleaning, running the coffee bar and general maintenance work. Volunteers normally work 6 hours per day, 6 days per week for periods of at least one month, mostly in the summer but sometimes also in Spring and Autumn.

Applicants must be aged over 18, and would find knowledge of more than one language an advantage. Free board and lodging are provided, but participants must cover their own travel costs to and from the centre.

For further details contact the Secretary at the above address.

### Centro Camuno di Studi Preistorici
25044 Capo di Ponte, Brescia, Italy. Tel: (364) 42091

The Centro is a research institute concentrating on the study of prehistory and primitive art and run by a non profit making cultural association. Up to 10 volunteers a year are needed to help with the exploration of sites in surrounding Valcamonica and to do laboratory work, research, mapping, bibliographical work and computerising data in the centre. The field-work takes place mostly in the summer, but the centre itself is open around the year. Volunteers are taken on for an initial period of three months.Board and accommodation are not provided but assistance is given in finding cheap basic accommodation. A few scholarships are available; candidates are selected after the initial trial period of three months.    Volunteers must be aged over 18 and be deeply interested in archaeology, primitive rock art, anthropology or the history of religions, but formal qualifications are not necessary. Those interested should contact the above address for further details.

**Companheiros Constructores**

Rua Pedro Monteiro 3 - 1, 3000 Coimbra, Portugal. Tel: 039 716747

This organisation recruits volunteers to assist with socio-economical projects in the poorest parts of Portugal. Volunteers are needed to work in international teams on construction work and agricultural jobs during short term workcamps, and in centres for physically and mentally under-priviledged children for longer periods. Between 150 and 200 volunteers are needed each year. The workcamps last from three to four weeks during the summer months, while volunteers wanting to work with the children must be prepared to stay for three months or more, all year round.

Workcamp volunteers must be in good health and at least 18 years old. Volunteers to work with the children must be at least 21 years old, have some experience in this field and have some knowledge of Portuguese. Volunteers pay a fee of about £100 which includes insurance. Board and lodging are provided.

Those interested should apply to the General Secretary at the above address.

**Fundo de Apoio aos Organisms Juvenis - (FAOJ)**

Rua Duque de Avila 137, 1 097 Lisboa, Codex, Portugal. Tel: 535081

FAOJ organises around 70 international workcamps in Portugal each summer. About 1,000 volunteers are needed to assist with construction and reconstruction work, protection of the natural environment and the protection and restoration of Portugal's cultural heritage. The workcamps last for around two weeks. No special skills are required to join a workcamp but volunteers must be aged 15 to 25 years old. Board and lodging are provided.

The workcamps programme is usually issued in February or March and sent to all members of Service Civil International. Volunteers should apply to Service Civil International in their home country.

**Gruppi Archeologici d'Italia**

via Tacito 41, 00193 Roma, Italy. Tel: 687 4028

This organisation arranges archaeological workcamps at sites in Italy. Between June and September around 1,000 volunteers of any nationality are needed to assist with the excavations. The workcamps are for a minimum of two weeks but the exact period may vary for different sites. Volunteers experienced in the techniques of excavation work are preferred but unskilled volunteers will be accepted. A certificate of vaccination against tetanus is required upon arrival at the workcamp and volunteers should be at least 16 years old. The fee for attending the camps varies between £122 and £180 but always includes full board and accommodation at a local youth hostel.

Enquiries should be sent to the Secretary for Foreign Volunteers at the above address.

**Instituto de la Juventud "Servicio Voluntario Internacional"**

Calle Ortega y Gasset 71, Madrid 6, Spain

This organisation arranges summer workcamps in Spain which involve archaeological excavations, the reconstruction of monuments, protection of the countryside, building work, nature studies and community work. About 2,000 volunteers take part in the camps each year which last from two to three weeks. There are no restrictions or special skills required. Board and lodging are provided.

Those interested should apply to the address above, or if possible to the affiliated organisation in their own country: Mouvement des Jeunes pour la Paix, 92 rue Stevrin, 1040 Bruxelles, Belgium; Mellemfolkeligt Samvirke, Hejrevej 38, DK 2400 Copenhagen NV, Denmark; Internationale Begegnung in Gemeinschaftsdiensten e V, 7252 Weil der Stadt Merklingen, Haupstrasse 64, Germany; Concordia, 28 rue du Pont Neuf, 75001 Paris, France; United Nations Association, Welsh Centre for International Affairs, Temple of Peace, Cathays Park, Cardiff CF1 3AP, UK.

### United Democratic Youth Organisation (EDON)
P. O. Box 1986, Nicosia, Cyprus

Every summer EDON organises international workcamps in Cyprus involving various types of community work. Each camp lasts for two weeks and all expenses are paid within Cyprus.

Further information can be obtained from the above address.

## Eastern Europe, Greece, Malta and Turkey

### Almatur: the Polish Students Association
00 953 Warsaw, 9, Ordynacka Street, Poland. Tel: 26 23 56

Every year Almatur receives around 50 volunteers from abroad who take part in various projects involving construction, conservation etc. These camps last for two to three weeks and take place in July and August. Volunteers are given full board and accommodation.

Participants must be aged between 18 and 30 and speak English, German or French. They must obtain a Polish visa and a participation fee of $25 (1988) is charged.

Volunteers should apply through voluntary organisations in their own country: British applicants should contact International Voluntary Service or the Christian Movement for Peace.

### American Farm School (Summer Work Activities Program)
1133 Broadway @ 26th Street, New York, NY 10010. Tel: 212/463 8433

Every summer from early June to July the farm school organises an international group of about 20 people to help man the agricultural and maintainance programmes at the school when regular staff and students are on vacation. The work involves a 35 hour week: a small allowance is paid. Other activities include a climb up Mount Olympus, trips into Thessaloniki and the islands, as well as a short stay with a family in a rural village. Accommodation and meals are provided by the school. Participants should be 18-26 years of age and are expected to pay their own fare to Thessaloniki.

Further information and application from the Programme Coordinator at the above address.

### CKM—Travel Bureau of Czechoslovak Youth and Students
Zitna 12, 12105 Prague 2, Czechoslovakia. Tel: 538 858

CKM organises international workcamps in Czechoslovakia which specialise in agricultural, conservation, and social work. About 500 people a year join these camps, which last for two or three weeks in July, August and September. There are between 15 and 25 people in each group, of whom no more than three may be of the same nationality. English tends to be the most widely spoken and understood language, although a knowledge of Russian would be handy in the light of an increasing participation from socialist countries. The five day working week allows time for organised cultural and leisure activities.

Applicants are expected to prepare for their trip: they should have a basic knowledge of Czechoslovakia, and some familiarity with the type of project undertaken by the camp they have chosen. Participants should be aged between 19 and 35, and are provided with food and accommodation.

Those interested should contact CKM through central voluntary organisations in their own country.

### Committee of Youth Organisations of the USSR (KMO)
Bogdan Khmelnitsky 7/8, Moscow, USSR

KMO organises international voluntary workcamps in the USSR and also sends volunteers from the USSR to other countries. Around 350 volunteers are needed to help with agricultural, construction and conservation work. Workcamps are only held during the summer and last for two weeks. No special skills are required but volunteers must be at least 18 years old and physically able.

Volunteers pay a registration fee but accommodation is provided, and the host organisation pays local costs. An invitation to attend a workcamp is sufficient to obtain a visa.

Application should be addressed to the Co-ordinating Committee for International Voluntary Service, 1 rue Miollis, 75015 Paris, France.

### Gençtur Turizm ve Seyahat Acentasi Ltd.
Ycrebatan Cad., No: 15/3, 34410 Sultanahmet, Istanbul-Turkey. Tel: (1) 526 54 09/(1) 512 04 57

Gençtur organises international workcamps in Turkish villages involving manual work such as constructing schools, village centres, digging water trenches, forestry, etc. Study tours, camp-tours, special interest tours and Turkish language courses are also arranged. No work permits are required but volunteers from socialist countries and Sweden need visas. English is the main language in the workcamps but some German and French is also spoken.

Approximately 600 volunteers a year attend the camps, which last for two weeks between June and October. The minimum age is 17 and the maximum is 35. Board and lodging are provided but volunteers must pay an inscription fee of £20. Those interested should apply to the address above or if possible to a workcamp organisation in their own country. Cheap accommodation and travel for young people and students are organised and a tourist information service with maps and leaflets is provided.

### The National Council of Hungarian Youth: Workcamp Commission
1388 Budapest, Pf. 72, Hungary. Tel: (01) 403 974

The Council organises work and study camps lasting for two weeks over the summer in Hungary. The work is manual, and most of the camps have a specific theme for discussion, such as "the role of youth in strengthening the atmosphere of cooperation and solidarity". Around 30 hours of work a week are expected of participants: in exchange they receive board, lodging and leisure-time activities.

Applicants must be aged between 18 and 30 and speak English. They will also need to obtain Hungarian visas. Applications should be made through a voluntary organisation in their own country. British applicants should contact Quaker Workcamps, International Voluntary Service, or the United Nations Association (Wales) before March.

### OHP: Federation of Unions of Polish Youth
International Workcamps, Nowy Swiat 18-20, 00-920 Warsaw, Poland. Tel: 32 43 99

OHP organises international workcamps and brigades to undertake social, preservation and conservation projects within Poland. Over 350 volunteers help each year by undertaking unskilled manual work, study and social projects. The workcamps and brigades are held during the summer and last from two to four weeks.

Volunteers must be English speaking, 18 to 35 years old, in general good health and have obtained a Polish visa. Board and lodging are provided.

Those interested should apply through a Service Civil International member organisation in their home country as no individual applications will be accepted by this organisation.

### Silatur
Emek Ishani (Gokdelen), Kat: 11, No: 1109, Kizilay, Ankara, Turkey. Tel: (41) 18 13 26

Silatur operate voluntary work camps in Turkey involving construction, gardening and environmental projects. The camps last for three weeks and take place in the summer, from June to September, with between 15 and 20 volunteers on each camp. Participants should be aged between 18 and 26; no particular qualifications, skills or experience are needed although good health is required. No registration fee is charged and people of all nationalities are welcome. All year round volunteers are also invited to help in Silatur's office for periods of three weeks. Volunteers receive free food while on the camp, and are occasionally given some partial help with their travelling expenses. Those interested should contact the above address for Silatur's annual workcamp programme.

**Youth Travel Bureau**
VYHA Head Office, 17 Tal-Borg Street, Pawla, Malta. Tel: (356) 229361

The Bureau operates the Malta Workcamps Scheme which gives people the opportunity to learn about the country while spending some of their time doing voluntary work. This involves spending around 20 hours a week doing office work, building, decorating and administration work in Malta's youth hostels. There are no set hours of work, but participants are expected to put in the full 20 hours a week. They will normally work either from the 1st to the 15th or the 16th to the 31st of each month. One may apply for periods of two to 12 weeks. Free accommodation and breakfast are provided.

No special qualifications or experience are required, but volunteers are expected to put a reasonable amount of effort into their work.

For further details send two International Reply Coupons to the above address.

**Zveza Socialisticne Mladine Slovenije (ZSMS)**
Commission for International Exchange of Volunteers, Dalmatinova ul.4, YU-61000 Ljubljana, Yugoslavia. Tel: (061) 312 381

ZSMS is a socio-political organisation which organises international workcamps to undertake various tasks in Yugoslavia. Around 600 volunteers per year are needed to assist with construction and renovation projects, maintenance work in parks and forests, programmes for children and mentally or physically disabled people, rural facilities, study camps, etc. Workcamps are mainly held from June to September and last for three or four weeks.

Most projects do not require any special skills or qualifications but volunteers must normally be at least 18 years old. Accommodation and food are provided at the workcamps but volunteers must pay for their other expenses.

If possible applicants should apply through Service Civil International member organisations in their own country. Otherwise volunteers may apply directly to the Co-ordinator at the above address.

# North, Central and South America

**American Hiking Society, Volunteer Vacations Programme**

1015 31st Street, N.W., Washington, D.C. 20007, USA. Tel: (703) 385 3252

About 250 volunteers are needed annually to maintain American hiking trails, as well as helping as fire lookouts, campground hosts, historical researchers, wildlife observers, backcountry guides and trail workers. Some of these jobs are especially attractive because of the scenic location or the unusually interesting work; as a result, positions are often filled by mid-February, however park and forest managers seek volunteers all the year round and welcome inquiries any time.

Accommodation is sometimes provided, however work is often carried out in remote wilderness areas where camping accommodation is necessary. Volunteers generally work for two weeks. Outdoor camping experience and a knowledge of backpacking equipment are very helpful. An international driver's licence, though not necessary, can be useful. Volunteers must be over 16 years of age and prepared for hard work in isolated places. Some applicants may be recruited by the US Forest Service through AHS. No work permits are needed by foreign volunteers. A directory *Helping Out in the Outdoors,* listing more than 1,000 of these volunteer jobs in 42 states, is published by the AHS, at a cost of $3.00.

Enquiries may be sent to the Director, VCC, at the above address.

**Amigos de las Americas**

5618 Star Lane, Houston, Texas 77057, USA

This organisation sends approximately 500 volunteers to Latin America each year to carry out a variety of public health assistance programmes. The programmes include dental hygiene instruction, eye care, immunisation, sanitation, veterinary programmes, and sanitary latrine construction. In 1988 they operated in Mexico, Costa Rica, the Dominican Republic, Ecuador, Paraguay and Honduras.

Volunteers must successfully complete a six month training programme which takes place in the evenings and at weekends from January to June. Correspondence courses are available. Programmes operate for four, six and eight weeks in June, July and August. Volunteers should be over 16 and in good health. All nationalities are welcome and the organisation secures any visas necessary. They are asked to pay part of the volunteer participation cost, but airfares, accommodation, food and travel within the country are provided.

Applications should be made to the Director of Training and Administration at the above address.

**Appalachian Mountain Club Trails Program**

PO Box 298, Gorham, NH 03581, USA. Tel: (603) 4662721

The Appalachian Mountain Club is a non-profit-making recreation and conservation group which is responsible for over 1,000 miles of trail in the northeast of the United States, including over 350 miles of the Appalachian National Service Trail. Every summer the club sponsors a variety of weekend and five to ten day volunteer trail, forest and park projects which are open to individuals, families and other groups. Volunteers may work on their own or in teams but are given training and tools to enable them to undertake all types of trail, shelter and other work. Over 500 volunteers are needed annually.

Volunteers must be at least 16 years old, in good health, willing to learn and work hard with others and have backpacking experience. All volunteers must have their own accident insurance. Room and board are provided but volunteers are charged £10 or more per week.

For further information contact the Trails Program Director at the above address.

### Betterway Inc.
612 Middle Avenue, Elytia, Ohio 44035, USA. Tel: 216 323 2431

This organisation provides group homes in Elyria, Ohio for young homeless or troubled people aged 13 to 18 years old. Around eight volunteers are needed to act as staff/house parents/big brothers or sisters in houses where about 15 young people live. Duties include caring for the young people, organising recreational activities and supervising and holding discussions with individuals or groups. A 40 hour week is worked year round. Volunteers willing to work for one year or more are preferred but placements for the summer months may be accepted.

Volunteers must speak English, be physically able to play active games, enjoy working with young people and have a driving licence. Preference is given to applicants aged 19 to 30 years old but volunteers up to 40 years will be accepted. Board and lodging are provided and depending on the needs of a volunteer, up to £50 per month may be paid.

Apply to the Director at the above address.

### Britain - Cuba Resource Centre
Carila, 29 Islington Park Street, London N1

The Centre organises and selects the British contingent of volunteers for the annual 250-strong Jose Marti International Work Brigade in Cuba. The aim of the brigade is to express solidarity with and to learn about the Cuban revolution. Of the month in Cuba, three weeks are spent working alongside Cubans on local construction and agricultural projects for $4\frac{1}{2}$ days a week. The rest of the time is spent visiting schools, hospitals, factories and other organisations and sightseeing to learn about Cuban society and politics. The timing of the brigade varies from year to year.

Only 25 to 30 people living in Britain and who are committed to learning about a socialist society are selected. Volunteers pay a fee of around £600 which covers the cost of accommodation, food and travel. The centre organises the required visa.

Write to the Brigade Co-ordinator at the above address for an application form and further information.

## Centre for Urban Archaeology, Baltimore City Life Museum

802 E Lombard Street, Baltimore, Maryland 21202, USA. Tel: (301) 396 3156

The Centre conducts archaeological research in the city of Baltimore, USA. Volunteers are needed to participate in excavations, laboratory processing of artifacts, archival research, photography, illustration, editing, data entry and secretarial work. Around 50 volunteers are needed all year round with the greatest demand being from April to September. A minimum commitment of four hours per month is required.

Volunteers must speak English, should have a desire to learn about archaeology and be willing to take direction. Physical fitness is required and if volunteers are younger than 13 years old they must be accompanied by an adult. Volunteers are responsible for organising their own visas.

Those interested should apply to the Archaeological Director at the above address.

## Community for Creative Non-Violence

1345 Euclid Street N.W., Washington D.C. 20009, USA

This Community meets the needs of the homeless in Washington D.C. Volunteers are needed to assist with cooking, serving soup, counselling, office work and campaigning on behalf of the poor. Board and lodging are provided. A minimum stay of six months is strongly encouraged.

Those interested in helping should write to the above address.

## Friends Weekend Workcamp Program

1515 Cherry Street, Philadelphia, PA 19102, USA

This organisation offers short term projects (2-10 days), within inner city Philadelphia which combine physical work with discussions on urban poverty. Approximately 200-250 volunteers are engaged annually, mainly between October and May, on a variety of work projects including painting, plastering and cleaning homes, work with senior citizens and outdoor community projects. All nationalities are welcome but must speak English and be at least 15. Board and lodging are provided but each volunteer is asked for a donation of $15 per weekend.

Those interested should apply to the Programme Organiser at the above address.

## Frontiers Foundation

2615 Danforth Avenue, Suite 203, Toronto, Ontario, Canada, M4C 1L6. Tel: (416) 690 3930

The Foundation organises workcamps which take place mainly during the summer months. The scheme involves sending five or eight volunteers to a low income community in Canada: these tend to be Indian communities in isolated northern areas. Under the leadership of one of their number, the volunteers live together as a group, and work with the local people on the construction either of housing or community buildings. There are about 100 participants a year in these projects; they may be of any nationality, so the

Foundation has adopted a policy of "mixing" to prevent any one nationality from dominating the programme.

All applicants must be over 18, and produce a doctor's certificate which states that they are capable of performing manual work in an isolated area. During the summer, the minimum period of work is from 30 June to 31 August (after summer, the period is 8 weeks). All living and travel expenses inside Canada are paid, and, in addition, pocket money is provided for those who serve for longer than the minimum period.

Applicants should write to Marco A. Guzman, Programme Co-ordinator at the above address.

### Genesis II Cloud Forest
Apdo 655, 7050 Cartago, Costa Rica, Central America

This organisation is responsible for preserving a cloud forest in the mountains of Costa Rica, (altitude 2,360 metres), for bird-watching, recreation and academic research. Volunteers are needed to help with the system of trails which are continuously being expanded and improved and other related work. Tasks include trail work, gardening, reforestation, transplanting and fence construction. Around ten volunteers are needed annually for a minimum period of one month.

Volunteers of all nationalities are welcome but a knowledge of Spanish is useful and preference is given to people experienced in construction or ecological work. Since conditions are rugged and work takes place at high altitudes, applicants with disabilities or poor cardio-vascular systems are not accepted. Accommodation is provided.

For more details contact the Co-Owner at the above address.

### Heifer Project, International Learning and Livestock Center
Route 2, Box 33, Perryville, Arkansas 72126, USA. Tel: (501) 889 5124

The Project in a non-profit-making organisation that supplies livestock and related technical information to low-income farmers in need throughout the world. The Project uses the Learning and Livestock Center near Perryville as a holding centre for donated animals, to breed animals for special projects, for bio-intensive farming, cheesemaking, office work, etc. Around 70 individual volunteers and around 400 people in workcamp groups are needed to undertake a variety of ranch and farming duties, from livestock assistance to farm construction, and to assist with conferences and workcamps held at the Center each year. The length of stay is variable but usually six to eight weeks, all year round. Preference for summer staff positions is given to those who will stay for the entire workcamp season, late May to mid-August. Both skilled and unskilled workers are welcome.

Individual volunteers should be at least 18 years old and in good health, while groups for workcamps should be of High School age or older. Board, lodging and in some cases, a small stipend are provided to individual volunteers. Workcamp volunteers must pay for their food and transportation as well as a £5 fee.

British applicants are advised to apply at least three and preferably six months before the desired time period to the Heifer UK Project, The

Amicable School House, 70 St. Marychurch Street, Rotherhithe, London SE16 4HZ for further details.

### InterSharing/Short Term Volunteer in Mission
Box 125, Colfax, Iowa 50054, USA. Tel: 515 674 3125

This organisation operates through the United Methodist Church to offer individuals, couples and work teams an opportunity to undertake volunteer projects in the United States of America, the Caribbean or other parts of the world. Tasks may include tutoring, teaching in Vacation Bible Schools, construction jobs or medical, social and agricultural service activities. Over 100 work teams and 50 individuals/couples are needed annually for periods of two days to two months. Each project co-ordinator specifies the length of their volunteer needs but many requests are for summer positions.

Volunteers must be in good health and in countries in which English is not spoken, it is useful but not essential if volunteers speak the local language. Accommodation is usually provided.

For further details contact the Administrator at the above address.

### Koinonis Partners
Route 2, Americus, Georgia 31709, USA. Tel: (912) 924 0391

Koinonis Partners is a self-supporting Ecumenical Christian community of 25 people working with the local poor. Groups of ten volunteers are taken on for three month periods every March, June and September.

A normal week consists of about 32 hours of work alongside members of the community and six hours of seminars. Work may be in the office or consist of gardening, youth tutoring, shipping and food preparation. Applicants must speak English but need not be Christians provided that they will openly consider the teachings of Jesus Christ.

Board, lodging and a small amount of pocket money for incidentals are provided, but volunteers must obtain a tourist visa for their length of stay.

Those interested should apply to the Volunteer Co-ordinator at the above address.

### Los Ninos
1330 Continental Street, San Ysidro, CA 92073, USA. Tel: (619) 690 1437

Los Ninos is a charitable organisation founded to provide food, clothing, shelter, education and affection to children in orphanages and poor communities in the Mexican border cities of Tecate, Tijuana and Mexicali. Approximately 1,200 volunteers of predominantly high school and college age take part in weekend or one month-long summer study programmes in July and August. Volunteers assist by undertaking jobs in education, nutrition, construction, as youth counsellors or in other areas of community development. Around 25 other volunteers help long term on the same jobs and stay for periods of over a year.

All volunteers must have a visa which allows them to cross the United States and Mexican border daily. Summer volunteers must be at least 16 years old. Long term volunteers must be at least 21 years old, proficient in Spanish, skilled in the specific areas mentioned above and hold a driver's licence. Summer volunteers receive accommodation but must pay about £50 per week while long term volunteers receive free board and accommodation and around £25 per month in pocket money.

Those interested should contact the Office Manager at the above address.

**Lubbock Lake Landmark**
The Museum, Texas Tech University, Lubbock, Texas 79409-4499, USA

The Lubbock Lake National Historic and State Archaeological Landmark is an archaeological preserve on the outskirts of Lubbock. The aims and activities of the Landmark are orientated toward the excavation of data and the interpretation of that data for the public through a number of public education courses. Around 50 volunteers a year are required to help with the excavation programme.

Volunteers must be able to read, write and speak English and are required to act as field and lab crew members during the excavations, collections workers for the care of the collections in the museum, or as leaders on tour programmes.

The minimum age for prospective volunteers is 18 years, and the period of participation is from six weeks to three months between June and August. Volunteers must pay for their own travelling and incidental expenses but receive free board and lodging in the field camp.

For further details contact the Director at the above address.

**The National Central America Health Rights Network (NCAHRN)**
853 Broadway, Suite 416, New York 10003, USA. Tel: 212 420 9635

NCAHRN sponsor a wide range of activities designed to promote health in Central America. In particular, NCAHRN offers a variety of short and long term volunteer opportunities for health workers, (doctors, nurses, midwives, etc.), in El Salvador and Central America. Around 100 volunteers are needed all year round to instruct in medical or health schools, teach skills in communities and health clinics and to provide health care to international work brigades. Placements vary from two weeks through to six months or one year.

All volunteers must speak Spanish, be qualified and have experience in their field and appropriate work permits. Accommodation is provided in some cases but expenses are not paid.

Contact the National Staff Officer at the above address for details on particular programmes.

**The Nature Conservancy**
1800 North Kent Street, Suite 800, Arlington, VA 22209, USA. Tel: (703) 841 5300

The Nature Conservancy protects the habitat of endangered species in the United States and Latin American countries. Volunteers are needed to help in various departments including science, development, administration, personnel and general office work, all year round.

Volunteers must be able to be legally employed in the United States and to show proof of residential status. Some field work may require strenuous outdoor activities or the ability to operate mechanical devices. Accommodation may be provided.

Those interested should obtain a listing of addresses from the Personnel Assistant at the above address before applying directly to the desired office.

## Nicaragua Network

2025 I Street N.W., Suite 212, Washington DC 20006, USA. Tel: (202) 223 2328

Nicaragua Network raises funds for their humanitarian aid programme in Nicaragua and recruits volunteers for coffee harvesting, tree planting and house building work brigades. Around 250 volunteers are needed for these brigades which last from two weeks to one month. The coffee harvesting brigades are held during winter and the other brigades usually during summer.

Volunteers of all nationalities are accepted as long as they are at least 16 years old. (Volunteers aged 16 and 17 years old must have parental consent). A knowledge of Spanish is helpful. Accommodation is included in the cost of joining a work brigade.

Those interested should apply to the Office Manager at the above address.

## Nicaragua Solidarity Campaign

23 Bevenden Street, London N1 6BH. Tel: (01) 253 2464

The Nicaragua Solidarity Campaign arranges and conducts work brigades to pick coffee and do building and reafforestation work in Nicaragua. Around 160 volunteers of any nationality are needed year round, as while the coffee brigades are conducted from November through to February, reafforestation brigades occur from May to August and building brigades are needed all year round. Coffee brigades last for six weeks, building brigades three months and reafforestation brigades one month. Usually one week of each brigade is devoted to a study tour.

Volunteers must be physically fit but apart from the building brigades where experience in building work is necessary, no special skills are required. Costs vary according to the brigade attended but are in the vicinity of £850 which includes return air fares to London, living costs while working and accommodation and some meals during the study tour programme.

Contact the Brigades/Tours Worker at the above address for further information.

## Old Sturbridge Village

Sturbridge, Massachusetts 01566, USA. Tel: (6177) 347 3362

The village is a recreation of a rural early 19th century New England community. People in historical dress demonstrate the daily work, community life and celebrations of early New Englanders for more than 500,000 visitors each year. An important part of the villages function consists of conducting research projects into life in this period, including archaeological excavations. Around 10 volunteers a year help with this during the year.

Volunteers help to catalogue, clean, draw and reconstruct artefacts and do preliminary work on them. Those with field experience may also get the opportunity to take part in the actual excavations. Volunteers must arrange and pay for their own accommodation. Participants should be healthy and aged over 18; previous laboratory or archaeological field experience is mandatory. Volunteers should apply to the Research Archaeologist at the above address.

### Overseas Development Network, Inc.

Box 1430, Cambridge, MA 02238, USA. Tel: (617) 868 3002

The Overseas Development Network is a national student organisation in America which provides opportunities for students to become involved in Third World development. Students or volunteers are needed all year round to work in the two offices at Cambridge, Massachusetts and Stanford, California and to assist with the annual summer cross-country bike-a-thon, 'Bike Aid'. Volunteers give whatever time they can. There are also opportunities for around 50 students to take part in overseas internship programmes lasting for around six months. Students are placed in indigenous grassroots development agencies to learn about development first hand. Countries offered are India, Bangladesh, the Philippines, Latin America and the Appalachian region of the USA.

Volunteers should be interested and preferably experienced in Third World studies, travel or issues. A knowledge of English is important for the work in the USA and Spanish is required for the Latin American internships but for other internships the language of the country is preferred but not necessary. Volunteers pay all internship programme costs but some fellowships are offered to financially needy students when absolutely necessary. Accommodation with staff or through staff contacts can be provided.

Contact the Regional Co-ordinator at the above address for information about all opportunities except for the Latin American Internship programmes, Bike Aid or voluntary work in the Stanford office where the appropriate address is ODN/West, Box 2306, Stanford, CA 94305, USA. Tel: (415) 725 2869.

### Short Term Evangelical Projects (STEP)

The Evangelical Union of South America, High Rising, Linton, Ross-on-Wye, Hertfordshire HR9 7RS. Tel: (098982) 323

STEPs provide opportunities for around 100 young Christians to undertake community based tasks in support of the Latin American church in Brazil, Peru and Bolivia. Projects vary from evangelical or graphic arts tasks to building or bricklaying work. STEPs can be from two to six months long with most occurring from July to September.

Volunteers must be in good health, aged 17 to 30 years old and committed Christians who can provide recommendations from their local church, although older people with specific skills will be considered. Some knowledge of Spanish or Portuguese is an advantage. Volunteers are responsible for all travel and living expenses (around £900). Accommodation is provided.

Apply to the Director of STEP at the above address.

## Sierra Club

730 Polk Street, San Francisco, CA 94109, USA. Tel: (415) 776 2211

The Sierra Club subsidises trips which combine wilderness outings with preservation projects in North America, although occasionally one or two trips are held in Europe. Between 300 and 500 volunteers are needed annually. Volunteers use their own camping equipment and camp out while helping to build or repair trails and restoring damaged wilderness areas. The trips last from one week to ten days with most of the trips being held in summer although some are conducted in spring and autumn, and all trips incorporate days free from work.

Volunteers must be physically fit and aged at least 16 years old, although some team leaders may make exceptions. No special skills are required but medical doctors may have their trip cost waived if they act as a staff doctor on an expedition. A typical trip costs around £70.

Contact the Publicity Manager at the above address for further information.

## Sioux Indian Young Men's Christian Associations

Box 218, Dupree, South Dakota 57623, USA

The Sioux Indian YMCA's organise spring and summer community projects and a summer camp in South Dakota. In the spring and summer projects the volunteers live and work in small isolated reservation communities under the direction of indigenous community YMCA organisations and help with informal recreation, leadership training and counselling. The projects last from April to June or mid-June to mid-August.

The summer camp takes place on the Oahe Reservoir of the Missouri River. It is a primitive camp without electricity or running water, and the campers are all from the small reservation YMCA's on the Sioux reservations.

Volunteers should be sensitive and mature, able to relate to people of other cultures and like working with children. All skills are welcome especially those connected with water safety, first aid, creative arts and crafts, games and sports. Those working on the Summer camp should have previous experience of camping life.

Volunteers should be in good mental and physical health and over 18. Board and lodging are provided, but volunteers are responsible for travel and personal expenses.

Applications should be made to the Director at the above address.

## Student Conservation Association

PO Box 550C, Charlestown, NH 03603, USA. Tel: (603) 826 5741

This Association offers internships for students and adults to work in national parks, forests and wildlife refuges across the United States, including Alaska, Hawaii, Puerto Rico and the Virgin Islands. The High School (HS) Programme enables around 350 students between 16 and 18 years of age to work on construction, maintenance and trail orientated projects in groups of six to 12 students. In the Research Assistant (RA) Programme around 750 older students and adults work in a professional capacity alongside other staff in resource management agencies. Placements are for four or five weeks during the summer for the HS Program, but for ten to 12 weeks, all year round in the RA Program.

All volunteers should be in good health and overseas applicants must pay for their travel to the United States. No special skills are needed for the HS Program but participants must pay for their personal equipment and transportation to the site. (Financial aid is available). The RA positions require either a specific academic background or an interest in conservation and an enthusiasm for performing this type of work. RA volunteers must be at least 18 years old and out of high school. They are paid for their travel expenses within the United States and receive accommodation and a food allowance.

For further information contact the Assistant Program Director in Recruitment at the above address.

**Tahoe Rim Trail Fund Inc.**
PO Box 10156, South Lake Tahoe, CA 95731, USA. Tel: (916) 577 0676

This volunteer organisation was formed in 1983 to build and maintain a 150 mile multi-purpose trail around the ridgetops of the Lake Tahoe Basin in California and near the Nevada border. The goal is to complete the trail by the end of 1990 but volunteers will still be needed for maintenance work. Between 400 and 1,000 English speaking volunteers per year are needed in all seasons for all aspects of the project, from office work and fund raising events to trail building and maintenance, but demand for volunteers is highest during the construction season which begins in May and ends mid-October. Volunteers specify the length of their service.

No special skills are necessary as training is given, but volunteers with rock blasting or engraving and surveying skills will be welcomed. Membership is not required but volunteers should be in good health and at least 16 years old. Accommodation and pocket money are not usually provided.

Write to the Director at the above address for an application form and further information.

**United Church Board for Homeland Ministries**
132 W 31st Street, New York, NY 10001, USA. Tel: 212 239 8700

This Church administers three voluntary programmes which are located in the United States and Puerto Rico. Volunteers may undertake short term, summer or one year voluntary service programmes. Tasks include undertaking community service, assisting with emergency shelters, helping with programmes concerned with peace and justice, etc. Of the 90 volunteers needed each year, up to 15 of these are overseas volunteers.

Volunteers must be at least 18 years old, English-speaking and willing to be placed by a Christian church organisation. Some projects may have specific health, professional or driving licence requirements. Overseas volunteers must pay their full round trip transportation costs and have a J-1 visa. Summer service volunteers receive room and bard while one-year volunteers also receive a stipend.

Those interested should apply to the Secretary for Special Programmes and Services at the above address.

**University Research Expeditions Program (UREP)**
University of California, Berkeley, CA 94720, USA. Tel: (415) 642 6586

UREP provides opportunities for people to participate in scientific discoveries by acting as field assistants on a University of California research expedition. Research topics offered in a large number of countries include animal behaviour, archaeology, anthropology, sociology, art, music, botany, ecology and marine studies. Over 200 volunteers are needed each year for over 20 different projects. Most projects are offered from February to September and last around two or three weeks.

Volunteers must be in good health, at least 16 years old, have a desire to learn, enthusiasm and willingness to undertake team work. Specific skills or experiences are not essential but may be an advantage. Volunteers pay an equal share to cover the project's costs. This contribution covers research equipment and supplies, preparatory materials, camping and field gear, ground transportation and meals and accommodation. Travel to the site is not included.

For more information contact the Secretary at the above address.

**Ventana**
339 Lafayette Street, New York 10012, USA. Tel: (212) 475 7159

Ventana is an organisation of cultural workers who sympathise with the workers of Central America. Ventana seeks to change the intervention policies of the United States government by fund raising, generating articles on Central American issues and culture, presenting music, dance and art exhibitions, lecturing and giving slideshows and video presentations and organising cultural exchanges with Central American institutions. Volunteers are needed all year round to assist with all of these activities in the United States or they may join one of the cultural delegations. (Delegations to Nicaragua cost approximately £200 from the United States. Accommodation is provided). A knowledge of Spanish is useful but volunteers need no other special skills.

Those interested should contact the Corresponding Secretary for more information.

**The Winant-Clayton Volunteer Association**
43 Trinity Square, London EC3N 4DJ. Tel: (01) 488 4772

This Association organises an annual exchange between the United Kingdom and the eastern states of the United States of America for a group of 20 volunteers. Selected volunteers work on community projects which include visiting house-bound people, working with children of all ages, psychiatric rehabilitation and running lunch clubs for the elderly. The exchange lasts for three months, the last month being free for individual travel, between June and September.

To be selected to travel to the United States, volunteers must be resident in Great Britain and over 19 years old. The average age of volunteers is between 22 and 28 years old but individual volunteers may be much older. Volunteers must have some experience of community or group work, an interest in people, a sense of humour, flexibility, stamina and a satisfactory way of dealing with stress.

The Association obtains the special work permit required and provides pocket money and accommodation for the two months of work. No other expenses are paid. Interviews are held each January.

Applications should be made to the Co-ordinator at the above address.

# Israel and the Middle East

### American Dental Volunteers for Israel (ADVI)
108-13 67th Road, Forest Hills, NY 11375, USA. Tel: (718) 263 4918

ADVI is a non-profit-making organisation which recruits volunteer dentists and dental hygienists of all nationalities to work for kibbutzim in Israel. Volunteers undertake reparative dentistry, stress the preventative approach and train dental assistants. Between 50 and 75 volunteers are needed for placements of three or four weeks, all year round.

Volunteers must be licenced dentists or registered dental hygienists with a minimum of one or two years experience and in good health. All volunteers are granted a temporary licence to practise in Israel upon presentation of copies of licences and diplomas to the Israel Ministry of Health. Accommodation is provided but volunteers must pay their travelling expenses.

For more details contact the Chairman at the above address.

### American Zionist Youth Foundation
Long Term Programs, 515 Park Avenue, New York, NY 10022, USA. Tel: (1) 212 751 6070

Sherut La'am (Service to the People) is a one year programme that provides an ideal opportunity to experience Israel from within. Working as volunteers, participants are given the chance to become integral members of the communities in which they live and work. Volunteers are able to aid in the growth and development of these communities, while contributing profoundly to their own personal fulfilment.

The programme also includes three months of intensive Hebrew and nine months work placement in one's profession or area of special skill. Volunteers should be college graduates up to age 35. Six month programme available if fluent in Hebrew.

The programme begins in July and October. Further information can be obtained from the above address.

### Center of Nautical and Regional Archaeology (CONRAD)
Kibbutz Nahsholim, Israel 30815, Tel: (06) 390 950

CONRAD is located in the grounds of the Kibbutz Nahsholim on the Carmel Coast, Israel. The Center is the home base of the Israel Department of Antiquities and Museums' maritime inspection team and the Tel Dor excavations. Volunteers are needed year round to help with all projects. Field work including diving, restoration, exhibit planning, publication preparation and general maintenance of the building goes on year round. The Tel Dor excavations take place during July and August and during autumn, spring and winter, inspection diving is at its peak with underwater surveys and rescue excavations being conducted. Volunteers to act as tour guides and to assist with clerical work are always needed. Placements are for as long as the volunteer wishes but for periods longer than three months work visas may be required.

Volunteers must be in good health, over 18 years old and be able to speak Hebrew or English. Diving volunteers must have diving licences. The volunteer is responsible for all costs including accommodation, meals and medical and accident insurance, although reduced rates for accommodation can be given.

Volunteers should apply to the Director at the above address.

### The Church's Ministry among the Jews
30c Clarence Road, St Albans, Herts AL1 4JJ. Tel: (0727) 33114

Every year the Church requires about 24 volunteers to work in its hostel in Tel Aviv and conference centre on Mount Carmel for periods of three to 12 months. The work usually consists of the preparation and serving of meals for guests, housework and maintenance of the grounds and buildings. No special skills are required and volunteers may be of any nationality provided they are over 17 years old and in good health.

Volunteers must pay for their own travel expenses but receive full board and lodging and pocket money. Visas are arranged in Israel.

Further details can be obtained from the General Director at the above address.

### Department of Antiquities and Museums
Ministry of Education and Culture, P.O. Box 586, Jerusalem, 91 004

A number of excavations in Israel accept volunteers each year. Details of most of them cannot be given very far ahead as final plans are not usually drawn up before spring. If applicants write to the Department early in the year they will be sent a detailed list of proposed excavations. It can however be said that Israel is a country rich in its history, and possessing archaeological remains from every period since prehistoric times.

The minimum age for prospective volunteers is 18 years, and the minimum period of participation is usually two weeks. The capability and willingness to do any work in the field connected with the excavation is required. Accommodation and food are provided by the expedition, but full or part payment may be asked for this, especially if archaeological tuition is involved.

Enquiries should be sent to the Assistant to the Director at the above address.

### Edinburgh Medical Missionary Society
14 Mayfield Terrace, Edinburgh EH9 1SA. Tel: (031) 667 2518

This Society assists the Nazareth Hospital in Nazareth, Israel to obtain volunteers for occasional medical, nursing, para-medical and general maintenance vacancies. Vacancies occur irregularly at any time of year. Volunteers may be of any nationality provided that they are in good health and have appropriate qualifications or experience in the relevant area. At least three volunteers a year are required for placements of one to two months, but longer stays are possible. Simple accommodation and the appropriate work visa are provided by the hospital. Travel expenses are not paid.

Write to Dr R. Martin, The Nazareth Hospital, EMMS, PO Box 11, 16100 Nazareth, Israel for further information.

## Ein Yael Living Museum

Israel Department of Antiquities, PO Box 586, Jerusalem, Israel. Tel: (02) 278601 227

The Ein Yael Living Museum is situated in the Rephaim Valley of Jerusalem. The project combines archaeological excavation of the 40 acre site, experimentation in the techniques of weaving, pottery, metallurgy and agriculture as practiced in various periods and research in an attempt to understand the way ancient man interacted with his environment. Over 2,000 volunteers are needed annually for both the excavation and the experimentation of ancient technologies for a minimum period of one week. The summer excavation season lasts from May through to September but volunteers can participate in experimentation activities all year round.

Volunteers of all nationalities are welcome provided they are at least 16 years old and in good health. No previous experience is required but volunteers must be prepared to work seven hours a day, five days a week in the hot sun. A registration fee of around £16 is required upon arrival and volunteers must arrange their own accident insurance in advance. Camping at the site is possible for a fee of £16 per week. Meals can be provided if required.

For further information write to Gershon Edelstein, Director, at the above address.

## Friends of Israel Educational Trust

25 Lyndale Avenue, London NW2 2QB. Tel: (01) 435 6803

The Trust has three basic functions. It directs around 4,000 young people a year towards various kibbutz placement agencies, it recruits 13 young people a year to work as medical auxillaries in the ALYN Childrens orthopaedic hospital in Jerusalem, and it runs a six month programme called "Bridge in Britain" for 12 people a year, providing an expenses paid opportunity to take part in kibbutz work, teaching, sports training, and archaeological work. Applications for work only in Kibbutzim are forwarded to Kibbutz Representatives (see below).

Applicants for work as hospital auxiliaries should be aged between eighteen and thirty, and will receive a small salary, but must pay their own travel costs. Those accepted in the "Bridge in Britain" scheme are provided with the cost of travel to and from Israel and living expenses while there, but not pocket money.

For further details contact the Directorate at the above address.

## Gil Travel Ltd.

65 Gloucester Place, London W1H 3PF. Tel: (01) 935 1701

This company arranges placements for volunteers who wish to work on moshavim in Israel. Volunteers of any nationality are welcome to work in all branches of agriculture from vegetable, fruit or flower growing to poultry or dairy farming in all stages of production. The working week is six days, with eight hours work per day.

Only healthy volunteers aged 18 to 35 years old and willing to spend a minimum of two months will be accepted. Workers on moshavim receive a number of benefits including free accommodation, social facilities and an allowance of about £160 per month. Gil Travel charges a registration fee of £20 to £30 and can provide prospective volunteers with a booklet about life and work in moshavim.

Send a SAE to the Managing Director at the above address or telephone for further information.

### Hebrew Union College - Jewish Institute of Religion
One West 4th Street, New York, NY 10012, USA. Tel: 212 674 5300

The School of Biblical Archaeology at the above institute, in co-operation with the Israel Department of Antiquities and the Semitic Museum of Harvard, has a long term ongoing programme of excavations at Tel Dan, Israel. Around 50 volunteers per season are needed to assist with the excavation process during summer. Volunteers must be at least 18 years old with an interest in archaeology but no special skills are required. The minimum placement is two weeks and all volunteers must submit a completed medical form. The cost of around £800 excludes travel but includes room and board.

Applications to Dr Paul M. Steinberg, Director, American Office, at the above address.

### Institute of Archaeology, Tel Aviv University
PO Box 39040, Ramat Aviv 69978, Tel Aviv, Israel. Tel: (03) 5411295

The Institute is involved with archaeological excavations in a scholastic setting. Lectures, field trips and other recreational activities are also organised outside working hours. About 300 volunteers are taken on every year, drawn from many different countries. Volunteers are mostly students or individuals interested in Biblical archaeology, field archaeology or the historical geography of Israel. There is also the possibility of work for graphic artists, surveyors and pottery restorers. Most work involves digging. No experience is necessary, but the applicant must be in good health. English and Hebrew are the basic languages, however groups may come with an interpreter. Excavations are generally carried out in the summer months and anyone over 18 who is capable of working in outdoor conditions may apply. The minimum stay is two weeks, going up to six weeks.

Accommodation is provided in camps or in a kibbutz. Three full meals and several breaks are also provided five days a week. Expenses above this are the responsibility of the individual volunteer.

Those interested should apply to the above address.

### Israel Youth Hostels Association
3, Dorot Rishonim Street, P.O. Box 1075, Jerusalem, Israel

Every year the Association takes on between forty and fifty volunteers to work in its 31 youth hostels for periods of between three and four months.

There are no age limits, but volunteers require certificates of good health and insurance. They receive full board and lodging and pocket money.

For further information contact the Director-General at the above address.

## Kibbutz Representatives

1A Accommodation Road, Golders Green, London NW11. Tel: (01) 458 9235

Each year working holidays on kibbutzim in Israel are organised for about 3,000 people aged 18-32 and in good health. The work may involve physical labour in the fields, orchards, fish ponds, cowsheds and gardens; or work in the kitchens, laundry, general services or factory. Applicants must pay for their own travelling expenses and insurance for their stay lasting from five weeks to three months, with the option of extending it up to one year, and then receive free board and accommodation, leisure and entertainment facilities and occasional excursions, plus a small amount of pocket money.

All nationalities are welcome, except those which do not hold diplomatic relations with Israel. One can arrange to travel either as an individual or with a group of 12-15 people, which will be organised by Kibbutz Representatives. Prospective participants are all interviewed by Kibbutz representatives and kibbutz life is fully explained.

Enquiries to the above address.

## Laboratory of Prehistory

Haifa University, Haifa 31999, Israel

Volunteers of over 18 years are required to assist with archaeological excavations in caves, open air and underwater prehistoric sites in the Mount Carmel and Galilee region. They must stay for a minimum of two weeks during the summer months. Accommodation is provided and participants pay a contribution towards living expenses which vary for different projects.

For further information please contact the Director of the Institute of Archaeology and Maritime Studies.

## Lahav Research Project

Cobb Institute of Archaeology, Drawer AR, Mississippi State University, Mississippi State MS 39762. Tel: (001) 325 3826

The project was created in 1975 with the objective of excavating the seven acre mound-site of Tell Halif near Kibbutz Lahav in Israel and has since conducted seven summer field seasons of excavation. The site is of great historical importance, containing evidence of occupation in the Early Bronze, Late Bronze, Iron II, Roman and early Byzantine periods. Approximately 35 volunteers a year assist the staff of 25 specialists to uncover and process materials. Another purpose of the project is to allow the volunteers to gain theoretical as well as practical experience, so the daily timetable includes training sessions, supplementary lectures, and rotation of work assignments. The project lasts for six weeks each year, from mid-June until the end of July, and keeps the weekends clear to allow time for travel. No excavations are planned for 1989, but excavation seasons are planned for 1990 and 1991.

There are among the volunteers each year a large proportion of American students who use the dig as a means of obtaining academic credit at undergraduate or graduate level through one of several participating universities. English speaking people of any nationality are welcome to take part, but those with previous experience in this field are given priority. As the work is very strenuous and in extremely hot conditions, volunteers over 40 must produce satisfactory medical evidence of their health. The accommodation consists of a camp with five or six to a tent, and the food is said to be good (and ample: there are two breakfasts, for example, but this is something of a necessity, as work begins at 4 a.m.). A $795 contribution has been required from each volunteer to go towards expenses.

Those interested should write to Dr. J. D. Seger, Director, at the above address.

### Project 67
36 Great Russell Street, London WC1B 3PP. Tel: (01) 636 1262/3

Organisers of three types of working holiday in Israel, which are taken by over 2,000 a year. These are: Kibbutz working holidays, which last from five weeks to three months; archaeological digs, from two weeks to two months; and moshav working holidays from two months. A non-political and non-denominational organisation, Project 67 arranges transport and placement on a "package holiday" basis. Accommodation is provided on all holidays, but pocket money is only given at kibbutzim and moshavim.

The age limits vary according to the work chosen: for the kibbutzim, applicants should be 18-35, for the digs, 18 or over. Although no work permits or visas are required for EEC/UK/Irish/Commonwealth nationals, certain nationalities may have visa problems; beyond that there are no restrictions.

For further details, send a SAE to the above address.

### Religious Kibbutz Movement
7 Dubnov Street, Tel Aviv. Tel: (03) 257231

The Movement accepts volunteers to work on its Kibbutzim which are situated in many parts of Israel, including the Beit Sh'ean Valley, Ashdod, Ashkelon, and the Jerusalem and Tel Aviv areas. It should be noted however that only Jewish young people who are ready to follow an orthodox way of life are taken on as volunteers. The minimum period of stay is two months. The volunteer works at least eight and a half hours each day, most of the work being seasonal and agricultural. The Movement also runs four Kibbutz-Ulpan programmes (five months in duration), which combine formal instruction in Hebrew with voluntary work in a Kibbutz. These programmes take place throughout the year.

Volunteers must be at least 18 years of age, and in good health. No special qualifications are needed, but people with diplomas in life-saving are appreciated. All nationalities are welcome. Accommodation and food are provided, and moderate pocket money is paid. Expenses are not paid, including those arising from travel. A tourist visa is required, but no work permit is needed.

Applications should be sent to: Bnei Akiva, 2 Hallswell Road, London

NW11 0DJ. Tel: (01) 209 1319; or to Kibbutz Representatives, 1a Accommodation Road, London NW11 8EP. Tel: (01) 458 9235. These organisations handle all the formalities required for entry into the religious Kibbutzim.

## UNIPAL
20a Plantation Road, Oxford, OX2 6JD. Tel: (0865) 310138

UNIPAL, the Universities Educational Fund for Palestinian Refugees, sends about 60 volunteers annually to work on short-term projects during July and August in the Israeli-occupied West Bank and Gaza Strip, and with Palestinian communities in Israel. Most projects involve teaching English. There are also opportunities for long-term work with children (relevant qualifications/experience required) and teaching English (after successful completion of summer project—RSA Prep. Cert. in TEFL required, minimum period one year).

Although personal qualities are considered to be as important as formal qualifications experience of teaching English or working with children is an advantage. Short-term volunteers are provided with food and accommodation but pay their own air fares and insurance. Long-term volunteers receive pocket money and may be given assistance in paying fares etc.

Send SAE for application form in January/February. Interviews in March, April and May. Briefing in June for those selected.

## United Kibbutz Movement (Volunteers Dept)
82 Hayarkon Street, PB 26131, Tel Aviv. Tel: (03) 655207/651710

This organisation accepts visitors, individuals and groups, as temporary workers on a Kibbutz for a period of at least one month. A basic knowledge of English is necessary for participation, and the age range is 18-32 years. A working visitor on a Kibbutz works an eight hour day, six days a week. Apart from Saturday, which is usually the day of rest, the visitor receives three extra days monthly. As a rule, working visitors must be prepared to do any kind of work allotted to them by the work manager. The kind of work involved is of a very diversified nature, and depends on the type of Kibbutz that the volunteer is sent to. It is still mainly agricultural, but tending to be industrial as well. As the Kibbutz is a self supporting community, with its own services, quite a proportion of volunteers also go into essential services. The Kibbutz provides rooms (for 2-3 persons), meals in the Kibbutz dining hall, laundry service, work clothes, medical care, entertainment and pocket money. Travel expenses are not paid.

The best way to ensure a place on a Kibbutz is by applying to Kibbutz Representatives in one's own country. For the UK the address is: 1A Accommodation Road, Golders Green, London NW11 8EP. Tel: (01) 458 9235. For the USA: 27 West 20th Street, New York, NY 10011. Tel: 212 255 1338. More detailed information can be obtained there as well. Alternatively, volunteers who are already in Israel may apply directly to the offices at the above address, but in this case a place on a Kibbutz cannot be guaranteed.

**The Workers' Moshav Movement in Israel (Volunteers Dept.)**
19 Leonardo da Vinci Street, Tel Aviv, Israel

The first Moshavim were founded in 1921. They are family based settlements which were originally mainly agricultural but are now becoming increasingly industrial. Unlike the Kibbutz the Moshav allows for private enterprise and members have their own land and property. They also contribute to the cost of equipment needed by the whole Moshav. There are about 450 Moshavim in Israel and over 100 of these participate in the Moshav Volunteers Scheme.

Volunteers must be in the 18-35 age group with a clean bill of health, prepared to work for at least two months. Accommodation varies from Moshav to Moshav, but there is generally a volunteers' house next to the farmer's home with a shower, kitchen, cooking facilities etc. In most Moshavim there is also a club for the volunteers with facilities for sport and social activities. The working week is six days, eight hours a day, with one day off extra a month. Any overtime is paid extra, over and above the allowance of about $300 a month. After two months volunteers get a trip bonus of about $40.

Volunteers are required to abide by various regulations regarding work and leisure and the Moshav is also required to fulfil its share of the mutual obligation.

Applications can be made directly to Israel to the office at the above address.

**WST Ltd.**
Israel-Egypt Dept., Priory House, 6 Wrights Lane, London W8 6TA. Tel: (01) 938 4362

Assorted agricultural, domestic and factory work on Kibbutzim and Moshavim can be arranged for volunteers willing to stay a minimum of six weeks. There are also opportunities for excavating, cleaning and cataloguing on archaeological digs in Israel. Kibbutz workers are paid a small allowance in addition to their accommodation, meals and other necessary expenses.

There are no restrictions on applicants, however letters of reference and a doctor's certificate of fitness are required. No visas are needed for British volunteers.

Enquiries may be sent to the above address.

# Africa

**Alliance des Unions Chretiennes de Jeunes Gens du Cameroon**
BP 13.183, Douala, the Cameroons. Tel: 42 70 99

The Alliance organises a number of workcamps every year concerned with helping the community: projects include establishing schools, dispensaries, bridges, roads, communal fields etc. Around 60 volunteers are taken on international camps, which last for less than three months per year. Volunteers should be aged between 18 and 40 and should be of good health. Knowledge of either French or English is necessary, but no other qualifications or experience are needed.

Applications should be made to the above address.

**Chantier des Jeunes Voloountaires**
CCP 169-87 Rabat, BP 558 Batha, Fes, Morocco. Tel: (06) 332 37

This organisation conducts study courses, cultural activities and disaster relief programmes in Morocco. International volunteers can assist with these activities by joining weekend and summer workcamps held mainly during July and August. Around 140 volunteers are needed each year for periods of two to 21 days.

Volunteers must be at least 18 years old, have no infectious diseases and able to undertake manual work. Board and lodging are provided, but volunteers must pay their own expenses.

Applicants should apply to the President at the above address.

**Chantiers Sociaux Marocains**
BP 456, Rabat, Morocco

CSM organises workcamps in Morocco which concentrate on projects intended to benefit the local community. About 300 volunteers a year are involved, spending two or three weeks of the summer on the sites with fellow workers from many European and African countries.

Applicants should be between 18 and 30 years old, and in good health. Food and accommodation are provided, but the volunteer is responsible for all his personal expenses.

Those interested can either apply through their national branch of the CCIVS (which is IVS in Britain), or directly to the President at the above address.

**FOCUS, Inc.**
Department of Ophthalmology, Loyla University Medical Center, 2160 South First Avenue, Maywood, Illinois 60153, USA. Tel: 312 531 3408

FOCUS recruits ophthalmologists as short term volunteers for eye clinics in Nigeria. The volunteers provide medical and surgical eye care services. Around 15 volunteers are needed for placements of three weeks or longer, all year round. Applicants must be certified ophthalmologists and need to obtain a Nigerian visa. Usually a US medical licence is required but this would be waived for UK ophthalmologists.

Board, lodging, laundry services and transportation within Nigeria are provided but volunteers pay for their international travel.

Write to the President of FOCUS at the above address for more details.

### Gormogor Agricultural Development Organisation (GADO)
c/o Njala University College, Private Mail Bag, Freetown, Sierra Leone, West Africa

GADO's primary concern is to promote community development in the 100 or so villages within the Dasse chiefdom of Sierra Leone. Most changes and improvements are needed in agricultural related areas but opportunities also exist for other community work such as conducting educational courses for various groups within the communities. Around five volunteers are needed each year with the volunteer specifying the length of service. Tasks for volunteers involved in agricultural work will vary according to the season but on-going tasks include conservation projects and erection of fences and huts. Other volunteers may teach, work in creches, undertake administrative work, etc.

All volunteers must be at least 15 years old and able to communicate in English. As volunteers live in remote African villages they should also be in good mental and physical health. No special skills are required but volunteers with agricultural experience will be welcomed. Accommodation in huts is provided but volunteers must pay their own travelling expenses and contribute towards the food which is provided for them. GADO will help volunteers to obtain the necessary work permit.

Those interested should write to the Programme Director at the above address for more information.

### Jeunesse et Cooperation
B.P. 19, Safi, Morocco

Every summer international workcamps are organised in several towns in Morocco to work mainly on projects to help the poor. The work involves construction and renovation, carpentry, painting, bricklaying, work with children and the maintenance of parks. Participants should speak Arabic, French, English or Spanish, be at least 18 and in good health. They usually stay for three weeks and board and lodging are provided.

Those interested should contact the President at the above address.

### Lesotho Workcamps Association
PO Box 6, Maseru 100, Lesotho. Tel: (050) 314 862

This Association organises workcamps within Lesotho for volunteers of all nationalities. Around 400 volunteers are needed to work in co-operation with local communities on manual tasks including soil conservation, afforestation, installing water supplies and building roads, foot bridges and latrines. Held in June, July, December and January, the camps last for two or three weeks and consist of up to 30 people from Lesotho and abroad who are prepared to work seven or eight hours a day for five days a week.

Volunteers must be at least 18 years old, physically fit, speak English and have attended any sort of workcamp or have experience in construction. Board, lodging, health insurance and local transport are provided.

Write to the Director at the above address for more information.

## Mission Aviation Fellowship
Ingles Manor, Castle Hill Avenue, Folkestone, Kent CT20 2TN. Tel: (0303) 41356

Mission Aviation Fellowship is a Christian organisation which provides an air service for churches, missions and development agencies working in remote areas. The United Kingdom branch currently has bases in Chad, Kenya, Tanzania and Uganda and also flies into other countries. Around 12 volunteers with professional qualifications in aviation, (commercial pilots, mechanics and aviation technicians), are needed each year. Often volunteers experienced in office work, building and ancillary services are also required. Placements may last from three months to two years.

Volunteers must be committed Christians, fit, in good health and have appropriate experience. Accommodation is provided but volunteers usually provide or raise their own sponsorship for each assignment. The Fellowship obtains any visas or work permits required by the volunteer.

Further information can be obtained from the Personnel Manager at the above address.

## Pa Santigie Conteh Farmer's Association (PASCOFAAS)
P.M.B. 686 Freetown, Republic of Sierra Leone, West Africa

PASCOFAAS is centred around Makarie and over 20 neighbouring villages in the Bombali district, and was founded in 1982 to promote increased agricultural productivity for food production and income generation in order to improve the living conditions of members (roughly 2,000) with special attention to women, children and young people.

Activities undertaken include agriculture, the planting of rice and trees, construction of houses, roads and so on. Opportunities open to volunteers include secretarial work in the head office, agricultural and construction work and training local people in different skills.

All nationalities may apply as long as they speak English. They are required all year round for periods of two weeks to two years. About ten international volunteers are taken on each year. The minimum age is 17. Expenses are not paid, nor is pocket money provided, but accommodation is.

The association also supplies information to anyone interested in farming in rural areas of Sierra Leone. For further details about this or the voluntary work, contact Andrew Conteh, the Director, at the above address.

## Pensee et Chantiers
B.P. 1423, Rabat R P, Morocco. Tel: (07) 536 99

Pensee et Chantiers organise work camps in Morocco for international

volunteers. The work camps last for 21 days during July and projects include forest management, gardening, construction and maintenance work. Volunteers need no special skills but the minimum age accepted is 18 years. Sleeping bags and tools used in the projects are provided. Volunteers must pay a registration fee of around £20, provide their own meals, and pay for their own travel expenses.

For further information write to the President at the above address.

### Union Marocaine Des Associations De Chantiers (UMAC)

BP 455, Rabat, Morocco (correspondence); or 37 Rue Al Hind, Immeuble Ghandouri Maison No. 3, Rabat, Morocco.

Morocco is a country with a young population: three out of four Moroccans are under 30 years of age. Workcamp organisations have come to play an important part in mobilising the energies of Moroccan youth, and encouraging a positive attitude to the problems of a developing country. The Moroccan workcamp movement grew out of local organisations and the first major project the latter undertook was helping with the construction of "La Route de l'Unité" joining the North and South of the country. This was shortly after independence. In 1960 six regional organisations were founded in Meknes, Rabat, Fez, Sale and Safi. Then a national co-ordination committee was founded in 1961, which became UMAC in 1963. It organises weekend camps throughout the year and about fifteen summer camps lasting three weeks to a month in July and August. Activities include construction work, welfare work, agriculture, and protection of the natural environment. At Easter there are training schemes. About 350 volunteers are recruited each year.

The summer camps are international, and all nationalities are welcome. No special qualifications are needed. Volunteers should however speak Arabic, French or English, and enjoy good health. The age limits are 18 to 35. A participation fee of about £40 is payable. Board and lodging are free and work insurance is provided. No pocket money is paid, however, and volunteers pay their own travel expenses.

Applications should be made to the individual organisations directly. Some of these are: Amis des Chantiers Internationaux de Meknes, BP 8, Meknes, RP; Association de Chantiers de Jeunes, BP 171, Sale; Jeunesse et Cooperation, BP 19, Safi; Chantiers Sociaux Marocains, BP 436, Rabat; Chantiers Jeunes Marocs, BP 1351, Rabat; Pensee et Chantiers, BP 1423, Rabat; Mouvement Twisa, BP 77, Khemisset; Association de Travail Volontaire et Culturel, BP 4537, Casablanca, Morocco.

### Voluntary Workcamps Association of Ghana (VOLU)

PO Box 1540, Aacra, Ghana. Tel: Accra 663486

VOLU organises workcamps in the rural areas of Ghana for international volunteers. Tasks involve mainly manual work; construction projects, working on farm and agro-forestry projects, tree planting, harvesting cocoa and foodstuffs, working with mentally retarded people, teaching, etc. Around 1,500 volunteers are needed for workcamps at Easter, Christmas, and from June to October. Volunteers can stay throughout each period.

No special skills or experience are required but volunteers should be over 16 years old and fit to undertake manual labour. Volunteers pay their own travelling costs and a £50 inscription fee but accommodation and food are provided at the camps. VOLU supplies official invitations to enable volunteers to acquire visas before leaving for Ghana.

Those interested should apply through Service Civil International member organisations in their own country or directly to the National Organising Secretary at the above address.

## Voluntary Workcamps Association of Sierra Leone
PO Box 1205, Freetown, Sierra Leone, West Africa

The Association organises weekend, Christmas, Easter and summer vacation workcamps, during which volunteers are sent out to rural communities to help build schools, hospitals, roads and assist with other local projects. It also runs Farm Centres in rural areas to train local farmers in modern farming methods. During the long vacation camps, which last six weeks, the Association recruits volunteers from other West African countries, the USA and Europe, of whom some 150 are needed. However, both short term (six months) and long term (at least one year) volunteers are taken on. No special qualifications are needed, but people with skills in building construction, nutrition, nursing and agriculture are appreciated. Volunteers must be physically fit, and preferably between 18 and 60 years of age. The summer camps are held from around 10th July to 31st August. For the summer camps foreign volunteers pay a fee of $3 per day, which covers all living expenses: food, excursions, medical facilities and accommodation. Pocket money is not provided. The Association can arrange for visitors' visas for foreign volunteers in the summer. If volunteers stay for longer periods their visas can be extended.

Applications should be made to the Secretary General of the Association at the above address.

# Asia and Australia

## Australian Trust for Conservation Volunteers (ATCV)

PO Box 423, Ballarat, Victoria, 3350, Australia. Tel: (053) 32 7490

ATCV places volunteers in ATCV workteams in Australia at any time of the year. The conservation work undertaken by ATCV teams may be farm fencing, seed collection, tree planting, historic building restoration, birdhide construction, walking trail construction or maintenance tasks, etc. About 3,000 volunteers each year live and work in teams of up to 12 people to undertake these tasks. The length of placements depend on the applicant but are usually nine to 13 weeks long.

Volunteers must be over 17 years old, physically fit and able to speak and understand English. Potential volunteers are offered holiday packages that cost from £240 for nine weeks in one state of Australia to £460 for 13 weeks in up to four states. These packages cover food, accommodation and travel expenses over that period but not international travel to and from Australia. Volunteers must also produce evidence of suitable health and medical insurance on arrival.

For further information contact the National Director at the above address.

## Bharat Sevak Samaj

22 Sardar Patel Road, Chanakya Puri, New Delhi, and Nehru Seva Kendra, Gugoan Bye Pass Road, Mehrauli, New Delhi, India. Tel: 374016/374248

The Samaj was founded by Shri Jawaharlal Nehru, the first Prime Minister of India, as a non-political national platform for mobilising people's spare time, energy and resources for national reconstruction as a part of the first Five Year Plan. It has a network of branches all over the country, with a membership of over 750,000, 10,000 members working on projects, and about 50 foreign volunteers helping each year. Any person who offers his services for a minimum of two hours a week can become a member of the Samaj. Its normal programme includes the organisation of urban community centres in slum areas, night shelters, child welfare centres, nursery schools, training camps for national reconstruction work, family planning camps and clinics, and publicity centres for the Plans. The work also encompasses relief and reconstruction work after natural calamities, such as famine, drought, cyclones and earthquakes as well as the construction of houses for the Schedule Caste (lowest caste) and tribes and low cost latrines in villages.

Both skilled and unskilled workers are welcomed. Foreign volunteers, who can serve for between 15 days and three months, should be prepared to live in simple accommodation and respect local customs and traditions. They must finance their own stay, and it is preferred that they speak English.

Applicants should contact the General Secretary at the above address for further details.

## BMMF Interserve

186 Kennington Park Road, London SE11 4BT. Tel: (01) 735 8227/8

Each year approximately 40 volunteers participate in the Missionary Education Programme in Pakistan. (Medical Electives can also be arranged in Nepal and India). Generally volunteers become involved in medical, educational and technical projects which last from two to three months. This is primarily a self-financing scheme. Accommodation while on the job is free, food expenses are the responsibility of the volunteer. Concessional air fares are obtained and volunteers pay £350-£450 for travel.

Volunteers must be committed Christians who have a desire to share their faith as well as their skills.

Further information may be obtained from the MEP Secretary at the above address.

## Christian Work Camps — Australia

c/o Australian Council of Churches, P.O. Box c199, Clarence Street, Sydney 2,000, Australia.

For three weeks after Christmas Christian Work Camps organise building projects constructing houses, halls etc. for causes such as drug rehabilitation centres, youth camps, or as housing for aborigines. Around 40 volunteers a year are needed to do the work on these camps, the materials for which are provided by the organisation concerned. The work involves carpentry, plumbing, bricklaying, tiling etc. and a certain amount of routine domestic work such as cooking and washing. There are also some smaller camps in May and August.

Volunteers must be aged over 18 and be reasonably fit. Previous building experience would be useful, but is not essential. Accommodation is provided free, usually in a school or church hall, but a contribution of around $150 is expected to cover the cost of food, insurance etc.

For details write to the N.S.W. State Convenor at the above address.

## FEBA Radio

Ivy Arch Road, Worthing, West Sussex BN11 2DT. Tel: (0903) 37281

FEBA owns and runs a Christian radio station in the Seychelles which broadcasts a variety of programmes and news to the Middle East, South West Asia and East Africa in 26 languages. Two volunteers are needed annually to work as electronic and electrical engineers in radio programme production.

Volunteers must be committed Christians with experience in radio programme production or students of electrical and electronic engineering. Applicants must raise their own funds but accommodation is provided. A 'gainful occupation' permit is required for the Seychelles.

For further information contact the Personnel Officer at the above address.

## Indian Volunteers for Community Service

36 Headstone Road, Harrow, Middlesex HA1 2PE. Tel: 863 9544

This organisation seeks to help and motivate young British Asians to gain an understanding of their cultural origin by enabling them to participate in rural development projects in India. Non-Asians can also partake in order to learn about Indian culture. Each year eight Asian and 15 non-Asian youths are sent as volunteers to different projects for periods of six months, all year round. There is no set programme for the duration of the stay as the volunteers spend the time learning about the project in assisting in any way that they are able.

Asian volunteers must be fluent in an Indian language and aged between 18 and 25 years old. They receive free board and lodging, and sometimes insurance but must pay for their own airfares and personal sightseeing expenses. Non-Asians need no special skills but must pay for their travel and around £30 for their board and lodging. All volunteers need a tourist visa.

Applications should be made to the General Secretary at the above address.

### Joint Assistance Centre
H-65, South Extn-1, New Delhi 110049, India

The Joint Assistance Centre is a small voluntary group for disaster preparedness and relief that has its headquarters in Delhi, India. International volunteers can help by participating in workcamps held all over India, undertaking office, editing and library work or developing useful training resource materials. Workcamp projects may be road repair, construction of community centres, reafforestation and conservation projects, etc. Around 100 volunteers are needed each year, all year round, although workcamps are held intermittently. Placements vary from one to 26 weeks long.

Volunteers may be of any nationality provided that India has diplomatic relations with their country. All volunteers must be at least 18 years old and English-speaking. Very basic accommodation with elementary facilities is provided but volunteers pay a contribution of around £50 per month of their stay.

For more information write to the Convenor at the above address, enclosing three International Reply Coupons.

### Lanka Jatika Sarvodaya Shramadana Sangamaya (Inc.)
98 Rawatawatta Road, Moratuwa, Republic of Sri Lanka. Tel: 507159/ 505255

The ideals on which this organisation is based are contained in its name: "Sarvodaya" means the awakening of all, and "Shramadana" means the sharing of labour. For over 30 years the movement has sought to improve the quality of life of those who live in the most deprived areas of Sri Lanka, placing as much stress on the spiritual and cultural elements of life as on purely material development. Construction work is undertaken in 8,000 villages around the country with about 30,000 volunteers lending their services every year. Small numbers of helpers are taken from those countries with which Sri Lanka has diplomatic relations, and those with qualifications in tropical agriculture and technological skills are preferred. Any familiarity with the fields of health, nutrition, education, and social welfare would also be useful.

Volunteers should be young and in good health. The usual period of service is three months: no expenses are paid, but limited accommodation in dormitories is available.

Those interested should write to the Co-ordinator, International Division

### The Leprosy Mission
Goldhay Way, Orton Goldhay, Peterborough PE2 0GZ, UK

The Mission sponsors about 10 medical students each year to spend an elective period of a minimum of eight weeks at one of its centres in Southern Asia. They receive a substantial grant towards travelling costs and free board and lodging at the centre, but no pocket money. Students must be in their final year of training, in good health, and practising members of one of the Christian churches.

Applications should be made to the Executive Director at the above address.

### Paschim Banga Samaj Seva Samity
191 Chittatanjan Avenue, Calcutta-700 007, India. Tel: 39 7631

This voluntary organisation maintains hospitals, health clinics and other social institutions in India. The range of jobs open to volunteers is very large: assisting with health care, creches and workcamps, maintaining libraries, etc.

Around 300 volunteers are recruited for three to four weeks from January to February, June to July, and October to December. Applicants must obtain

a visa for their stay and should be English speaking, aged 16 to 28 years and in good health. Board, lodging and some pocket money are provided.

Write to the Treasurer at the above address for more details.

**Retarded Citizens Welfare Association of Tasmania**
GPO Box 1385 P, Hobart, Tasmania, Australia 7001. Tel: (002) 73 1149

This organisation runs a number of centres for retarded citizens in Tasmania, Australia. Voluntary workers are needed to help run the four branches of the association, to conduct fund raising activities and to help in the day centres, hostels, community homes, workshops and adult training centres around the state. Most of the 240 volunteers needed each year are active in fund raising while approximately 40 are needed all year round in the various centres.

An empathy for the retarded people is vital but any skills required and the length of placements will depend on the nature of the job undertaken. Accommodation is not normally provided.

Those interested should apply to the Office Manager at the above address.

# Other Short Term Opportunities

The following organisations are mostly concerned with long term voluntary work, but they also cater to some extent for volunteers for periods of under a year. They will be found listed in the *Long Term* chapter above.

ATD Fourth World Voluntariat
Bureau for Overseas Medical Service
Benediction Lay Volunteers
Catholic Medical Mission Board
Centro Studi Terzo Mondo
Christians Abroad

Direct Relief International
Habitat for Humanity
International Liaison of Lay
Volunteers in Mission
Missions to Seaman
Project Ladywood

# Non-Residential Work in the United Kingdom

The need for this section of the book is illustrated by a speech given by the Home Secretary Douglas Hurd on June 25th, 1988, in which he said that the "strong and able" should take responsibility for the less fortunate. With "increased leisure time and earlier, generally healthier, retirement, we should be looking to the active citizen and volunteer to play a greater part in enriching our neighbourhoods and communities".

But even before recent public spending cuts there were many jobs for which it was either impractical or impossible to employ professional workers. Among this category are "befriending" jobs with the old and disabled. A paid health visitor may be able to ensure that an individual has the necessities of life, such as food and clothing, but is unlikely to be able to spare enough time to meet the more intangible needs, such as reading aloud or simply providing company on a regular basis. Although volunteers involved in health and social work may be relegated to these unskilled jobs, their work can still be of vital importance. In the probation service, for instance, a full time probation officer may have the job of keeping a regular watch on prisoners and parolees, but it is the volunteer who has the chance of actually befriending an individual: his unofficial status is a positive advantage.

Volunteer work in the UK is not only available in the general area of health and social services, however. There are a large number of pressure groups, conservation groups and others who require assistance in their administrative duties as well as in their research, campaigning (whatever methods they use) and their fund-raising.

The work listed in this section may be pursued on a full-time basis, but since few of us are lucky enough to have no other commitments, the majority of opportunities described below are more of a part-time nature. Some of these part-time duties involve a fairly heavy time commitment of several hours a week; others merely require a degree of regularity or consistency. Some may continue for several years; others may last only for a weekend or for a couple of weeks during the summer.

In attempting to categorise the different types of voluntary work available in the UK, it has not been possible to draw distinct dividing lines, although it is to be hoped that the classification system will act as a general guide. There are obvious overlaps, for instance between the section of *Disease and Disability* and the sections on *Children* and *The Elderly*. At the beginning of several sections, an attempt is made to cross-refer readers to other relevant sections, but is assumed that the general areas of overlap will be easily deduced from a glance at the table of contents. It should also be mentioned that several sections, notably *National and Local Volunteer Organisations, Community Projects* and *Fund Raising and Office Work* describe organisations that cut across the general classifications system.

# National and Local
# Volunteer Organisations

Unbeknown to the general public, the UK's voluntary resources are carefully monitored by several complex and overlapping networks of official and semi-official organisations. At the national level, these organisations are concerned with collecting and interpreting data, and producing new plans and programmes in response to both national and local needs. The local offices are in charge of implementing these plans, and acting as recruitment and referral agencies on behalf of the prospective volunteers, and of the local bodies that require volunteers.

As far as individual applicants are concerned, the national offices that are described below are of little practical value, other than as a source of information and referral to the appropriate local office. Local branches— whatever title they adopt—act more or less in the same way as labour exchanges. However, they vary a great deal in their policies, and some are more actively involved in recruitment than others. All can at least offer information on local volunteer needs, and can refer enquiries to the appropriate local organisations.

The people who run local volunteer bureaux should be in touch with all nearby organisations and institutions concerned with voluntary work, and be aware of the type of help that they need. For example, a conservation group may need people with a knowledge of architecture, an old people's home may want car drivers with their own cars, or a youth club may require a bricklayer to help build a new clubhouse.

There is normally a short informal interview before a volunteer is sent on to an agency. This is to make sure that the volunteer will be used in a situation where his interests and abilities will be put to the greatest use, and to tell him what exactly his job will entail. There is a big difference between vaguely wanting to "do something useful", and being prepared, for example, to give up every Monday evening for an indefinite period in order to drive people to and from a hospital. Of course, not all voluntary work involves a regular commitment of time, but there are many cases, especially those which concern befriending people, where some degree of regularity is essential.

## National Associations

### National Council for Voluntary Organisations
26 Bedford Square, London WC1B 3HU. Tel: (01) 636 4066

The object of the Council, which was founded in 1919, is to act as the central voluntary agency for the maintenance and promotion of voluntary social service by individuals and groups in urban and rural areas. It aims to do this by developing co-operation between voluntary organisations and statutory authorities, by providing information on social service, and by taking initiatives in the field of social action where appropriate. The Council provides information, training, legal and advisory services for voluntary organisations in general and for local counterparts such as County Community Councils and Councils for Voluntary Service.

In conjunction with a network of over 200 local and regional bodies, the Council can respond to each community's new needs either by establishing a new organisation (past examples include Age Concern, National Children's Bureaux and the National Association of Citizens Advice Bureaux) or by working with existing organisations to meet such emergency needs as unemployment, inner city deprivation, etc.

The National Council is not in a position to help individuals find suitable voluntary work in their area, but for 85p (including postage of amendment sheets), they will send a list of addresses of the local and regional offices with whom they are connected. Alternatively, these can be found in local telephone directories, or by enquiring at Citizens Advice Bureaux. A local organisation may be called a *(County) Community Council, Council for Voluntary Service, Council for Social Service, Rural Community Council* or *Federation of Community Associations;* the name of the town or county will be included in the organisation's full title. Although these offices do not recruit volunteers direct, they should prove useful sources of information on local volunteer requirements. People living in Wales should contact the Council of Social Service for Wales, Llys Ifor, Crescent Road, Caerphilly, Mid Glamorgan. Tel: (0222) 869224/5/6.

### National Youth Bureau

17-23 Albion Street, Leicester LE1 6DG. Tel: (0533) 471200

The National Youth Bureau is a non-departmental public body offering information and support to those engaged in social education work with young people. The Bureau does not itself place volunteers, but provides information about voluntary work opportunities in England and Wales. In particular it publishes *Sparetime Sharetime,* a resource pack on voluntary work opportunities in England and Wales. *Sparetime Sharetime* is free, but include a cheque or postal order for 50 pence to cover postage and handling costs.

### The Volunteer Centre UK

29 Lower King's Road, Berkhamsted, Herts. HP4 2AB. Tel: (044 27) 73311

The Volunteer Centre UK is a national agency looking critically and constructively at current practice in volunteer involvement. It gives information and advice to people working with volunteers in both voluntary and statutory sectors. The Centre is an independent charity funded by the Voluntary Services Unit of the Home Office and by charitable trusts.

The Volunteer Centre UK operates an enquiry service (there is an information bank of 10,000 items on volunteering), a consultancy service, runs training courses, and produces publications and case studies on the policy, theory and practice of volunteering, plus regular publications including a quarterly journal. These services are aimed not only at voluntary service co-ordinators, but also paid workers working alongside volunteers (for example, social workers, nurses, teachers) and policymakers and managers in central and local government and voluntary organisations.

If you wish to get involved in voluntary work locally, contact your volunteer bureau, or contact the Centre's information unit at the above address.

# Local Volunteer Bureaux and Councils

Prospective volunteers are recommended to consult one of their local associations or councils for advice on voluntary work opportunities within their area. Not all local associations are actively involved in recruiting volunteers, but all are prepared to at least refer applicants to an appropriate local recruiting body.

A few of the more active local volunteer bureaux and councils are described below, but it must be emphasised that these are only included as examples, and their activities are typical of many such bureaux up and down the country.

### Advance (Advice and Development for Volunteering and Neighbourhood Care in London)
14 Bloomsbury Square, London WC1. Tel: (01) 831 9873

Advance is an independent organisation that offers advice, information, training and consultancy services to both volunteer organisers and those who work with volunteer organisers. Their work is mainly with those in Greater London but they do undertake some work outside this area.

Those interested contact the above address.

### Bournemouth Voluntary Workers Bureau
167 Holdenhurst Road, Bournemouth, BH8 8DT. Tel: (0202) 293300

The Bureau recruits, interviews and places between 150 and 200 volunteers a year in statutory and voluntary agencies in the Dorset area. The main types of work are servicing an agency as an administrator or fundraiser and working directly with those who need help and conservation work. Those interested should contact the Bureau at the above address.

### Bristol Council for Voluntary Service
The Southville Centre, Beauley Road, Southville, Bristol BS3 1QG. Tel: (0272) 662676

The Bureau acts as a clearing house of volunteers and an information service on voluntary work in the Bristol area. Around 200 local and national organisations are served each year.

For further information contact the Volunteer Bureau Organiser at the above address.

### Clywd Voluntary Services Council

Station Road, Ruthin, Clywd, North Wales LL15 1BP. Tel: (082 42) 2441

The Clywd Voluntary Services Council collects information about the opportunities for voluntary work that exist within the county of Clywd in Wales. Potential volunteers are given advice and information before being referred to appropriate organisations. Around 300 volunteers are recruited each year to help with mentally disabled people, clerical work, sporting and church activities, holiday play projects, animals, etc.

Those interested should apply to the Director at the above address.

### Dyfed Association of Voluntary Services (DAVS)

11/12 King Street, Carmarthen, Dyfed SA13 1BH. Tel: (0267) 236 367

DAVS is a registered charity formed by the amalgamation of local voluntary organisations and statutory bodies. It provides support and assistance to all volunteer bodies throughout the county of Dyfed in a variety of ways, including recruiting volunteers who are then placed in contact with appropriate schemes and organisations.

Those interested in participating in voluntary work in Dyfed should contact the Information Officer at the above address.

### Gwent Volunteer Bureau

8 Pentonville, Newport, Gwent. Tel: (0633) 213 229

This Bureau recruits, places and provides support for volunteers in Gwent. There are around 200 mostly non-residential positions offered each year. The minimum age for volunteers is usually 14 to 15 years and special or useful skills such as having a driver's licence may be required for some jobs, but not for most. The length of time for which volunteers are required varies widely.

Those interested should contact the Volunteer Bureau Organiser at the above address.

### Leeds Volunteer Bureau

229 Woodhouse Lane, Leeds 2 9LF. Tel: (0532) 448 921

Leeds Volunteer Bureau recruits volunteers for all types of voluntary work in the Leeds area and also supplies information on voluntary work opportunities in other areas. Around 1,000 volunteers are recruited each year usually for placements of a month or more.

Volunteers must normally be over 16 years old and most jobs do not require any special skills. Many organisations pay for volunteers' expenses but accommodation is not usually provided.

Prospective volunteers should apply to the Organiser at the above address.

### Leicester Volunteer Bureau

32 De Montfort Street, Leicester LE1 7GD. Tel: (0533) 553333

The Leicester Volunteer Bureau recruits for both statutory and voluntary organisations in the Leicester City area. Opportunities are available during daytimes, evenings and weekends and are long term and short term. As with other Volunteer Bureaux there is a wide variety of openings available from helping with children in playschemes through to elderly people at Lunch Clubs, local groups on outings and holidays. Practical help is also needed from drivers with their own cars, people to help with basic woodwork, metalwork or painting at a workshop, people to service in charity shops and so on.

Special qualifications may be needed for some jobs, but not for most. The minimum age is normally 14. Organisations recruiting volunteers are encouraged to pay expenses. The length of time for which volunteers are required varies widely.

Applications should be sent to the above address.

### Rochdale Voluntary Action

158 Drake Street, Rochdale, Greater Manchester OL16 1PX. (0706) 31291

The Council for Voluntary Service for Rochdale Metropolitan Borough co-ordinates the work of over 360 local organisations involved in voluntary activities with disabled, elderly, young or disadvantaged people, etc. It also represents the interests of the voluntary sector and seeks new initiatives in voluntary work such as a silk screen workshop.

The Council has an extensive library with a computer, and provides a limited duplicating and typing service for member organisations.

Further information may be obtained from the General Secretary at the above address.

### Scottish Community Education Council

Atholl House, 2 Canning Street, Edinburgh EH3 8EG. Tel: 031-229 2433

The Scottish Community Education Council promotes and co-ordinates community involvement throughout Scotland. It provides an information service on topics related to community education and refers volunteers to appropriate agencies and organisations. The council also issues an annual information sheet "Summer Opportunities" which lists addresses of voluntary work programmes in Scotland.

For more information or referral, contact the Personnel Officer at the above address.

### Strathclyde Regional Council: Community Education Department

218 Ayr Road, Newton Mearns, Glasgow. Tel: (041) 639 7160

Around 100 volunteers a year are needed to help run youth clubs, holiday playschemes and community improvement projects for the Council. The play-schemes take place in July: the other activities take place around the year. Non-local volunteers could be found accommodation in local homes if they can pay for their own food, etc. Those interested should contact the Area Community Education Officer at the above address to learn how they can help.

### Tameside Volunteer Bureau

300 Stamford Street, Ashton Under Lyne, OL6 7NW. Tel: (061 339) 2345/ 9797

The Bureau operates as a general clearing house of volunteers and information service on volunteer work in the Tameside region. Every year it helps around 300 volunteers to find suitable work with over 50 local voluntary and statutory agencies according to their interests, abilities and availabilities.

Those interested should contact the organiser at the above address.

### Youth Volunteer Action

7, Chilston Road, Tunbridge Wells, Kent. Tel: (0892) 315 84

Youth Volunteer Action recruits volunteers aged between 13 and 25 for a range of voluntary work with different organisations in the Tunbridge Wells area. These include working with the elderly, the handicapped and children, decorating, conservation, fund raising etc.

Those interested should contact the Youth Volunteer Action Organiser at the above address.

# Other Nationwide Organisations

The organisations listed and described above, whether at the national or local level, are all inter-related through official and semi-official networks. The entries below refer to organisations and schemes that are nationwide in their scope and also cover such a wide spectrum of voluntary work opportunities that they defy classification elsewhere. Other national bodies that are more specific in their activities and volunteer needs will be found under the other divisions of this chapter.

### Active Christian Training Scheme

Glenburn House, Glenburn Road South, Dunmarry, Belfast BT17 9JP, Northern Ireland. Tel: (0232) 620611

This organisation has a middle-man role in that it refers interested volunteers to other agencies and missionary groups. Active Christian Training Scheme also publish FACTS which informs Christians about world evangelism.

Copies of FACTS may be obtained by writing to FACTS Magazine at the above address with prepayment of £3.50 annually.

### Association for Jewish Youth

50 Lindley Street, London E1 3AX. Tel: (01) 790 6407

The Association for Jewish Youth is the umbrella organisation for Jewish Youth Clubs in the UK. It is also the parent organisation for the Jewish Youth Voluntary Service which operates a number of schemes throughout the country in which teenagers and young adults work for the disadvantaged. Volunteers act as helpers in youth clubs, with senior citizen's groups and the Meals on Wheels service.

Applicants should contact the Executive Director at the above address.

### British Association of Settlements and Social Action Centres

13 Stockwell Road, London SW9 9AU. Tel: (01) 733 7428

This Association unites 63 member organisations around the country doing many types of local community work. These need volunteers to work with young people, the mentally and physically handicapped and the elderly.

A list of the member organisations can be obtained from the above address and applications should be made direct to them.

### Christian Service Centre

2 Dukes Avenue, London N10 2PT. Tel: (01) 444 6326

The Christian Service Centre acts as an information centre and counselling service for people wishing to undertake voluntary work with Christian organisations and missionary societies both in Britain and abroad. The Centre also carries out a preliminary vetting of most applicants before recommending them to other organisations. A new project is a skills register to match available people with skills to various short term Christian projects requiring those skills. The Centre also produces the "Short Term Service" folder which advertises vacancies in over 30 different Christian organisations.

For more information contact Barbara Patching at the above address.

### Family Service Units

National Office: 207 Old Marylebone Road, London NW1 5QP. Tel: (01) 402 5175/6

The aims of Family Service Units are to undertake intensive and comprehensive welfare work among families who require special assistance, and to develop community resources. The contribution of voluntary workers has had a far-reaching influence on the work of Family Service Units, as the genesis for the organisation was the activities of a group of volunteers during the Second World War. Today there are at least three times as many volunteers, including committee members, as paid staff in the 23 Units in England and Scotland.

There are five broad categories of volunteers working in the units: (1) committee members who manage local and national business; (2) those who provide services to clients, such as transport to clinics or holiday homes, running children's groups, playschemes and mothers' groups; (3) those who bring practical skills such as fund raising or decorating, and who usually are not in direct contact with clients; (4) those who give free advice to Unit committees and staff, based on their professional experience, e.g. teachers, doctors, psychiatrists and social workers; (5) clients and ex-clients who are able to offer practical help to either a Unit or to other clients.

Those who would like to help should contact their local Unit; the address should be in the telephone directory.

### League of Jewish Women

5th Floor, Woburn House, Upper Woburn Place, London WC1H OEP. Tel: (01) 387 7688

The League of Jewish Women is the leading national Jewish Women's Voluntary Service organisation in the UK. It provides all types of service to the whole community regardless of race, colour or religion. Membership is approximately 6,000 and almost 75% of these actually carry out voluntary work such as working with the young, in hospitals, for the physically and mentally handicapped, the elderly, and with and for other organisations including the WRVS, the Red Cross, Adult Literacy, Marriage Guidance Council, Counselling and Council of Christians and Jews.

Membership is open to all Jewish women resident in the UK who are over 15 for a minimal annual subscription. There are groups throughout the UK which meet regularly. No special skills are required, all are welcome, and expenses are paid where necessary.

Applications for membership should be made to the General Secretary at the above address and will be forwarded to the relevant Group Secretary.

### National Council of YMCAs
640 Forest Road, London E17. Tel: (01) 520 5599

The Council operates some 250 Youth Centres, Hostels and Outdoor Centres in England. Volunteers are used to organise work with the young unemployed, help with clerical work and administration at both central and local level, etc. There are at present over 8,000 voluntary Youth Leaders involved with some 600,000 members.

There are no special restrictions and skills required depend upon the job undertaken. Accommodation is sometimes provided where necessary.

Those interested should write to the above address.

### REACH (Retired Executives Action Clearing House)
89 Southwark Street, London SE1 0RD. Tel: (01) 928 0452

REACH enables retired professionals, business people and executives to find appropriate work with voluntary organisations which need assistance but cannot afford to pay for it. The service is provided free to both parties and opportunities for varying periods arise all year round. During 1987, 468 retired people were placed in voluntary jobs which made use of their skills and experience.

REACH only places skilled retired people. The voluntary organisation joined meets volunteers' out-of-pocket expenses.

For further information contact the Director at the above address.

### Salvation Army
101 Queen Victoria Street, London EC4P 4EP. Tel: (01) 236 5222

The Salvation Army performs a greater variety and volume of social service than any other voluntary organisation in the world. It has 25,000 Officers in 84 countries who have dedicated their lives to the service of God in the Army; but their work is made even more effective by the support of individuals who give voluntary help in hostels, homes and centres. In Britain alone the Army has nearly 1,000 centres of worship, evangelism, and community activity, as well as 125 social centres, all of which operate varying programmes for helping others.

There now exists in Britain a nationwide network of homes, hostels and other centres caring for people in physical and moral need. Although much of the work is done by Officers, volunteers can provide valuable ancillary services.

For further details contact the Leader of Social Services, 105-109 Judd Street, Kings Cross, London WC1H 9TS. Tel: (01) 383 4230.

## Willing Hands Service
W H Smith Limited

The WHS consists of the distribution of leaflets describing the possible range of local voluntary work and giving the address of a local volunteer bureau to contact. The scheme has proved to be a great success; it is estimated that since it began in 1972 it has introduced almost 23,000 people of all ages to voluntary work. Volunteers need no formal qualifications to take part and there is a wide range of jobs open to them.

Willing Hands leaflets, describing local volunteer opportunities are distributed from special dispensers located at cash points in selected W H Smith shops.

## Women's Royal Voluntary Service
234-244 Stockwell Road, London SW9 9SP. Tel: (01) 733 3388

The WRVS assists Government Departments, Local Authorities and other voluntary bodies in organising and carrying out welfare and emergency work for the community on a nationwide network operated through area, county, district and London Borough organisers.

Activities include work for elderly and handicapped people: residential/day clubs, meals on wheels, books on wheels, visiting schemes; for young families: children's holidays, playgroups, mother and baby clubs; for prisoners and their families; non-medical work in hospitals including shops/canteens and trolley services; clothing stores which provide clothing for distribution to the needy; drivers for rural transport; welfare work for HM Forces and for Service families; trained members to assist local authorities in emergencies including food, rest centres and information services.

Women and men of all ages, who can provide a few regular hours of help, are welcomed. Local office addresses are in telephone directories, or for further information write to the above address.

# Advice and Counselling

The organisations in this section all require volunteers to help the general public with problems that arise in their everday lives. Volunteers should be dedicated enough to undergo specialised training and to make a definite regular commitment of their time (for at leat five years, in the case of the National Marriage Guidance Council); they should also be intelligent enough to give the correct advice and mature enough to cope with the personal crises of others; and should be able to respect the confidence of their clients. Those who are not willing to become so deeply involved can still be of use by helping with the administration and office work involved with running such large national organisations. Obviously those who know how to type or have experience of office procedure can be of the greatest use here, but there may still be scope for those whose main qualification is enthusiasm.

## CRUSE - Bereavement Care
Cruse House, 126 Sheen Road, Richmond, Surrey. Tel: (01) 940 4818

Cruse was formed in 1959 to help widows and their children, and extended its service to widowers in 1980 and now offers help to all bereaved people. It provides counselling support by trained and selected counsellors, advice on practical problems and opportunities for social contact. There are now 140 branches in Britain which are normally run entirely by volunteers. Each branch organises a programme of social meetings and activities.

Those who would like to help should contact the Information Officer at Cruse House for details of their nearest branch.

## Family Planning Association
27 - 35 Mortimer Street, London W1N 7RJ. Tel: (01) 636 7866

The FPA needs volunteers both nationally and regionally to answer routine telephone enquiries about clinic hours, to man bookstalls at conferences and to administer information centres. Less casual volunteers may wish to train as speakers and discussion group leaders. Volunteers usually receive expenses, refreshments and a Christmas bonus.

No special qualifications are needed since training for the allotted task will be given. Participants may wish to work for a short time or indefinitely.

Applicants may enquire for details from the Personnel Manager at the above address.

## The Family Welfare Association
501-505 Kingsland Road, Dalston, London E8 4AU. Tel: (01) 254 6251

The Association is a registered charity that offers counselling and advice on personal and emotional problems both to individuals and families in Greater London, Milton Keynes and Northampton. Voluntary help is needed both to offer assistance to social workers on various counselling projects and also to take part in fund raising activities. Expenses are paid. For further information contact the Resources Department, at the above address.

## Lesbian and Gay Switchboard
BM Switchboard, London WC1N 3XX. Tel: (01) 837 7324

Lesbian and Gay Switchboard provides a 24 hour telephone information, advice and support service for gay men and women. As well as having detailed information on clubs, pubs, discos, befriending and counselling organisations in London and UK (incuding information on specialist groups such as disabled and married gays); they also operate a free accommodation service for those gay people seeking somewhere to live as well as those wishing to let, within the Greater London Area. They have about 120 volunteers at any one time to answer the telephone lines, produce publicity, carry out fund raising and administration.

Volunteers usually stay for about two years, are of either sex and are welcomed on the basis of being lesbian or gay and willing to undertake a short, supervised training aimed at expanding their knowledge of the London gay scene, AIDS and the law. Travelling expenses are reimbursed for unemployed volunteers.

Applications initially to the Training Group at the above address.

**Marriage Counselling Service**
24 Grafton Street, Dublin 2, Eire

The service provides marriage and family counselling, marriage preparation courses, counselling in schools, marital sexual dysfunction clinics and training of personnel in related agencies in the Republic of Ireland. Volunteers are welcomed to assist with the provision of these services all the year round. There are no special qualifications required. Expenses are paid.

Those interested can obtain further information from the above address.


**National Association of Citizens Advice Bureaux**
115/123 Pentonville Road, London N1

The Association is the central servicing body for the 1,156 Citizens Advice Bureaux throughout the UK. These provide information, advice, guidance, support and representation to any individual on any subject. Many have special legal and/or financial advice sessions with experts on hand; all help is supplied free and in complete confidence. Over 90% of the 15,000 people working in the bureaux are volunteers. Some of these have special skills, such as legal or financial knowledge or experience of administration or social work, but they should all be mature, understanding and sympathetic. The range of jobs to be done include interviewing, tribunal work, secretarial, clerical, filing and organising. Each interviewer is asked to work for at least four hours a week.

Skills are developed by training and in-bureau experience. All new workers are required to undergo a ten week course of information sessions, practical work and visits for one day a week which should provide a basic knowledge of procedure. After this course trainees are generally offered a three month probationary attachment to a bureau. Training is a continuing process and all workers are expected to attend courses for experienced workers, refresher courses, training on new legislation, and special courses on particular topics. The service expects an equal quality of work from paid and unpaid workers. Any travelling or personal expenses incurred by voluntary workers in attending courses are reimbursed.

Those interested in offering their services should contact their local bureau: the address should be in the telephone directory.


**RELATE, National Marriage Guidance**
Little Church Street, Rugby, Warwickshire CV21 3AP. Tel: (0788) 73241

Counselling is skilled work demanding much warmth, tact and perseverance, but it can be done very well by part-time volunteers.

Men or women who wish to work as marriage and personal relationship counsellors for RELATE have to undertake a part-time training course and commit about seven hours of their time per week for 40 weeks in the year. The timing of the work and the training can to some extent be adapted to meet the volunteer's own circumstances. An informal commitment to work for RELATE for five years is looked for. Volunteers are not normally accepted below 25 years of age.

Out-of-pocket expenses are paid, and in many RELATE centres some payment is made to counsellors who work substantially more than the basic voluntary commitment.

Local RELATE centres are happy to give more information to interested people; their addresses are listed in telephone directories under RELATE, National Marriage Guidance.

### Samaritans

17 Uxbridge Road, Slough SL1 1SN. Tel: (0753) 32713

The Samaritans exist to befriend the suicidal and despairing, by means of telephone, letter, or face to face meetings. There are 182 branches throughout the UK which make use of over 21,000 volunteers, and at each branch there are at least two volunteers manning the phones at any one time. The organisation is frequently the last straw at which a troubled person can grasp for assistance, so the recruitment system for volunteers is very selective to ensure that the applicant is suitable. The initial procedure of interviews and classes may take three to five months; thereafter, volunteers are expected to work three or four shifts per month.

Applicants should be 17 or over, and possess good hearing. They need not own a phone, and expenses will be paid to cover travel, other than ordinary commuting to and from the centres.

It is preferred that applicants write to their local branch (the address is in the phone book). Similar organisations outside the British Isles are affiliated to Befrienders International (Samaritans Worldwide), c/o The Samaritans at the above address.

# Children and Youth

The organisations in this section are not all necessarily involved in looking after children in need, as such: many are concerned with helping children to make constructive use of their time, and in some cases the person being assisted is the mother, who has her children safely taken off her hands for a time. In other cases the organisations provide help for children with special needs, such as a physical handicap or a deprived background. The entries below reflect the wide range of volunteer involvement that is required—from scout leaders or playgroup staff to flagsellers—in the cause of child and youth care. Most of the work is directly involved with looking aftr the young, but there are also jobs in the general area of fund raising, as well as indirect help like maintenance of toy libraries.

Voluntary help is normally welcomed at the many playschemes run by local Councils over the school holidays, especially in the summer. These playschemes are intended to keep children aged between 5 and 13 occupied and entertained from Mondays to Fridays while their parents are at work. They are normally staffed by paid workers, but additional assistance from volunteers should be appreciated whether it is given on a regular or irregular basis. People with any artistic, musical or sporting abilities would be especially useful. For further information contact the Recreation Department or Section of the relevant local authority, which will be co-ordinating playschemes in the area.

Other voluntary opportunities connected with child care and youth work will be found under *The Sick and Disabled, Hospitals,* and *Education.*

## Army Cadet Force Association

Cheltenham Terrace, London SW3 4RR. Tel: (01) 730 9733

The ACF is a voluntary youth organisation sponsored by the Army taking part in both military and community activities. It is open to boys between 13 and 18 years of age and a limited number of girls can be accepted in detachments where suitable facilities can be provided. Adult volunteers are needed to lead in the ACF and supervise activities such as shooting, sport, games, training for the Duke of Edinburgh's Award and visits abroad. They should be in good health, aged between 18 and 55 and British citizens. Training is provided for supervisors at the Cadet Training Centre in Surrey.

Those interested should contact the General Secretary at the above address.

## Association of School Care Workers

Inner London Education Authority, Social Work Service, The County Hall, London SE1 7PB. Tel: (01) 633 3289

The ASCW works with the Education Social Work Service to ensure that children living in Inner London benefit in the widest sense from the education provided. School care workers are involved in visiting families who find it difficult to cope with problems which may harmfully affect their children's education, families whose children may have special educational needs, and those with children starting or transferring school. Volunteers may join at any time but their services are required particularly during the school terms. Training is given. Travelling expenses, postage and telephone calls are paid for.

Applications should be made to the Director of Education Social Work Service at the above address.

## Bristol Association for Neighbourhood Daycare

c/o Office 1, 75 West Street, Oldmarket, Bristol 2

BAND co-ordinates 22 afterschool and holiday care schemes for 5-13 year olds throughout Bristol during the school holidays. Volunteers who have an interest in children are required to assist with playing games, arts and crafts sessions, drama, swimming and escorting them on outings.

Anyone interested should contact the Co-ordinator.

## Cheyne Holiday Club for Handicapped Children and Centre for Spastic Children

61 Cheyne Walk, London SW3. Tel: (01) 352 8434

The Holiday Club requires volunteers to assist during the school holidays with general care and feeding of the children, outings and as bus escorts. The Centre also needs them during the school terms to work one-to-one with the children under supervision, help with swimming, general care and in the office.

There are no restrictions except that bus escorts must be 18. Free lunches are provided.

Those interested should apply to the Principal at the above address.

### Children's Country Holidays Fund (Inc.)

1 York Street, Baker Street, London W1H 1PZ. Tel: (01) 935 8371

Every year the Fund provides holidays in the country, at the seaside, in private homes or established camps, for almost 3,500 disadvantaged London children. The arrangements for the children's holidays are undertaken by voluntary workers, under the umbrella of a small administrative staff in Head Office. Volunteers are also needed to act as train marshals supervising the children's travel to and from London.

There are no special requirements for camp supervisors, beyond a minimum age of 18, good health, and the ability to supervise children aged between nine and thirteen. The holiday periods vary between ten to fourteen days, and holidays always take place during the six weeks of the school summer holidays.

Those interested should write to the Director at the above address to find out how they can help.

### Church of England Children's Society

Edward Rudolf House, Margery Street, London WC1X 0JL. Tel: (01) 837 4299

Founded in 1881, the Society has developed the care it provides for children and families in need as problems have changed. Today, the Society's main aim is to prevent the break up of families. It has more than 40 family centres and neighbourhood projects throughout England and Wales. Volunteers play an important role developing projects and activities and working with children, teenagers and parents. Many of the centres run holiday schemes which rely heavily on volunteers.

A number of the Society's residential centres and community projects for children in trouble have links with voluntary organisations such as Community Service Volunteers and welcome regular voluntary visitors. Residential projects work with handicapped young people as well as children with special problems and needs.

Anyone wishing to offer their services should write to the Social Work Director at the above address who will then put them in touch with the nearest regional office.

### City of Bradford Playscheme Association

c/o Community Recreation Office, Baildon Recreation Centre, Green Lane, Baildon, Bradford, W. Yorks. Tel: (0274) 593234

At present the Association organises playschemes throughout the whole of the Bradford district which operate during the summer holidays for children aged between 6 and 15. There are about 70 schemes in operation, many of which include children from different racial backgrounds. Most of the schemes run for around three weeks.

Participants must be 16 or over, and like hard work and children! A small sum is usually paid to cover expenses.

Applicants should write to John Bedford, Community Recreation Officer, at the above address.

## Contact a Family
16 Strutton Ground, Victoria, London SW1P 2HP. Tel: (01) 222 2695/ 3969

Contact a Family aims to form local self-help groups with the help of full time workers in London and elsewhere, for both physically and mentally disabled children. Volunteers are needed to help in these and promote neighbourhood playschemes, weekend clubs, family holidays and special activities and events which provide very necessary help and support for families who live in the more urban, deprived and multiracial areas where children and their families are particularly isolated and under extreme pressure.

For further information contact the above address.

## The Cotswold Community
Ashton Keynes, Nr. Swindon, Wiltshire SN6 6QU. Tel: (0285) 861239

This community provides care, treatment and education for 50 severely emotionally deprived boys aged 9 to 18. The community consists of five separate households, a school and a farm. Around six volunteers are needed each year to teach and care for the boys. Placements are for a minimum of four months and may be up to a year long.

Volunteers may be of any nationality provided that they are at least 20 years old, speak English well and are in good health. Full board and lodging and about £15 pocket money per week are provided.

For further information contact the Principal at the above address.

## Dr. Barnardo's
Tanners Lane, Barkingside, Ilford, Essex IG6 1QG. Tel: (01) 550 8822

Dr. Barnardo's is a child care charity which helps handicapped or deprived children, young people and their families. There are five main areas of child care work: day care and services for young families; youth and community; residential; family support services; fostering and adoption. Volunteers over 18 years old are needed for child care work and fund raising activities.

The child care work is organised from local child care divisions and fund raising from the relevant appeals region. Those interested in helping should contact their nearest office as follows:

Divisional Director, London Division or Regional Appeals Director, London and East Anglia Region, Tanners Lane, Barkingside, Ilford, Essex IG6 1QG. Tel: (01) 551 0011 (Child Care) or (01) 550 8822 (Appeals).

Regional Appeals Director, Southern England Region, Summerfold House, 152 Leylands Road, Burgess Hill, West Sussex RH15 8JE. Tel: (04446) 43489

Divisional Director, Midlands Division or Regional Appeals Director, Midlands Region, Brooklands, Great Cornbow, Halesowen, West Midlands B63 3AB. Tel: (021) 550 5271

Divisional Director, North East Division, Orchard House, Fenwick Terrace, Jesmond, Newcastle-upon-Tyne NE2 2JQ. Tel: (091) 281 5024

Regional Appeals Director, North East England Region, Four Gables, Clarence Road, Horsforth, Leeds LS18 4LB. Tel: (0532) 582115
Divisional Director, North West Division, 7 Lineside Close, Liverpool L25 2UD. Tel: (051) 487 5313
Regional Appeals Director, North West England Region, Golden Hill, Leyland, Preston, Lancs. PR5 2NN. Tel: (0772) 453929
Divisional Director, Yorkshire Division, Four Gables, Clarence Road, Horsforth, Leeds, West Yorkshire LS18 4LB. Tel: (0532) 582115
Divisional Director, South Wales/South West Division or Regional Appeals Director, Wales and West Country Region, 177 Newport Road, Cardiff CF2 1UD. Tel: (0222) 485592 (Child Care); (0222) 493387 (Appeals)
Divisional Director, Scottish Division or Regional Appeals Director, Scottish Region, 235 Corstorphine Road, Edinburgh EH12 7AR. Tel: (031) 334 9893
Divisional Director, Northern Ireland Division or Regional Appeals Director, Northern Ireland Region, 414 Antrim Road, Belfast BT15 5BA. Tel: (0232) 370811
Director, Republic of Ireland, 244/246 Harold's Cross Road, Dublin 6. Tel: (0001) 977276

**Duke of Edinburgh's Award**
5 Prince of Wales Terrace, Kensington, London W85 5PG. Tel: (01) 937 5205/9

The Award is a programme operating in nearly 50 countries, of adventurous, cultural and practical activities undertaken voluntarily by young people. All participants are required to complete a Service Section which is intended to encourage them to realise that as members of a community they have a responsibility to others and that their help is needed. This Service Section involves practical work in one of the following fields (after some initial training): first aid; coastguard service or mountain rescue; work with the WRVS; or care of the mentally handicapped. For the Gold Award the participant must give practical service over a minimum period of 12 months, as well as reaching the required standard in the course of instruction and the service to which it is related. The scheme relies on an estimated 40,000 adults in the UK, who assist as leaders, organisers, instructors, fund raisers and committee members.

The Award programme is open to all young people between the ages of 14 and 25. Adults who help as instructors and assessors must be qualified persons nominated by the appropriate bodies.

Applications should be made to the Operations Officer at the above address, who will pass them on to the appropriate Regional Officer.

**Erdington Y.M.C.A.**
300 Reservoir Road, Erdington, Birmingham B23 6DB. Tel: (021) 373 1937

The YMCA operates a two week summer scheme all over the country for children aged 5-14 in August. Volunteers are needed from Mondays to Fridays during the day. Around 10 volunteers are needed to work as activity leaders, in the coffee bar etc. Volunteers must be aged over 18; those with skills in art, crafts or sport would be useful. Possession of a driving licence would be a great asset. A limited number of rooms are available for accommodation (which should be applied for well in advance), and pocket money is provided each week. There is also the possibility to work all year round.

Those interested should contact the Youth and Community Worker at the above address.

## Gingerbread: The Association for One Parent Families
35 Wellington Street, London WC2E 7BN. Tel: (01) 240 0953

Gingerbread was founded in 1970 by a woman who was experiencing difficulties in keeping a home together for her sons and herself. The authorities told her that the boys should be taken into care whilst she found a home, which would not only have been far more expensive for the state, but would also have broken up the family. The organisation grew as a result of the initial publicity, and there are now more than 300 self-help groups operating throughout England and Wales, with separate organisations covering Scotland and Ireland. Although the organisation runs largely on a self help basis, volunteers are also needed, especially to assist with child care. This ranges from baby sitting for individuals to running full and part-time holiday playschemes and after school care for 5 to 11 year olds. Help may also be needed by lone parents who are ill and therefore unable to take their children to school, go shopping, or perform household jobs.

Those interested should contact the national office at the above address, who will put them in touch with their local branch.

## Girl Guide Association
17-19 Buckingham Palace Road, London SW1W 0PT. Tel: (01) 834 6242

Guiding aims to help girls to learn self-reliance and self-respect. It teaches them to be resourceful, responsible and to think for themselves. It develops their sense of tolerance, kindness, justice and honour and shows them the importance of family and community values.

Guiding offers fun, friendship and adventure. The eight-point programme tailored to age groups—Brownies 7-10; Guides 10-14; Rangers 14-18; Young Leaders 15-18;—provides a framework within which a young girl can, by setting her own goals and working at her own pace, pursue new interests, show personal initiative and generally broaden her horizons.

Membership of the GGA is voluntary and open to any girl over the age of seven provided only that she is willing and able to make the Guide Promise of Service to God, the Queen and other people and to accept the code of living embodied in the Guide Law.

There are 778,131 members in the United Kingdom and $8\frac{1}{2}$ million Girl Guides and Girl Scouts in more than 100 countries. Guiding depends on volunteer adults. Women, especially those who have been Guides themselves, are always needed to run units. Men and women who are able to give occasional or regular help with the paperwork, fund raising, transport, publicity, training and badge testing are also welcomed.

To make contact with Guiding in your area contact Communications at the above address.

**Handicapped Adventure Playground Association Ltd**
Fulham Palace, Bishop's Avenue, London SW6. Tel: (01) 736 4443

There are five adventure playgrounds for handicapped children in London maintained by this association. Each has four full time paid playleaders with extra temporary workers in the Easter and Summer holidays. Volunteers are also welcomed to help both with caring for the children and the playground. The charity shop in Fulham, run entirely by volunteers, raises money for the playgrounds. Volunteers can also help with administration, office work etc. They are needed all the year round and all skills and experience can be put to good use. Travelling expenses are given to regular volunteers if necessary.

Those interested should apply to the Administrative Secretary at the above address.


**Hawksworth Hall School: The Spastic Society**
Guiseley, Leeds, West Yorkshire. Tel: (0943) 870058

This is a residential school for severely handicapped children which uses many part-time volunteers each year for care and classroom work and taking the children on outings. Volunteers are needed all the year round except in the main school holidays, and there are no restrictions except that they should be in good health and physically strong.

Those interested should write to the Headmaster at the above address.


**Holicare (North, Central and East Bournemouth Schemes, and Verwood (Dorset))**
c/o Mrs Val Bass, Chairman, Flat 3, 7 Cavendish Place, Bournemouth, Dorset. Tel: (0202) 290235

Holicare is a playscheme for children aged 5-11 with working parents that is operated during all school holidays in three areas of Bournemouth and Verwood, a few miles to the north. It provides supervised activities in small groups, with a varied programme that includes craft work, games, outings and trips to the beach and the New Forest.

Around five volunteers are needed to help run each playscheme. The schemes operate from 8.45 a.m. to 3.45 p.m. Applicants must be aged over 18; the possession of a driving licence by people aged over 25 would be an advantage. For further details contact Mrs Val Bass, chairman of the Management Committee, at the above address.


**Hospitals for Sick Children**
Great Ormond Street, London WC1N 3JH. Tel: (01) 405 9200 Ext. 5258

The Hospitals for Sick Children organise non-residential voluntary work at two children's hospitals in London. The hospital has a minimum age limit of 18 and asks for a commitment of one day per week for at least three months.

For further details, please contact the Voluntary Services Organiser at the above address.

**Lothian Play Forum**

Lothian Region Education Department, Community Education Service, 40 Torphichen Street, Edinburgh. Tel: (031) 229 9166 Ext. 2145

About 150 volunteers are needed each year, mainly in the summer, to organise such activities as outings, camping, games, painting, etc. for children of primary school age. Volunteers should be at least sixteen, preferably have some experience in helping with children and be prepared to work for three to six weeks. Pocket money is provided but no accommodation is available.

Those interested should write to the Administrative Officer.

**Meldreth Manor School**

Meldreth, Near Royston, Herts. Tel: (0763) 60771/5

Meldreth is a residential school for Cerebral Palsied young people most of whom have multiple handicapping conditions and moderate to severe learning difficulties.

Volunteers are required to do a wide range of jobs from working with students to maintenance of the site. Many volunteers are taken on each year. Expenses are sometimes paid and accommodation can be provided if necessary.

Those interested should apply to the Head Teacher.

**National Association of Young People's Counselling and Advisory Services**

17-23 Albion Street, Leicester LE1 6GD

NAYPCAS is an independent association of individuals and agencies providing counselling, advice and information for young people. Anyone interested in volunteering for this type of work with young people should contact the Association which can forward their enquiries to the relevant address.

**National Elfrida Rathbone Society**

The Rathbone Society, 1st Floor, Princess House, 105/107 Princess Street, Manchester M1 6DD. Tel: (061) 236 5358

At the beginning of the century, Elfrida Rathbone was a pioneer in providing care for educationally disadvantaged young people. In 1919 she set up an occupational centre in North London for children excluded from special schools, and worked until her death in 1940 to prove that these children could be helped to lead active, useful lives. The Society has branches throughout the country which organise Youth Training Workshops (nationally, and especially Manchester), a Drop In Centre (Derby), and a Hostel (Leigh), school and family support schemes and an employment support scheme (Manchester).

Volunteers are seen as having a unique contribution to make. They bring fresh ideas, new skills and a non-professional friendliness to people whose lives would otherwise be threatened with narrowness. Using volunteers involves the community in supporting children and young people who can feel alienated and lack confidence. Volunteers are needed all year round to give one to one support in social/communication skills and literacy/

numeracy. Only a few hours a week are needed but a regular commitment is important. No accommodation is provided.

Enquiries may be sent to the Volunteers' Organiser at the National Office as above.

### National Playbus Association/Mobile Projects Association
Unit G, Arnos Castle Estate, Junction Road, Brislington, Bristol BS4 5AJ. Tel: (0272) 775375

Playbuses and mobile community resources are any vehicle, normally double decker buses, which provide a range of services in isolated areas both rural and urban. These range from playgroups for the under fives, holiday playschemes and afterschool work, youth club work, exhibition and welfare rights work, education projects and work with pensioners. The Association provides information, publications and support services to the 400 projects operating in the United Kingdom.

Anyone interested in helping with one in their area or seeking advice on how to organise one should contact the headquarters at the above address.

### The North East Children's Society
1a Claremont Street, Newcastle upon Tyne NE2 4AH. Tel: (091) 2323741

The Society was founded in 1891 and its main concern is the welfare of children (and their parents) in the North East of England, principally the Tyneside area. It possesses a highly motivated and experienced team of social workers, and runs a home visiting scheme with more than 200 trained volunteer parents who befriend families in their own homes. Volunteers also help with residential care for teenagers with the view to preparing them for independent living. Their other facilities include: a Family Resource Centre and Day Nursery.

Any volunteers interested in helping in these fields, generally being of help and support to families, should apply to the General Secretary at the above address.

### Play Matters (National Toy Libraries Association)
68 Churchway, London NW1 1LT. Tel: (01) 387 9592

Play Matters is the parent body for over 1,000 toy libraries in the United Kingdom; it is a Registered Charity.

The first toy libraries were set up by parents to loan toys to children with physical and/or mental handicaps. Now a growing number of toy libraries (over 50%) are open to all children in the community. Many toy libraries are run wholly by volunteers; those which have a paid organiser are also dependent on voluntary help. There are toy libraries in schools—nursery, infants' and junior—attached to public libraries and some loan to groups such as childminders and play groups.

Each toy library is autonomous—the need for voluntary help can vary from one to another. Anyone wishing to offer their services should contact Play Matters who will put them in touch with the nearest toy library. If there is not a toy library in the area, help and advice is available to anyone wanting to start one. Please write to the Director at the above address.

## Sailors' Children's Society
Newland, Hull HU6 7RJ. Tel: (0482) 42331/2

The Society cares for the children of seafarers from all parts of the country. Up to 56 children and young people are in residential care at the Newland Homes in family groups of not more than eight. A further 400 are supported with their widowed mothers in their own homes in different areas around the country. As well as its work for children the Society provides or supports homes for aged seafarers or their widows in Hull and South Shields. The Society has a considerable number of fund raising committees in various parts of the country, staffed by voluntary helpers.

Those interested in helping should contact the General Secretary at the above address.

## Saturday Venture Association
66 Clarendon Road, London W11 2HP. Tel: (01) 727 0670

This association is concerned with the provision of activities for disabled or terminally ill children. It works with councils to ensure that the most is made of entertainment and sports centre facilities and conducts Saturday clubs for the children and their friends. The Saturday Venture Association also has a charity shop and furniture shop in Richmond. All interested volunteers are needed to assist with the various projects; surveying areas to establish local needs and then setting up autonomous clubs, working in the charity and furniture shops, helping with Saturday activities in the clubs and helping on holiday projects which occur during Easter, Christmas and summer vacations. Any commitment, from one month to 12 months will be accepted.

Volunteers should be non-smoking and preferably have a driver's licence. Typing and other skills are useful. Depending on the project accommodation may be provided but pocket money is always paid.

Those interested should contact the Chairman at the above address.

## St. Basil's Centre
Heath Mill Lane, Deritend, Birmingham B9 4AX. Tel: (021) 772 2483

This youth organisation based in the city centre of Birmingham needs about 50 volunteers to help in the running of night shelters, hostels, information and housing aid and counselling services. Most of the young people who seek assistance are aged 16-25, and come from backgrounds of tension, frustration, fear and violence. They need to be helped in finding accommodation, and in learning to adjust to a more stable environment through acquiring appropriate social skills.

Applicants of all races and nationalities are welcome, provided they speak fluent English and are over 18 years of age. Experience of working with youths in informal settings would be an asset, although not essential.

Enquiries and applications may be sent to Mr. Les Milner, Warden and Team Leader, at the above address.

## Scout Association
Baden-Powell House, Queen's Gate, London SW7 5JS. Tel: (01) 584 7030

The Scout Association aims to prepare young people to take a constructive place in society by providing interesting and enjoyable activities under voluntary adult leadership. Scouting began in 1907 based upon Lord Baden-Powell's ideas and book, *Scouting for Boys*. The Movement quickly spread and the world Scout population is now 16 million in 150 countries. In the UK there are some 658,000 members—Cub Scouts (8-10$\frac{1}{2}$ years), Scouts (10$\frac{1}{2}$-15$\frac{1}{2}$) and Venture Scouts, which includes young women (15$\frac{1}{2}$-20). There is a pre-Cub facility, Beaver Scouts, from 6-8 years. The three principal sections offer Progress Awards culminating in the Queen's Scout Award for Venture Scouts which calls for the highest standards of self-discipline, personal achievement and a substantial record of community service.

The Scouting and Unemployment Programme gives advice and guidance to out of work members to help them to use time to their own and the community's benefit. Through government agencies it often initiates job opportunities for non-members as well as members of the Movement. During summer there are sometimes opportunities for voluntary service, with expenses paid, as instructors and assistants at local camp sites and activity centres. Those interested can obtain the address of their local branch from the above address.

### Youth Clubs UK
Keswick House, 30 Peacock Lane, Leicester LE1 5NY. Tel: (0533) 29514

Youth Clubs UK (formerly the National Association of Youth Clubs) provides a range of services to support youth club work throughout the UK. There are over 45,000 youth workers including part-time workers and volunteers, involved in over 7,500 affiliated clubs.

Volunteers are welcome, whether they bring a specific practical skill or simply enjoy working creatively with young people. Volunteers should contact their local youth club or Local Association of Youth Clubs, or the Director of Publications and Information at the above address.

# Community Projects

The organisations in this section perform many functions and owe their origins to a variety of different causes—perhaps a church, a local authority, or the combination of a group of like-minded individuals coming together. Their aims may be to start play-groups, provide advice for unemployed or those in financial difficulty, or looking after the local elderly. What they all share is that they are all run for the community by the community.

Anyone thinking of starting a community project in their own area should first contact the National Federation of Community Organisations (see entry below). The first problem will be finding suitable premises from which to operate, preferably with a telephone. With the right array of talents, skills and enthusiasm, it should be possible to start and run a successful community project. Most projects find that, after slow beginnings, their schemes snowball and their range of activities multiplies. Publicity is one of the keys to the success of this type of project: once a scheme is established and proves to be useful, it will generate its own publicity. Local press coverage and distribution of leaflets in public places (libraries, information centres, citizens advice bureaux, etc.) are invaluable in the early stages.

Many community projects exist in towns and cities up and down the country but community projects need not be solely in urban areas: residents of country villages isolated by reductions in bus services may now legally pool their resources and run a minibus service for those without cars, for example. It is hoped that prospective co-workers will enquire whether a community scheme exists in their neighbourhood. It is also hoped that a few readers will have the know-how, money and/or enthusiasm to start their own scheme if one does not exist in their neighbourhood.

### Ashram Community House
23/25 Grantham Road, Sparkbrook, Birmingham B11 1LU. Tel: (021) 7061 773

This Christian community runs a number of projects in the multi-racial and inner city area of Sparkbrook, Birmingham. All projects undertaken seek to respond to the problems in the predominantly Muslim/Pakistani district; poverty, unemployment and racism. Volunteers have the chance to live as members of the community, be involved in current projects, share in the social life and help with household chores. Over 100 volunteers are needed throughout the year to help with tasks such as cleaning, gardening, cooking, decorating, building, animal husbandry and organising social events and publicity. Placements are for a minimum of two weeks but vary according to the projects undertaken.

All volunteers are welcome provided they are mature, over 20 years old and understand and have some commitment to the aims of the projects. Volunteers skilled in horticulture, animal care, driving, Asian languages and office work are particularly welcome. Disabled people are welcome but the building is not suitable for wheelchair use. Volunteers are expected to contribute towards their expenses according to their financial position. Accommodation is provided.

Those interested should apply to the Co-ordinator at the above address.

### The Birmingham Settlement
318 Summer Lane, Birmingham B19. Tel: (021) 359 2113

The Settlement is an independent organisation which runs a number of projects using volunteers in the inner city area of Birmingham. It also operates a number of national Associations which use volunteers extensively. One of the most important of these is an advice centre for those in financial difficulties. The Housing Debtline Project is a national telephone counselling service for those faced with the possible loss of their homes. Their other projects include running play schemes and after-school clubs, and visiting old people's homes. Around 150 volunteers are used by the Settlement each year.

It is preferred that volunteers make a regular commitment of their time to whichever project they become involved with. People with any knowledge of legal or financial matters are especially needed to help advise about money. There is a limited amount of accommodation, usually reserved for volunteers from abroad. Travel expenses may be paid, depending on the circumstances of the applicant.

Those interested should contact the Volunteer Officer at the above address.

### The Centaur Project
313/315 Caledonian Road, London N1 1DR. Tel: (01) 609 3328/9639

The Centaur Project is a grass-roots initiative to regenerate the inner city. The project is strongly independent and non-political, and is principally involved with activities to do with employment; setting up and running skill-training workshops in a broad range of office disciplines, and providing support and advice. In particular the Project is cataloguing onto computer a vast and extensive reference collection on every old building and tourist site in the British Isles. Volunteers are especially needed to help with this, (an interest and knowledge in old buildings and computers is an advantage), with reception and administrative work, (secretarial, word processing, typing skills are useful), and to help with renovation programmes, (do-it-yourself and building skills). About 70 volunteers are needed around the year; the time given depends on the nature of the activity undertaken. Travel expenses and lunches are provided but not accommodation.

It is recommended that anyone interested visits the Project before committing themselves. For further details write to Mr McNiel at the above address.

### Free Form Arts Trust
38 Dalston Lane, London E8 3AZ. Tel: (01) 249 3394

Free Form is a registered charity which promotes the use of arts, crafts and decoration to improve the environment and develops opportunities for the participation of community groups and individuals in school and local projects around the country. Work may be either interior or exterior and examples are mosaic wall panels, landscaping and planting and decorative wall murals. For school projects every attempt is made to organise the work so that children, teachers and parents all have a chance to help. Depending on the project work, around 10 to 20 volunteers are needed per year to assist with all aspects of environmental regeneration from workshop activities to the production of written information material. Projects begin at Easter and may last through to October.

Volunteers must speak basic English, have writing, creative, architectural, landscaping or planning skills. Drivers are preferred. Reasonable expenses or pocket money may be paid.

For further information apply to the Administrator at the above address.

### Fulham Good Neighbour Service
378 Lillie Road, London SW6. Tel: (01) 385 8850/8308

The Service provide assistance through volunteers to those who need it and supplements statutory services in Fulham. About 100 volunteers are used annually in a variety of ways: driving, shopping, gardening, decorating, pushing wheelchairs, doing household jobs, electrical repairs, escorting, etc.

There are no restrictions or special skills required. Travel, expenses and on-the-job expenses are paid.

Anyone interested in helping should contact the Organiser at the above address.

### International Flat
20 Glasgow Street, Glasgow G12. Tel: (041) 339 6118

The International Flat is a community centre situated in a multi-racial area of Glasgow that aims to bring people of different races and cultures together. It contains a common room, library, childrens room, kitchen and office in addition to accommodation for a community worker and two overseas students. There are various activities such as weekly sewing, cookery and keep fit classes, monthly meetings intended to help people share their religious faiths, and an annual playscheme for children in July, for which voluntary help is required.

Help is needed from volunteers either for one or two hours per week around the year or for three weeks in July while the playscheme operates. Basic accommodation can be provided for volunteers on the playschemes. For further details contact the Community Worker at the above address.

### London Diocesan Board for Social Responsibility (formerly Wel-Care)
30 Causton Street, London SW1P 4AU. Tel: (01) 821 0950

The Board, a Church of England voluntary agency, employs professional social work staff in 16 local offices all over London north of the Thames. There are specialist residential and day care projects, and they assist over 2,000 people each year, dealing with family and personal problems arising from homelessness, inadequate housing, unemployment, poverty, family conflicts, bereavement, addiction, loneliness and difficult personal relationships.

Voluntary help is needed by local committees in management of practical projects, fund raising, book-keeping, typing and advertising. Volunteers who help with home visiting and counselling are given training and supervision.

Those interested should contact the Director of Social Work.

### The National Federation of Community Organisations
8/9 Upper Street, Islington, London N1 0PQ. Tel: (01) 226 0189

The Federation exists to provide advice and information to local community organisations on running voluntary organisations, managing community centres, identifying and meeting community needs, working with statutory authorities and other voluntary organisations etc. Help is needed from around ten volunteers per week who are able to conduct research, do general clerical work and provide legal advice. Some volunteers give regular help perhaps once a week, others just occasionally to help with specific jobs such as mailings. Expenses are covered where necessary. Applications to the Information Officer at the above address, who can also advise on the addresses of community organisations around the country.

**Student Community Action**

3 Round Church Street, Cambridge CB5 8AD. Tel: (0223) 350365

Student Community Action acts as an advisory agency linking student volunteers in Cambridge with community bodies, as well as organising its own projects. Students returning to Cambridge are also required for Student Action Community's annual August playscheme. The playscheme is conducted in an adventure playground for two weeks in the middle of August. Children between the ages of 5 and 18 years attend between the hours of 9 a.m. and 5 p.m. on weekends and weekdays. Skills in arts, crafts, music or sports are useful.

Volunteers must be at least 18 years old and competent in English. Accommodation is not usually provided nor are expenses guaranteed.

Those interested should apply to the Co-ordinator at the above address.

**Student Community Action Development Unit (SCADU)**

Oxford House, Derbyshire Street, London E2 6HG. Tel: (01) 739 9001

The Unit encourages, promotes and develops the voluntary community work of students through approximately 100 local Student Community Action Groups in Great Britain. Altogether there are some 15,000 volunteers involved with these autonomous local groups which have different priorities, perhaps concentrating on work with the mentally handicapped, children, young people, the disabled, welfare rights, women's centres, etc.

These groups are not volunteer bureaux; most members are students who become involved with the groups attached to their place of study and who state the level of involvement they are able to give to its activities over the academic year. It would be helpful if the area of the country in which involvement is wanted could be stated. There is no payment for this voluntary work: arrangements for travel expenses, board and lodging will depend upon the individual groups.

Those interested should send a stamped addressed envelope for a list of Student Community Action Groups in Britain.

# Conservation and the Environment

At first glance the organisations in this section have little in common, from preserving industrial architecture to protecting rural England. But they all share a goal of restoring, protecting and preserving the environment against the ravages of progress.

The term "environment" is used in its widest sense, but most organisations interest themselves in a specific aspect of our natural or man-made heritage, such as Victorian architecture, national parks, wildlife, etc. Some organisations are also specific about the types of social evil they are actively opposed to, e.g. industrial pollution, cruel sports, seal culling, urban expansion, etc. Methods of protecting the former against the latter are equally diverse. Direct positive and practical action like renovating old houses or picking up litter is one method; direct action against certain elements of society, such as property developers, etc., is another. Indirect action, for example doing research into alternative energy also works towards the same ends. Volunteers are required to take part in all these activities, as well as the more humdrum office work, research in libraries, surveys and fund raising activities.

The largest voluntary body concerned with nature conservation is the Royal Society for Nature Conservation, the national association of 46 regional Nature Conservation Trusts in the UK. The Society itself has only a limited need for volunteers, to perform clerical and administrative work in its offices at the Green, Nettlesham, Lincoln LN2 2NR. The regional Trusts, however, have wide needs for skilled and unskilled volunteers to perform practical conservation work on nature reserves and other land of conservation interest, to work as wardens on the reserves and to help with their office work. Each Trust recruits its own volunteers, and needs may vary from region to region: the addresses of individual Nature Conservation Trusts can be found in local telephone directories under the county or area name.

### Animals' Vigilantes
James Mason House, 24 Salisbury Street, Fordingbridge, Hampshire SP6 1AF. Tel: (0425) 53663

This international Trust promotes an interest in the care and welfare of animals and teaches young people to respect all animal life. People from more than 40 countries and of all ages may join in the work of the Trust.

Enquiries may be sent to the Membership Secretary at the above address.

### Association for Industrial Archaeology
The Wharfage, Ironbridge, Telford, Salop. Tel: (095 245) 3522

The Association provides advice on the conservation or restoration of industrial archaeology and related activities in the UK. Volunteers should write to the Secretary at the above address who will forward enquiries about local activities to the relevant regional group.

### British Butterfly Conservation Society
Tudor House, Quorn, Near Loughborough, Leics. LE12 8AD. Tel: (0509) 412870

Several projects devoted to the conservation of both common and endangered species of butterfly are carried out with the help of volunteers. Members are needed to volunteer for work on butterfly habitat surveys over a period of five years, in order to discover how habitat and climate affect certain breeds.

Participants with a considerable knowledge of British butterflies, larval food plants, wild flowers and trees are needed to carry out the work of the Society. Surveys are organised between April and October each year.

Enquiries may be sent to the Chairman, at the above address.

### British Naturalists' Association
23 Oak Hill Close, Woodford Green, Essex

The Association was founded in 1905 (as the British Empire Naturalists' Association) in order to bring nature lovers in all parts of the UK and from overseas into contact with each other. It encourages and supports schemes and legislation for the protection of the country's natural resources, and organises meetings, field weeks, lectures and exhibitions to extend and popularise the study of nature. The Association does not supplement the activities of local and regional bodies, some 150 of which are at present affiliated to it.

Volunteers who wish to offer practical help on such projects as clearing a village pond should join their local branch, if possible. These are at present operative in the following areas: Buckinghamshire, Dorset, Essex, Hampshire, Hertfordshire, Kent, Lancashire, London, Greater Manchester, Middlesex, Norfolk, Shropshire, Somerset, and Surrey.

The subscription rate for members is at present £7.50 per annum, which includes three issues of the Association's journal, and the Bulletin, which provides details of branch activities. Applications for membership should be sent to the Hon. Membership Secretary at the above address.

### Council for the Protection of Rural England
4 Hobart Place, London SW1 0HY. Tel: (01) 235 9481

The Council was formed in 1926 to organise concerted action to improve, protect and preserve the rural scenery and amenities of English country villages and towns. There is a branch office in every county, which acts as a watch-dog on planning applications. Research is carried out on any plans which pose an unreasonable threat to the countryside and, if necessary, formal opposition can be organised. Volunteers are needed for all stages of this process.

Enquiries may be addressed to the Secretary at the above address.

### Future Studies Centre (FSC)
c/o The Birmingham Settlement, 318 Summer Lane, Birmingham B19 3RL
Tel: (021) 359-3562/3563

The Future Studies Centre is a resource centre with a network of contacts in the United Kingdom and abroad. It collects and disseminates information on present trends and developments and alternative options for the society of the future. The help of volunteers is welcome in many areas. The flow of incoming publications has to be continually integrated into the extensive Future Studies Centre Library. Volunteers can also help with staffing and maintaining the Library. There is the possibility too of surveying and cataloguing special areas of interest within the collection.

There are places for self-financing full-time or part-time volunteers. The Centre can provide lunches on working days and reimbursements for local travel. At times, accommodation can be negotiated. For further information please contact the Administrator at the above address.

### National Canine Defence League
1-2 Pratt Mews, London NW1 0AD. Tel: (01) 388 0137

Volunteers are needed at rescue centres for mistreated and abandoned dogs throughout the country to help with the exercising of the dogs and especially to help raise funds to keep the centres open, running coffee mornings and stalls at local venues etc. In addition, clerical help is always welcomed at the head office in London. Volunteers should be at least 18 years of age. A list of centres is available from the above address.

## National Trust for Scotland
5 Charlotte Square, Edinburgh EH2 4DU. Tel: (031) 226 5922

The National Trust for Scotland runs over 80 properties and more than 80,000 acres of land in Scotland which are open to the public. Approximately 500 volunteers are needed during the tourist season (from April to October) to help with the presentation of these properties to visitors. Some knowledge of history, environmental studies, natural history, or art and design would be useful.

There are no restrictions as to age or nationality, although applicants must speak reasonable English. A knowledge of foreign languages might be of use when dealing with tourists from abroad. An allowance to cover expenses may be given if the applicant's circumstances demand it.

Those interested should write to Margaret Cameron at the above address for further details.

## North Norfolk Railway
Sheringham Station, Sheringham, Norfolk NR26 8RA. Tel: (0263) 822045

The North Norfolk Railway is a preserved railway running along the North Norfolk coast. Nearly all of the staff are volunteers and are involved in operating steam and diesel trains, restoring and renovating rolling stock and working outside on extending the line. Around 150 volunteers are needed, with any training given depending on the experience of the volunteer and the length of service offered—from a few hours to several weeks at a time, all year round.

Volunteers must be over 16 years old and while there is no upper limit, elderly volunteers may be restricted to the platform and souvenir shop duties. Drivers and firemen must acquire a certificate of competency which the Railway will provide after the volunteer has been suitably trained. Only in special cases will accommodation be provided.

Those interested should apply to the General Manager at the above address.

## North York Moors National Park
The Old Vicarage, Bongate, Helmsley, York YO6 5BP. Tel: (0439) 70657

The North York Moors National Park covers 553 square miles in North Yorkshire. Between Easter and October of each year, 120 volunteers are needed to act as rangers throughout the park. Tasks include providing information to visitors, patrolling the park and carrying out both conservation work and improvements to the public rights-of-way network. Weekend and day-long training sessions for prospective rangers are held during winter. Voluntary rangers are required to work a minimum of 12 sessions, lasting for six hours between 8 a.m. and 8 p.m., during the opening season.

Volunteers should be between 18 and 65 years old, able to get on well with people and reasonably fit. Applicants with a knowledge of the area and driving licences are preferred. No accommodation is available but a mileage allowance is paid.

Applicants should apply to the Principal Assistant in Land Management at the above address.

### Peak Park Conservation Volunteers

Peak National Park Office, Aldern House, Baslow Road, Bakewell DE4 1AE. Tel: (062 981) 4321

Each year thousands of volunteers help to protect the wildlife habitats and areas of outstanding natural beauty in the Peak District National Park over weekends, bank holidays and during school and college holidays around the year. Types of work to be done include building and repairing footpaths, stiles, steps, footbridges, fencing, walling, hedgelaying and tree planting, pond clearance, and collecting litter.

No specific requirements are expected of volunteers except that they be between 14 and 65 years old. No accommodation is available so applications from local volunteers are preferred; but tools, materials, training and drinks are provided.

Those interested should contact the Volunteers Organiser at the above address. There are sufficient applicants for 1989 but a need is anticipated in future years.

### River Thames Society

Side House, Middle Assendon, Henley-on-Thames, Oxon RG9 6AP. Tel: (0491) 571476

The aims of this Society are to encourage an active interest in the history, current affairs and future of the River Thames and its whole environment. Volunteers are needed to preserve and extend the river's amenities, to protect its natural beauty and to promote nature conservation. The Society with its 2,533 members, all of whom are volunteers, also assists in the development of art, science, sport and recreation associated with the Thames and its surroundings. There are no special requirements or restrictions for volunteers beyond a sound knowledge of the river.

Applications to become a member should be made to the Administrative Officer at the above address.

### Suffolk Wildlife Trust

Park Cottage, Saxmundham, Suffolk IP17 1DQ. Tel: (0728) 3765

The Trust undertakes practical land management work for wildlife conservation in Suffolk, England. Local volunteers are needed to help with a variety of duties including ecological surveys and research, photography, illustration and graphics for leaflets and reports, fund raising, local event organising and sales. The majority of the work takes place during winter and over 1,000 volunteers give their time; volunteers are normally residents of Suffolk but others are welcome as long as they speak English and arrange their own accommodation. Volunteers must be aged 18 to 60 years and have tetanus protection. Only very limited expenses are available and no pocket money is given.

Write to the Project Officer at the above address for more details on individual projects.

# Education

Although a high standard of free state education is available for all, there are still a large number of people who for one reason or another manage to pass through the system without learning basic skills: two million adults in Britain can hardly read, and half a million are totally illiterate. There are also a large number of immigrants living in ethnic communities in Britain who have never learnt to speak English, and are thus isolated from the bulk of the population. Volunteers are greatly needed to work as teachers in this field: the job requires a sympathetic approach, and patience, but no formal qualifications.

### Commission for Racial Equality

Elliot House, 10/12 Allington Street, London SW1E 5EH. Tel: (01) 828 7022

There are more than 100 Councils for Racial Equality in the UK, many of which can use voluntary help in such areas as running youth clubs, arranging publicity, and language tuition. The most important of these is teaching English, especially to Asian women, as many Asians are unaware of their rights simply because they cannot speak English. A regular commitment, even of only a few hours a week, is essential in this field as those learning English may forget what they have learnt or simply become disillusioned if their tutors arrive irregularly or simply give up.

The needs of Councils vary from area to area; prospective volunteers should contact their local Councils directly, either by finding their address from the phone book or through the Information Officer at the above address.

### The Marine Society

202 Lambeth Road, London SE1 7JW. Tel: (01) 261 9535

The Marine Society provides libraries for merchant ships and educational facilities for merchant seamen. About twenty teachers a year act as voluntary tutors by correspondence. One or two other volunteers are also used at the London office. Tutors can work either for short periods or indefinitely all the year round.

Postage for their correspondence is paid for and possibly pocket money to office volunteers. There are no restrictions except that volunteers should be fluent in English.

Enquiries should be sent to the General Secretary at the above address.

# The Elderly

The average age of a British citizen is now increasing as the products of the post World War 2 "Baby Boom" age, and they have not been replaced by an equally large younger generation. Average life expectancy has also steadily increased this century. There are therefore steadily increasing pressures on the social services to look after an older population, and there is more and more need for support from voluntary organisations to help them, a situation that can only increase by the end of the century.

It can make an immense difference to the life of an old person if they are visited by a volunteer, even if it is for only an hour a week. There are many simple practical jobs which a volunteer can do to improve the quality of life of an old person, from shopping, gardening or going to the library, to simply changing a light bulb. But the most important job that the volunteer can do is simply to provide companionship, whether the old person lives alone or in an institution: this is a job at which the young are particularly successful. For many housebound people the volunteer is their only visitor, someone to talk to over a cup of tea, and someone who is there because they care, not because they are just doing their job.

There are many ways of entering this field of voluntary work: Age Concern, the British Red Cross and the WRVS are the principal national organisations which are active on a local scale; alternatively, you can simply phone up the matron of a local old people's home and ask if you can help in any way.

Apart from the entries below, other voluntary work concerning the elderly is discussed in the sections on *The Sick and Disabled* and *Hospitals*.

### Abbeyfield Society

186-192 Darkes Lane, Potters Bar, Herts. EN6 1AB. Tel: (0707) 44845

The Abbeyfield Society is a national voluntary organisation which provides a special type of accommodation for lonely elderly people. Ordinary domestic properties are converted into a number of private bed-sitting rooms which are furnished and looked after by the occupants. There are now over 1,000 such houses throughout the UK. A resident housekeeper cooks and serves two main meals and provides materials for breakfast, which is prepared by residents in their own rooms. Houses are purchased, converted and managed by some 600 local Abbeyfield Societies all over the UK; members of local societies are all voluntary workers, with the exception of the resident housekeepers.

Local societies need a wide range of skills in order to function effectively. Executive Committees usually have a solicitor to deal with legal matters, a book manager or accountant to handle finances, a builder or surveyor to advise on properties and maintenance, and a doctor to liaise with the medical profession and advise on medical matters generally. It also needs several members who are available during the day to be responsible for the day-to-day administration of the Society's houses. Besides these voluntary committee members, whose responsibilities require fairly specific amounts of time, there is also always a need for volunteers whose time cannot be given on such a regular basis. These contributions may take the form of visiting, taking the residents on outings, gardening, organising jumble sales or coffee mornings, or deputising for the housekeeper on her days off.

Those interested should contact the Chief Executive at the above address for the address of their nearest local Society.

### Age Concern England
Bernard Sunley House, 60 Pitcairn Road, Mitcham, Surrey CR4 3LL. Tel: (01) 640 5431

Age Concern is the largest association in the country concerned with the retired, co-ordinating over 1,400 local groups around the country. It began in 1940 as the Committee for Welfare of the Aged, became known as the National Old People's Welfare Council in 1955 (a name which remains its official title as a charity), and adopted its present name in 1971. The general aims of the organisation are to study the needs of the retired and the elderly, to provide services for them at local level and to campaign on their behalf.

The activities for which volunteers are needed may differ slightly from area to area according to differing local circumstances and priorities. They include visiting the lonely, helping to run day centres and lunch clubs, providing a transport service for old people in isolated areas, and decorating and gardening. Most people should be able to provide some sort of help to their local Group.

The address of the nearest Age Concern Group can be discovered from the telephone directory.

### Counsel and Care for the Elderly
131 Middlesex Street, London E1 7JF. Tel: (01) 247 9844

Counsel and Care for the Elderly is a registered charity that with the help of volunteers offers a free advisory and individual counselling service, particularly concerning care, for those of pensionable age who are facing problems, and provides financial assistance to help with the cost of nursing care in a registered home or a home. The charity is expanding its network of fund raising Regional Organisers and help is also needed in this vital field. For further information contact the General Secretary at the above address.

### Help the Aged
St. James's Walk, London EC1R 0BE. Tel: (01) 253 0253

Volunteers can undertake a wide variety of roles with Help the Aged throughout the UK. Many of these opportunities arise within fund raising and can range from participating in or organising a local event to canvassing the support of local industry for a particular campaign. Local committees run by volunteers also carry out a programme of fund raising activities to help elderly people at home and overseas.

Other opportunities include giving talks, research, helping out in a charity shop, secretarial and administrative work.

There is no age limit for helpers, and those interested should apply to the Volunteer Co-ordinator at the above address, or to Help the Aged, Rutland House, 38/42 Call Lane, Leeds LS1 6DT. Tel: (0532) 430632.

### Jewish Welfare Board
221 Golders Green Road, London NW11 9DW. Tel: (01) 458 3282

For over 125 years, the JWB, a Voluntary Organisation, has served the Jewish Community in London and South England. Their objective is to meet the needs of elderly people and their families by maintaining elderly people in the community, supporting and encouraging families and the community to care for their elderly, reducing isolation and loneliness, and helping people prepare for and adjust to old age.

Volunteers are needed to assist Social Workers by providing a back-up service, which involves visiting and befriending people in their own homes (this can be done in their own locality). Other ways of being of service include driving, escorting and shopping. There are no recruitment restrictions; however volunteers of the Jewish faith will be preferred.

Enquiries may be sent to Mrs Rachel Frankel, Voluntary Services Co-ordinator, at the above address.

**Pensioners Link**
17 Balfe Street, London N1 9EB. Tel: (01) 278 5501

Elderly people who are no longer able to do much gardening, decorating or practical repairs are often in need of assistance from local volunteers. Pensioners Link which operates in 11 boroughs throughout London, undertakes to organise voluntary visits to pensioners to bring companionship as well as practical help. Out of pocket expenses are provided.

The minimum age of volunteers is 14 years and there is no maximum. Practical skills are always valuable.

Enquiries may be sent to the Director at the above address and are then forwarded to the appropriate local centre.

# Fund Raising and Office Work

There is hardly an organisation in this book that would turn down an offer of either money or administrative help from a volunteer. The organisations in this section have many different specific objectives, but all have in common the fact that their greatest need for voluntary help is with raising money and doing office work.

It must be stressed that the list of organisations requiring this type of help is almost endless, and the few entries below are merely examples. If a volunteer wishes to help a specific organisation, then he should find the address of the local branch from the phone book and offer his services. Alternatively, many organisations advertise in local and national newspapers for help with some specific project; for example the British Legion appeal for poppy sellers in early autumn. Often the media have pet projects: a local paper may run an appeal to buy a body scanner for a hospital, or a children's television show like "Blue Peter" may be saving to buy facilities for the disabled. Most "good causes" have some established machinery for fund raising, such as flag days or jumble sales, but they should also welcome new ideas, such as an offer from a school to organise a sponsored swim. The most dramatic fund raising schemes, such as wind surfing around Britain or running across the Himalayas, are normally the result of individual enterprise, someone feeling that he or she has some special way of attracting the attention of the public. It is always advisable to contact the relevant organisation before arranging any project, as it may be possible to link it with some publicity drive; at the very least, they should be able to provide some publicity material such as leaflets or T-shirts to increase its impact.

Clerical and administrative work is equally essential in any organisation whether commercially or voluntarily run. The examples of office work include below range from routine filing and letter-writing to organising complete surveys and investigative research studies. Although it may seem mundane, it is work that must be done if the organisation's overall aims are to be successful.

### ASH (Action on Smoking and Health)
5-11 Mortimer Street, London W1N 7RH. Tel: (01) 637 9843

ASH is an information campaign which aims to prevent the disability and death caused by smoking. It urgently needs volunteers in its office to help service the thousands of requests for information received each year; and to assist with projects on the many different aspects of smoking control, including smoking in public places, children and smoking, and passive smoking. Volunteers are paid travelling expenses and £1 to cover lunch. Anyone interested should contact the Volunteer Co-ordinator at the above address.

### Birth Control Trust
27-35 Mortimer Street, London W1N 7RJ. Tel: (01) 580 9360

The principal aim of the Trust is to advance medical and sociological research into contraception, sterilisation and legal abortion and to publish the results of this research. Around ten volunteers are needed to help with the office work at the above address, filing and sorting press cuttings. Volunteers normally help once per week or per fortnight.

Applications should be made to the Information Officer at the above address.

### The British Association of The Experiment in International Living
Upper Wyche, Malvern, Worcs. Tel: (06845) 62577

The Association exists to promote understanding between people of different cultures and countries throughout the world. It does this by enabling anyone over the age of 17 to stay as a member of another family in over 45 countries. In becoming part of that family they learn something of the customs and culture of that country. Host families are volunteers as are the local representatives who administer the programmes in each country. The National Office with 11 paid staff also recruits volunteers during busy periods. Volunteers are always needed to meet Experimenters arriving in this country at a variety of airports, and to act as advisors on how to recruit outbound participators. There are no restrictions or special requirements and the period for which volunteers are recruited depends upon the job. Host families receive expenses as do local representatives. Travelling and out of pocket expenses are provided for London work and generous expenses are given to recruiters of out-bound participators.

Further information can be obtained from the National Director at the above address.

### British Heart Foundation Appeal
102 Gloucester Place, London W1. Tel: (01) 935 0185

Volunteers are always needed to help with fund raising events throughout the United Kingdom.

Enquiries should be made to the nearest Regional Offices which are listed in all telephone directories.

### British Theatre Association
Regent's College, Inner Circle, Regent's Park, London NW1 4NW. Tel: (01) 935 2571

The British Theatre Association is a charity concerned with promoting the British theatre in Britain and around the world. Help is needed from volunteers to deal with mail outs, help with publicity, and to work in the library repairing books and stocktaking. Volunteers are needed around the year: travel expenses to and from work are paid for. For further information contact the Director at the above address.

### BUFORA (British UFO Research Association)
16 Southway, Burgess Hill, Sussex RH15 9ST. Tel: (04446) 6738

BUFORA depends entirely on the voluntary participation of its members for its research, investigations and administrative activities. The association, founded in 1964, aims to encourage, promote and conduct unbiased scientific research of UFO phenomena in the UK. It also co-operates with other researchers throughout the world. The research findings and theories are published in the bi-monthly BUFORA Bulletin and presented in a series of monthly lectures in London. Volunteers, sufficiently interested and informed, are needed to carry out, collate and document research. Voluntary help is also required in editing reports, summarising news, writing articles, translating relevant foreign journals and letters, and interviewing eye-witnesses, where the qualities of tact, perseverance, initiative and common sense are essential. BUFORA publishes an Investigator's Manual for instruction in researching and interviewing techniques. Some form of transport is usually needed by volunteers, since sightings can be reported in remote areas of the country. Sometimes expenses are reimbursed, although the majority of investigators bear their own expenses.

Enquiries, enclosing a self-addressed envelope, may be sent to the Hon. Secretary at the above address.

### Cancer Research Campaign
2 Carlton House, Terrace, London SW1Y 5AR. Tel: (01) 930 8972

As the largest single supporter of research into forms of cancer, including leukaemia, in the UK, the Cancer Research Campaign needs an unlimited amount of help with fund raising activities. There are 1000 local committees throughout the UK who co-ordinate the efforts of several thousand volunteers every year; in 1987 approximately £25,000,000 was raised from voluntary efforts, donations and legacies. This money is used to support over 600 projects in universities, medical schools, and hospitals throughout the country. It is impossible to do more than generalise about the range of fund raising activities which are organised, as volunteers are encouraged to use their initiative to find original means of attracting money.

Anyone seeking the address of their local Area Appeals Organiser should consult the local telephone directory under Cancer Research Campaign.

## CARE Britain
35 Southampton Street, London WC2E 7HE. Tel: (01) 379 5247

CARE Britain is a Third World development agency operating in 40 countries but voluntary positions are only available within the London office. Around three volunteers are needed to assist with fund raising activities such as mail-outs and special events at various times. Volunteers are normally recruited for periods of one to four weeks, all year round.

No special skills are required and volunteers may be of any nationality. Reasonable travel expenses within London and lunch are provided.

Those interested should contact the National Director at the above address.

## The Centre on Environment for the Handicapped
35 Great Smith Street, London SW1P 3BJ. Tel: (01) 222 7980

The Centre provides guidance to architects and planners of buildings on how they can take into account the needs of disabled people. Voluntary help is needed with routine office work, such as ordering publications, filling envelopes and filing. The hours of work depend both on the volunteers circumstances and the requirements in the office. Travel expenses are reimbursed to volunteers.

For further information contact the Information Officer at the above address.

## CHANGE
PO Box 824, London SE24 9JX. Tel: (01) 274 4043

CHANGE researches and publishes reports on the condition and status of women all over the world, organises exhibitions, meetings and book stalls and lobbies the Government. Around six volunteers are needed to help with all aspects of this work; basic administration, book production, writing press releases or other materials, organising meetings, exhibitions and book stalls and research. The duration of particular projects can vary from one month to one year.

Volunteers of any nationality with skills in any of the above areas are welcome. Fares within London are paid and short term accommodation for one or two volunteers may be provided.

Contact the Director at the above address for more information.

## Friends by Post

6 Bollin Court, Macclesfield Road, Wilmslow, Cheshire SK9 2AP. Tel: (0625) 527044

The aim of the organisation is to alleviate loneliness in all those who have no one to talk to. They seek to find for them compatible friends to write to and give them hints on how to transform a regular weekly letter exchange between strangers into a written conversation between friends. The service is free. Volunteers are asked to devote about eight hours a week to bringing these people into contact with one another for a weekly letter exchange.

For further information write to Conversation by Correspondence at the above address, enclosing an SAE.

## Green Deserts Ltd

Rougham, Bury St. Edmunds, Suffolk IP30 9LY. Tel: (0359) 70265

Green Deserts organise an educational "green leaf" project in Sudan. To support aspects of this work, about 15 volunteers are needed at the English office to help expand the tree nursery and environment centre and to assist with office administration and fund raising.

Volunteers must have initiative and be skilled in computing, horticulture, education, silviculture, administration or fund raising, and a few overseas opportunities for volunteers fluent in Arabic do exist. Work continues all year round but volunteers may specify the period of their service. Basic accommodation can be provided.

Those interested should apply to the Information Officer at the above address.

## Imperial Cancer Research Fund

PO Box 123, Lincoln's Inn Fields, London WC2A 3PX. Tel: (01) 242 0200

The Fund operates throughout the United Kingdom and recruits volunteers to help with all aspects of fund raising. Between 500 and 1,000 volunteers are needed annually to assist with the Fund's administration and to help run the Fund's network of charity shops. Volunteers of all nationalities are needed the year round for varying lengths of time.

No special skills are required but volunteers must be between 16 and 75 years old. Expenses may be offered to key volunteers.

Those interested should apply to their nearest regional office.

## Index on Censorship

Writers and Scholars Educational Trust, 39c Highbury Place, London N5 1QP. Tel: (01) 359 0161

The Trust is a charity that publishes manuscripts that have been banned and gives details of writing that has been censored anywhere in the world. There is a constant need for help in the office both with research and general clerical work. Volunteers are needed to work on a regular basis even if only for half a day per week.

For further details contact the editor at the above address.

**Jewish Child's Day**
1 Dennington Park Road, London NW6 1AX. Tel: (01) 435 8027

This organisation needs occasional clerical help with its fund raising. With the money it raises it provides equipment for a wide variety of children's homes, mostly in Israel, but also in the UK, France, Yugoslavia, Morocco and Tunisia.

Applications should be sent to the Director at the above address.

**National Society for the Prevention of Cruelty to Children**
67 Saffron Hill, London EC1N 8RS. Tel: (01) 242 1626

Although the society's active work is conducted only by professionally qualified staff, volunteers are always needed to start fund raising groups. The society has around 4,000 branch and district committees that raise money through house to house collections, organising functions and flag days, etc. Many individuals and groups of people help by running their own fun activities in aid of the Society.

Those willing to help should contact the National Appeals Dept. at the above address.

**OXFAM**
Oxfam House, 274 Banbury Road, Oxford OX2 7DZ. Tel: Oxford (0865) 56777 Ext. 2466

OXFAM volunteers work in the UK and Republic of Ireland to help OXFAM carry out its objective of relieving poverty, distress and suffering in any part of the world. As well as raising funds, this involves campaigning and educating the public in order to help tackle the causes of poverty. OXFAM is committed to an Equal Opportunities Policy and welcomes offers of help from people of all backgrounds and abilities.

OXFAM does not send volunteers overseas but around 30,000 people are involved in OXFAM's work throughout the UK and Ireland. They run over 800 shops and work in 36 area and district offices all over the country. Some help organise fund raising events, others are involved in campaigning and educational work. In the area offices, help with clerical and administrative work is often needed too. People with special skills such as book-keeping, design and typing can often put their talents to good use with OXFAM, but there are lots of opportunities for people without any particular qualifications.

In the Oxford headquarters over 100 volunteers work with 450 staff on a range of duties from routine packing and mailing through to research projects. Local OXFAM groups also exist in Rome, Bonn and Hong Kong. They do not provide accommodation or pocket money, but do reimburse travel expenses and meals, depending on the number of hours the volunteer works each day. Many areas offer a local one-day "Knowledge of Oxfam" course as an introduction to the organisation.

A booklet, *HELP! Ways you can help OXFAM as a volunteer,* gives more details and lists the addresses of area offices.

For further information, look up your local OXFAM office in the telephone book, or contact the Volunteers Personnel Officer at the above address.

## Population Concern

231 Tottenham Court Road, London W1P 9AE. Tel: (01) 631 1546

Population Concern raises funds for overseas population and development programmes, provides an information service and campaigns on population and related issues in schools and amongst the public. Projects are being undertaken in many developing countries in Africa, the Caribbean, Asia and the Pacific but volunteers are only required in the London office. Volunteers may work on a regular basis or just for short intensive periods, all year round. The work available depends on the applicant's interests and skills but include such areas of work as information, education, fund raising, and occasional project work.

Special skills such as typing, word processing and artwork skills are desirable but not essential. Students or recent graduates in Demography and related disciplines are very welcome.

Payment of travelling expenses is negotiable but accommodation is not provided.

Those interested should apply to the Information Officer at the above address.

## Royal National Lifeboat Institution

West Quay Road, Poole, Dorset BH15 1HZ. Tel: (0202) 671133

The operator of the lifeboat service throughout Britain and the Irish Republic, the RNLI is supported entirely by voluntary contributions. It is impossible to estimate the number of volunteers who assist the service; most of the crews of the life boats run from the 200 lifeboat stations are unpaid, and there are also some 2,000 fund raising branches around the UK.

There is an important distinction between these two forms of voluntary work; while anyone who is willing will be welcomed to assist with the raising of money, only those who are qualified seamen and live in the vicinity of a lifeboat station can be accepted as crew.

It is preferred that those interested should apply to their local branch of the RNLI, but if there is any difficulty about obtaining the relevant address, please contact the Public Relations Department at the above address.

## SOS Childrens Villages UK

32 Bridge Street, Cambridge CB2 1UJ. Tel: (0223) 65589

SOS Childrens Villages is an international charity caring for orphaned and abandoned children all over the world, and SOS Childrens Villages UK was formed to help fund SOS projects. Volunteers are needed to staff two shops in Cambridge which sell top quality third world crafts. Around 50 volunteers act as shop assistants throughout the year. No special skills are required but volunteers should have common sense and be reasonably active. No accommodation is provided but local bus fares are refunded.

For further details contact the Trading Manageress at the above address.

## Survival International

310 Edgware Road, London W2 1DY. Tel: (01) 723 5535

Survival International is an organisation working for and publicising the rights of threatened tribal societies. Approximately ten volunteers are needed in London each year to help with routine clerical work and other duties in all departments of Survival International including press, publications, projects, membership and administration. Duties include filing, typing, photocopying and mailing. Volunteers are needed year round and ideally give a regular commitment of a certain number of days per week.

No special skills are needed but there is no access for people in wheelchairs. Up to £2 per day is provided for travel expenses.

Enquiries to the Administration Director at the above address.

**War On Want**
37-39 Great Guildford Street, London SE1 0ES. Tel: (01) 620 1111

This organisation undertakes development and relief work to alleviate famine in the Third World. A national network of groups throughout the United Kingdom raise funds and campaign in their local areas. Volunteers are needed to join these local groups and also 100 volunteers are required annually for office and administrative work in the head office in London. Work continues all year round and volunteers give whatever time they can.

Any special skills that volunteers have will be utilised but none are essential. All volunteers are welcome but there is no access for disabled people at the London office. London office volunteers have their travelling expenses within London paid and receive a £2 lunch allowance per day. Local groups make their own arrangements.

Those interested in obtaining a list of local groups or wishing to work in the London office should contact the Volunteer Co-ordinator at the above address.

**World Development Movement**
Bedford Chambers, Covent Garden, London WC2H 8HA. Tel: (01) 836 3672

The World Development Movement campaigns for political changes in Britain's aid, trade and debt policies needed to help Third World countries. A small number of staff work on research and publications which together with the membership attempts to influence key decision makers. Volunteers are needed in the London office to help with general office work, all year round. No special skills are required and volunteers may be of any nationality. No accommodation is provided but travel expenses to and from the London office and a lunch allowance of £1.20 are paid.

Those interested should apply to Jo Collinge, Groups Officer, at the above address.

# Hospitals

Although hard-pressed professional hospital staff do their best to attend to their patients, there are still many ways in which a volunteer can help to make a patient comfortable. It must be stressed that the range of activities a volunteer can do is strictly limited, as they must not encroach upon the professional's preserve, and in many cases the number of hours a volunteer can help will be limited.

For example, it is permitted to drive a patient's relatives to and from hospital, but driving an out-patient home would encroach on the work of the ambulance service so would not be permitted. Nearly all of the work involving hospitals is concerned with direct contact with the patients and their families, although some Leagues of Hospital Friends also run a lot of fund raising activities. On the wards, volunteers can visit patients and befriend them on a one-to-one basis or can take part in entertainments and activities for the patients. In other situations, the hospital volunteer can go shopping for patients, visit patients' relatives at home, and drive friends and relatives to the hospital in visiting hours. Volunteers can also be of use in preparing a patient's home for his return.

Nearly three quarters of Britain's NHS hospitals have their voluntary work organised by a League of Hospital Friends. These Leagues of Friends are in turn co-ordinated by the National Association of Leagues of Hospital Friends, whose activities are described in the entry below. Other hospitals' voluntary services are either run by another organisation such as the Red Cross or the WRVS, or an increasing number of them have their own Voluntary Service Department. The individual hospitals described below are examples of the latter system. It should be stressed that they are only examples, and they are typical of many hospitals up and down the country. The best way to find out about volunteer needs in local hospitals is to telephone the hospitals themselves.

Other work involving hospitals and hospital patients will be found in the sections on *The Sick and Disabled, Mental Health, Children and Youth* and *The Elderly.*

### Amandus Club

Atkinson Morley's Hospital, Copse Hill, Wimbledon SW20 0NE. Tel: 946 7711 Ext. 41048

Volunteers are used to assist in a small workshop twice a week engaged on re-cycling greeting cards, printing, knitting, making toys etc.

Also to provide a hot midday meal for those who attend the workshop and tea and coffee for visitors. Some secretarial help is also needed. Anyone interested in helping should contact the Secretary at the above address.

### Ida Darwin Hospital

Fulbourn, Cambridge. Tel: (0223) 248074

The Ida Darwin Hospital is home for some 150 adults with profound mental handicaps, many of whom are also physically handicapped. Many volunteers, both short and long term, join with trained staff to improve the residents' quality of life, primarily in developing their leisure opportunities. No special qualifications are needed, but it would be helpful if applicants had some experience of working with people with a mental handicap. Volunteers should be at least 16 years old.

Those interested should write to the Voluntary Services Organiser at the above address.

**National Association of Leagues of Hospital Friends**
2nd Floor, Fairfax House, Causton Road, Colchester CO1 1RJ. Tel: (0206) 761227

The National Association acts as a support, resource and advice centre to some 1,350 Leagues of Friends in England, Scotland and Wales. Together these have 470,000 members and 80,000 volunteers who give about $6\frac{1}{2}$ million hours of voluntary time to their Leagues. About £15 million pounds is raised each year of which £$6\frac{1}{2}$ million is spent on patient comforts and £$8\frac{1}{2}$ million on medical equipment needed by the hospitals.

The aim of the charity is to improve the life of patients and ex-patients from hospitals and health care establishments by offering service and support facilities. The work of the volunteer is very varied and can stretch from patient befriending, through help in canteens, shops or ward trolleys to chaperoning on patient outings etc. The emphasis is now also changing to help within Community Care Homes.

The work can be rewarding and interesting with as much variety as the individual volunteer wants. For more details ask at the local hospital for the League of Friends contact or write direct to the National Association at the above address.

**St. Pancras Hospital Voluntary Help Department**
4 St. Pancras Way, London NW1. Tel: (01) 387 4411  ext. 368

The range of jobs for volunteers at St. Pancras Hospital is very varied: chatting to patients who never have visitors, writing letters, helping with arts, crafts and pottery, doing the shopping for patients, playing cards and board games in the ward games room, accompanying wheelchair patients to parks or on other outings, etc. There is a well organised voluntary programme for the large number of helpers under the direction of a full time Voluntary Help Organiser. The patients at St. Pancras are primarily geriatrics, but there are also psychiatric, general and tropical diseases wards and a Stroke Rehabilitation Unit. Many of the patients have been in hospital for a long time and are in particular need of contact with ordinary people leading ordinary lives. Personal attention to lonely patients, whether in the capacity of listener or entertainer, is invaluable.

Volunteers are provided with overalls and free meals, but no accommodation. All volunteers must commit themselves to three hours per week for at least eight weeks. Volunteers of any nationality over 18 years of age can bring pleasure to a person in hospital. The most important requirement is the possession of a cheerful and relaxed personality. All talents, both serious and frivolous, can be put to use in some way.

Applications may be submitted to the Voluntary Help Organiser at the Hospital.

**South Western Hospital Voluntary Service Department**
Landor Road, Stockwell, London SW9. Tel: (01) 733 7755 ext. 319

The South Western Hospital is an example of a hospital which has its own Voluntary Service Co-ordinators, instead of relying on the assistance of one of the national organisations. Some 70 volunteers are involved in the usual activities of meeting the social and practical needs of elderly residents.

No special skills are usually needed in the volunteer; if needed, training is given. Volunteers should be in good physical and mental health. Any expenses incurred by the volunteer during an assignment may be refunded.

Applicants should contact the Voluntary Service Co-ordinators at the above address.

### University College Hospital Voluntary Help Department
Main Hall, Gower Street, London WC1. Tel: (01) 388 6866

The Department co-ordinates the voluntary services in the North Bloomsbury Hospitals Unit. Around 200 volunteers give up their time to help patients, some for only a few months, others for years. There are no particular requirements beyond a willingness to make a regular commitment of time and effort, but any special qualities, such as the knowledge of a foreign language or an interest in craft work, are noted and used whenever the need arises. As always, the possession of a car is a valuable asset. Volunteers serving for three or more hours a day are given a voucher for refreshments of up to 85p in value, and small travel expenses are paid in certain cases.

Enquiries should be made to the Voluntary Services Co-ordinator at the above address.

### Whittingham Hospital Volunteer Scheme
Whittingham Hospital, Whittingham, Preston, Lancs. PR3 2JH. Tel: (0772) 865531

This volunteer scheme operates in two psychiatric hospitals, one of 650 beds and one of 45 beds. Some volunteers provide direct assistance by helping on wards and in the hospital library, befriending patients, providing entertainment for residents, driving cars, etc. Volunteers should be aged 15 or over; those with driving licences or special skills such as playing a musical instrument or speaking a foreign language are especially appreciated. In exchange they receive travelling expenses and luncheon vouchers.

For further information contact the Co-ordinator of Voluntary Services at the above address.

# Pressure Groups

The organisations in this section may have many disparate aims, from stopping blood sports to fighting for the rights of prisoners of conscience abroad, but they share a desire to help to change and motivate public opinion. Clearly, a prospective volunteer is required to share the views of the organisation he would like to help. Involvement with an organisation such as the Hunt Saboteurs Association may call for conviction deep enough to motivate someone to risk physical danger or arrest and so people should examine their motives carefully before becoming involved in the more controversial organisations. We have not included organisations that are protesting against specific local developments, such as the extension of a motorway or the closing of a village school, because such groups normally receive full coverage in the local media.

### AIM Group for Family Law Reform
PO Box 738, Dublin 4, Eire. Tel: (0001) 616478

AIM works in Ireland as a pressure group campaigning for reforms in laws and the legal system as they relate to the family and providing support, legal information and a referral service for people with problems following the breakdown of a family. In addition to the headquarters in Dublin, AIM has contacts in Limerick, Dundalk and Waterford. Volunteers are needed to provide counselling and to deal with research, help decide policy, apply political pressure by joining delegations to Government Ministers etc., and help with administration and fund raising. Experienced volunteers assist by giving talks to interested groups on AIM, family law, women's rights etc. No definite skills are needed as training is given, but the ability to drive or type, or knowledge of the law, social work, psychology, medicine, and languages would be useful. Applications should be made to the Administrator at the above address.

### Alcohol Concern
305 Gray's Inn Road, London WC1X 8QF. Tel: (01) 833 3471

There are many local councils on alcoholism around Britain, most of which employ volunteers to provide counselling for problem drinkers. The function of Alcohol Concern is to advise the councils on their recruitment and training and, where necessary, to train them over a period of at least a year. New volunteers are taken on every year.

Volunteers are carefully screened before selection: if they are ex-alcoholics they must have maintained sobriety for 2 years. They are expected to commit themselves to offering voluntary help on a part time basis for 5 years.

For further information contact the Director at the above address.

### Amnesty International
British Section, 5 Roberts Place, off Bowling Green Lane, London EC1R 0EJ. Tel: (01) 251 8371

Amnesty International won the Nobel Peace Prize in 1977. It works for the release of men and women imprisoned for their religious, political or other conscientiously held beliefs, their colour, language or ethnic origin. Only those prisoners who have either used or advocated violence are excluded from the cause. It actively opposes the death penalty as well as torture and cruel or degrading punishement for all prisoners. Between 50 and 100 volunteers are needed to do routine clerical work: stuffing envelopes, typing, wrapping parcels, etc. Travelling expenses are reimbursed for office helpers and luncheon vouchers are provided.

Enquiries should be sent to the Volunteer Organiser, Amnesty International, at the above address.

## Campaign for Nuclear Disarmament
22-24 Underwood Street, London N1. Tel: (01) 250 4010

The aim of CND is to persuade the Government to abandon nuclear weapons, and all foreign policy based on their use. The membership of 250,000 is distributed among 1,500 local groups which collect signatures for petitions against nuclear warfare, hold meetings, and recruit people to join in nationally organised marches and demonstrations, and help organise them. Specific weapons recently campaigned against include Trident, the Cruise Missile, Polaris and the Neutron Bomb as well as Russian SS20s. Membership is optional: any supporter is welcome to join in the activities of the organisation.

Those interested should apply to the organisation at the above address to find out the address of their local group.

## The Cats Protection League
17 Kings Road, Horsham, West Sussex RH13 5PP. Tel: (0403) 65566

The objects of the League are to rescue stray, unwanted and injured cats, to provide information on the care of cats and kittens, and to encourage the neutering of all cats not required for breeding. The practical work of the League and fund raising are carried out by voluntary workers through a system of 170 local branches and groups, with some 27,000 members. For further information those interested should contact the above address.

## Child Poverty Action Group (CPAG)
1-5 Bath Street, London EC1V GPY. Tel: (01) 253 3406

CPAG works to draw attention to the problems of the impoverished and to provide these people with advice concerning their rights. They accomplish this by publishing research pamphlets, such as *The National Welfare Benefits Handbook* and *The Rights Guide to Non-Means-Tested Benefits*. Volunteers are needed to carry out the clerical work of sending out the literature. Travelling expenses are paid and an allowance is given for lunch.

Enquiries may be addressed to the Publications Distribution Worker at the above address.

## FREGG (The Free Range Egg Association)
37 Tanza Road, London NW3 2UA

FREGG is involved in inspecting farms which claim to produce free range eggs and then putting them in touch with retail outlets. FREGG also runs publicity stalls and distributes information on owning hens. Volunteers are needed to help with all of these activities from inspecting the farms (particularly outside the southeast area where FREGG has contacts already) to helping with clerical work and writing to the local press on issues relating to egg production. Clerical help is needed mainly during spring and autumn but other work continues all year round.

Volunteers should be mobile and keen and a driving licence or clerical skills would be useful. Expenses are paid.

Those interested should contact the Honorary Secretary at the above address.

**Farmers' Third World Network**

Pentre Cefn, Craigllwyn, Oswestry, Shropshire SY10 9BJ. Tel: (0691) 70247

The Farmers' Third World Network is a collection of farmers and people with agricultural connections which seeks to promote awareness within the United Kingdom farming community of the problems of developing countries and the relationship between European and Third World agriculture. Volunteers are needed to join local groups which have specific action committees, assist volunteers going to Third World countries and host farmers and students from overseas on their farms.

Volunteers need a knowledge of agriculture or food production but no other restrictions apply.

Those interested should contact John Jones at the above address.

**Friends of the Earth**

26-28 Underwood Street, London N1 7JQ. Tel: (01) 490 1555

Friends of the Earth is an international environmental pressure group committed to the conservation, restoration and rational use of the environment. It has 220 local groups in the UK which work with the National Office on issues such as acid rain, pesticides, safe energy, water pollution, tropical rain forests and cities for people. Throughout the country these groups need help with their campaigns on a voluntary basis. Help is especially needed to cope with office work.

There are no age or health restrictions. Reasonable travel expenses are paid. All nationalities are welcome.

For further information please contact Judy Skeats at the above address.

**Greenpeace (London)**

5 Caledonian Road, Kings Cross, London N1. Tel: (01) 837 7557

The London Greenpeace Group is a non-violent libertarian pressure group which has recently gained much public attention with its opposition to the destruction of the environment, particularly by militarism and big business. Campaigns with which it is associated include protests against the continued development of nuclear technology, the misuse of science for military and commercial ends and the unnecessary mistreatment of animals and especially the development of everyone's personal responsibility for the way we relate to our eco-system. Other activities include the maintenance of a library of press clippings for use by interested parties, leafletting, pickets, street theatre, meetings, demonstrations and the production of periodic fact sheets and pamphlets on various subjects such as the chemical industry, pollution, pesticides, animal conservation and nuclear technology.

At any one time there is a minimum of 20 people actively involved with the group: weekly meetings are open to all those who share their point of view. There is scope for an unlimited supply of support when a campaign has been organised, as well as for general help regularly in the office. There are no restrictions or preferences concerning the type of person who is needed to help; indeed, the wider the cross section of society represented the better.

Those interested in helping should contact the group at the above address.

## Hunt Saboteurs Association
PO Box 87, Exeter, Devon EX4 3TX

This unique organisation was formed in 1963 and is engaged in a continuing campaign on non-violent direct action style campaigning which both saves the lives of hunted animals and brings to the public's attention the atrocities inflicted upon wild animals in the name of sport. The HSA is an animal rights organisation and is opposed as much to angling and shooting as it is to hunting deer, hare, mink and fox with hounds.

The HSA has nearly 5,000 members of which nearly 1,000 are active on a once weekly basis, normally Saturdays, throughout the winter months. Less activity takes place during the summer months. The Association will advise on the tactics to be employed in the saving of lives and welcomes enquiries from interested people.

The HSA employs no staff and has a decentralised structure; volunteers may offer their services for as long as they like; it is preferable that active members are over 16 years of age. The annual membership fee is £5. Further details are obtainable from the above address.

## International Broadcasting Trust
2 Ferdinand Place, London NW1 8EE. Tel: (01) 482 2847

International Broadcasting Trust is a television production organisation making programmes on Third World and development issues for transmission on television stations all around the world. Volunteers are needed to act as researchers in the pre-planning stages when developing television programme proposals, and occasionally to help with financial work and activities such as mailing out their newsletter three times a year. Around 15 volunteers are needed throughout the year for periods of six to eight weeks as researchers and from one to four weeks for the other jobs.

No special skills are required for most tasks but a knowledge of computerised spreadsheets for financial work is an advantage. The Trust aims to give work to British residents but volunteers of other nationalities will be accepted. Disabled people will find it difficult to reach the office. Travelling expenses and a lunch allowance are paid.

Volunteers should apply to the Assistant to the Director at the above address.

## The International Shakespeare Globe Centre Ltd
1 Bear Gardens, Bankside, Southwark, London SE1 9EB. Tel: (01) 602 0202

This Centre is an educational and cultural centre with a small theatre and museum containing Shakespeare memorabilia. The Centre is involved in fund raising in order to rebuild Shakespeare's Globe Theatre at Bankside, Southwark. Several volunteers are needed each year to help with public events or fund raising and to assist the Educational and Events Officer or Development Officer. Work project continues all year round but the length of each varies.

Volunteers may be of any nationality provided they have Arts qualifications and an interest in the Centre. Young students are preferred.

Accommodation is not provided but volunteers are reimbursed for any expenses incurred while working on a project.

Applicants should apply to the Administrator at the above address.

### Japan Animal Welfare Society Limited
RMC House, Townmead Road, London SW6 2RZ. Tel: (01) 736 9306

The Society exists to improve public standards of social and moral education regarding the welfare of animals, particularly in Japan. Voluntary help is needed around the year with office work and fund raising. No special qualifications are needed, but a knowledge of Japanese would be extremely useful. For further information contact the Office Manager at the above address.

### Minority Rights Group
29 Craven Street, London WC2. Tel: (01) 930 6659

MRG is concerned with the research and publication of human rights reports about minority groups around the world. Volunteers, including those of minority cultures, are welcome to assist with publicity, selling reports to bookshops and individuals contacts with local organisations and schools and general office work. Luncheon vouchers and travelling expenses are paid plus commission on sales of the reports.

Those interested should contact the Secretary at the above address.

### National Council for Civil Liberties
21 Tabard Street, London SE1 4LA. Tel: (01) 403 3888

NCCL is a pressure group which works to defend and extend civil liberties throughout the UK. Volunteers at the London office help prepare publications, assist with research or perform routine administrative tasks. Volunteer lawyers assist with legal casework.

A luncheon allowance is provided for volunteers and travelling expenses are paid inside London.

Enquiries should be sent to the General Secretary at the above address.

### National Peace Council
29 Great James Street, London WC1N 3ES. Tel: (01) 242 3228

The National Peace Council is at the centre of a network of over 170 peace organisations and related movements, including trade unions and religious peace associations. The council's task is to provide an exchange of information between its member organisations to facilitate co-operation among them. It also acts as a pressure group on behalf of its affiliates. A small number of volunteers are needed to look after the correspondence and mailing services, and to do continuing research into current events which pertain to disarmament issues. Typing and office experience would be an asset for those volunteers wishing to apply.

Enquiries may be sent to Al McLeod, Co-ordinator, at the above address.

### National Council for the Welfare of Prisoners Abroad
82 Rosebery Avenue, London EC1R 4RR. Tel: (01) 833 3467

This charity works for the welfare of British prisoners in foreign jails. The specific work done for individual prisoners varies enormously; dealing with foreign and British lawyers, and prison and other authorities, writing personally to prisoners and organising penpals, providing funds for prisoners to buy essentials like blankets and medicines, etc. Around 20 volunteers are needed all year round to help with all office activities; typing and other clerical work, answering both telephone and postal queries, word processing and writing letters to prisoners. Volunteers normally help for three months or more on a regular basis, with full days of work being preferred to half days.

Volunteers of all nationalities are welcome. Good communication skills are important and languages are an advantage but not necessary. All other skills will be put to good use. As the office is located on the second floor of the building with no lift disabled people will find access difficult. Travelling expenses and a lunch allowance are paid.

Volunteers should apply to the Administrator at the above address.

## One World Week
PO Box 100, London SE1 7RT. Tel: (01) 620 4444

One World Week in October of each year is a chance for churches and other groups to get together, celebrate and learn about issues of justice, peace, the environment and development. The London office provides support for this by supplying study materials and suggestions for activities and providing local contacts. Volunteers are needed to help existing groups celebrate the week or to organise their own activities. Fund raising is not encouraged.

Those interested should contact a Programme Worker at the above address for more information.

## Railway Development Society
48 The Park, Great Bookham, Surrey KT23 3LS. Tel: (0372) 52863

The RDS was formed in 1978 by an amalgamation of earlier societies. It is a pressure group fighting for the retention and improvement of Britain's railway system as a vital environmental issue. It maintains contacts with British Rail, Ministers, MPs, Local Authorities and other bodies. It produces Railguides, other booklets and leaflets and publishes a quarterly journal and branch newsletters. It needs approaching 100 volunteers a year to help with its activities, and makes use of a wide range of experience. Involvement can be at national or branch level or with help in the organisation of local rail users' groups to encourage local communities to take an active interest in their rail services.

There are no restrictions on applicants and no special qualifications are required apart from an interest in the aims of the Society.

Enquiries should be sent to the Administrative Officer at the above address.

## Survival International
310 Edgware Road, London W2 1DY. Tel: (01) 723 5535

Survival International is a London-based charity for the rights of threatened tribal peoples that aims to deflect the destructive influence of civilised society on native tribes in South and Central America, Indonesia, Philippines,

Bangladesh and Australia. They lobby international organisations, governments,and multi-national companies and support practical realistic field projects with the aim of assisting the survival and self-determination of tribes.

Volunteers are required as translators (Spanish, Portuguese, French, German), and to assist with clerical and secretarial work, library duties, visual aid materials and fund raising activities. A commitment of anything from half a day to five days per week is preferred. There are no restrictions, but skills in languages would be very useful.

Those interested should contact the Director at the above address.

### Teetotal Support Groups

'Jordans', 1c Grassington Road, Eastbourne, East Sussex BN20 7BP. Tel: (0323) 638 234

Teetotal Support Groups aim to offer support to anyone who wishes to totally abstain from alcohol. Social contact with others on the nationwide Teetotallers' Register of local support groups will be encouraged, especially for members who move to other areas.

Help is needed to form new groups in different localities. Groups may choose to launch a juice bar, or coffee "shop" project run by volunteers and based in a school, comunity house or spare room of a local church.

Anyone interested in joining or forming a local group should write to the above address for advice and addresses, or telephone.

### Tools for Self Reliance

Ringwood Road, Netley Marsh, Southampton SO4 2GY. Tel: (0703) 869697

Tools for Self Reliance is a charity which collects and refurbishes basic hand tools in Britain and then provides tool kits to co-operative work schemes in Africa and Central America. Volunteers are needed to help with all aspects of this work: office work, building maintenance, gardening and general site maintenance, refurbishing tools and preparing and packing tools. In addition to work undertaken by the various local groups around Britain, Tools for Self Reliance hold workcamps lasting for up to two weeks at their national headquarters in Netley Marsh. The workcamps cater for up to 12 volunteers at any one time and are designed for volunteers who cannot help regularly throughout the year.

Volunteers need no special skills. There are facilities for people in wheelchairs at Netley Marsh and accommodation and food are provided during the workcamps. Smoking is restricted.

Contact the Workshop Supervisor at the above address for further information.

### The Vegetarian Society (UK) Ltd

Parkdale, Dunham Road, Altrincham, Cheshire WA14 4QG. Tel: (061) 928 0793

This Society promotes the vegetarian way of life. More than 15 volunteers are needed each year to help at their headquarters. Tasks include administrative duties and helping with talks, cooking demonstrations and stalls. Volunteers give whatever time they can.

Volunteers must be vegetarian or very sympathetic, to the cause as no meat, fish or fowl are allowed on the premises. No special skills are required but volunteers skilled in typing, designing, cooking or languages would be very welcome. Accommodation is not usually provided but travel and other expenses incurred while working are paid.

Those interested should contact the Publications Officer at the above address.

# Prisons and Probation

For a prisoner a volunteer can provide a vital, and perhaps the only, link with the outside world. Volunteers have had a long and fruitful connection with prisoners and their families: indeed, the statutory Probation Service itself was begun when the authorities realised how successful voluntary involvement had been in re-integrating prisoners into society. The special value of volunteers in this work lies in the fact that they are not a formal part of 'the system', and so offenders respond more readily and openly to them than they would to paid and officially appointed officers. Volunteers may be acting on their own, having approached the governor of a prison individually; or they may be part of a voluntary organisation such as the New Bridge, or working in co-operation with the Probation and After-Care Service. Prison visitors are subjected to rigorous entry procedures, and their final appointment is subject to Home Office approval.

By visiting a convicted prisoner, a volunteer can be of use either by simply providing companionship, or by maintaining a link with the prisoner's family, as a period of imprisonment can prove a strain on marriages. The need for the help of a volunteer does not end with the release of an offender; the support of a known and trusted volunteer can be of a great help in finding a job and somewhere to live. This is especially valuable in time of high unemployment, as prisoners will experience more difficulty than most people in finding work.

Other functions performed by volunteers include organising and supervising community work for those sentenced to community service orders, and teaching illiterates to read and write (many of Britain's two million illiterates are driven to crime by their inability to get a job). Volunteers also perform a valuable function in the probation service, where they are used to befriend probationers on a one-to-one basis.

### Apex Trust
1-4 Brixton Hill Place, London SW2 1HJ. Tel: (01) 671 7633

The Apex Trust is a registered charity providing advice, special training and education facilities to ex-offenders and others facing particular difficulties in the job market.

The Trust operates an employment placing agency for ex-offenders and other disadvantaged unemployed people and also acts as a training and advisory service for people working with them. A network of Apex Employment Resource Centres is in operation in various parts of the country which provide pre-employment training, advice on job search techniques, training in the basic skills required for work or further formal training, and a job placement service operates for volunteers. Unemployed Centre participants are particularly encouraged to engage in voluntary work of benefit to their own Community. Further to this, voluntary help is very welcome at all of the centres from members of the community who may have time to spare, or who may be unemployed themselves, but can offer skills to pass on to others. Voluntary assistance will also be appreciated in general areas such as industries and employer liaison, public relations, assistance with pre-employment training and job search, clerical help etc.

For further details please contact the above address.

**Catholic Social Service for Prisoners**
189a Old Brompton Road, London SW5 0AR. Tel: (01) 370 6612
1c Chapel Street, Preston, Lancs. Tel: (0772) 21215

CSSP assists prisoners, ex-offenders and their families of any religion or none, and employs five full-time social workers. They work in close collaboration with statutory bodies, particularly the Probation and Prison Services and other relevant voluntary organisations. Ex-offenders are helped towards rehabilitation with advice and counselling and spiritual and material needs are taken into account. Where possible the help of local volunteers is called upon as appropriate to take a personal interest in an ex-offender. Much help and support is also given to the families and dependants of serving prisoners. In addition to the London and Preston offices there are voluntary groups in Durham, London, West Yorkshire and South Devon. Volunteers are invited to assist in the local social work undertaken by these groups and the annual holiday on the south coast for prisoners' families.

Anyone who is interested in supporting or becoming involved in the Society's work should get in touch with either the London or Preston Office.

**Inner London Probation and After-Care Service**
73 Great Peter Street, London SW1P 2BN. Tel: (01) 222 5656

The Service undertakes a wide range of activities with voluntary helpers within the 12 Inner London boroughs. These relate to most aspects of the Probation Service's work and would entail, for example, one-to-one contact with clients, group work, adventure activities, or practical help on a regular or single task basis.

Applicants should be at least 18 years old and under most circumstances it would be helpful if they could offer their services for at least 12 months. The personal qualities needed are sound common sense, tolerance and kindness. Applicants must also be prepared to work closely with supervising Probation Officers.

Those interested should, in the first instance, contact Mr P. M. Rogers, Senior Probation Officer, Camden House, 199 Arlington Road, NW1 (North of Thames) or Mr G. A. Porterfield, Senior Probation Officer, 2 Kimpton Road, SE5 (South of Thames).

**National Association for the Care and Resettlement of Offenders (NACRO)**
169 Clapham Road, London SW9 0PU. Tel: (01) 582 6500

NACRO runs housing, employment, youth training, education and advice projects for offenders and others; provides research, information and training services for people concerned about crime and offenders; and contributes to the development of crime policy and the prevention of crime. Over 2,000 staff work in some 200 projects and other services throughout England and Wales. Opportunities for voluntary work are limited to a small number of projects providing education for unemployed adults and activities for young people, which are organised on a local basis. NACRO aims to be an equal opportunities employer and to eliminate unfair discrimination against anyone in its selection process.

For more information, contact NACRO's Information Department at the above address.

**National Association of Prison Visitors**
46B Hartington Street, Bedford. Tel: (0234) 59763

In the UK prison visitors are officially appointed. Normally they make an appointment to see the governor of the prison nearest them. If this interview passes satisfactorily they are accepted for a probationary period of three months. After this they must be appointed by the Home Office. It is important that people in prison (and in other penal institutions) should not lose contact with the outside world. Prison staff and visiting probation officers have a part to play, but the prison visitor has a unique contribution to offer, working alongside this team rather than as a member of it. Although appointed by the Home Office and subject to the regulations of the prisons, he or she is a volunteer, not an "official", and this independent status has an appeal to the prisoner. The main role of the visitor is to establish a one-to-one, impartial, non-authoritarian relationship with the prisoner. There are 550-600 visitors in the UK and 8-10% of prisoners have prison visitors. The Association wishes to expand its activities and new recruits will be welcome. (N.B. Prison visitors should not be confused with Voluntary Associates, who work in co-operation with the Probation and After-care service.)

Visitors must be at least 21 and not over 70, and are normally expected to retire at 75. To be of value, visits must be made at frequent intervals, normally weekly or fortnightly, early in the evening, and at weekends. Both men and women are taken on, and women visitors can visit men's prisons. Visitors usually visit their nearest prison.

Those interested should apply to the Governor at their nearest prison.

**National Association of Probation and Bail Hostels**
78 Stanhope Grove, Beckenham, Kent BR3 3HP. Tel: (01) 650 2942

The Association is a co-ordinating body for the one hundred probation hostels throughout England and Wales. The period of residence within the total framework of a probation order is entirely at the discretion of the Court, the referring officer, the hostel and the client. Some volunteers are taken on to help with the day to day running of the hostel, getting involved with the residents on a personal level. Some are also needed on the voluntary committees of the voluntary managed hostels (which are about one-third of the total.)

Volunteers are usually accepted at the request of other organisations who know the hostel or the warden concerned. They are expected to pay their own way. Accommodation is provided where possible, but this is arranged at local level and varies from hostel to hostel.

Applications should be made to the Secretaries of the individual hostel committee. The Association will forward enquiries.

### The New Bridge

Room A, 1 Thorpe Close, Ladbroke Grove, London W10 5XL. Tel: (01) 969 9133

The New Bridge operates two schemes: a nationwide befriending scheme for people who are in prison, and an employment service for those who have left prison in the greater London area. Some 150 volunteers lend their time to the organisation, of whom the majority are involved in the befriending scheme. This means that the volunteer keeps in touch with a prisoner both by personal visits and by letters while he is in prison, and offers help and encouragement in starting a new life on his release.

The only specific requirement is that volunteers should be over 18; but anyone living in London with time to spare during the day would be welcomed to help with the employment service, which involves making contact between prospective employers and released prisoners. Expenses in London may be reclaimed.

Those interested should write to the Befriending Scheme Organiser at the above address for further details.

# Problems, Emergencies and Housing

There are many people who fall through society's safety nets, often through no fault of their own. For example, there are those who cannot get a job because they do not have a home, and they cannot get a home because they do not have a job. This is one of the crisis areas in which the volunteer may be able to provide assistance.

Many of the organisations listed below deal with individuals who are facing a rapid succession of linked problems, such as bereavement, poverty, homelessness, unemployment and poverty, and are unable to cope with the pressure. Without some assistance many such cases may end up with suicide or crime. Some of the organisations are concerned with prevention, such as offering advice and friendship to those who are nearing breaking point, while others set out to pick up the pieces afterwards by such actions as offering refuge to alcoholics or battered wives. Often all that is needed is a friendly voice for someone to speak to: it is significant that the suicide rate has dropped since the Samaritans began operating. In other cases skilled help is needed, to liaise with council housing departments, for example.

The voluntary work associated with these types of operations may involve direct contact, sometimes for long periods, with the people in crisis situations.

It follows that the volunteer must be of a stable mental condition, as he/she could be exposed to prolonged confrontation with tragic circumstances such as broken homes, violence, suicide and despair.

Other organisations that deal with emergency social crises of this nature include the Salvation Army and WRVS (see under *National and Local Volunteer Organisations*). Some of the organisations listed under *The Sick and Disabled, Children and Youth, The Elderly* and *Prisons and Probation* also contain provisions for dealing with crises within their respective areas of activity.

### Alone in London Service

West Lodge, 190 Euston Road, London NW1 2EF. Tel: (01) 387 6184

This service provides advice, counselling and accommodation for homeless men and women. Volunteers assist full-time staff in the advice centre, the two residential settings managed by the project and with administrative work. Often adolescents in distress are referred to ALS by social service agencies. Training of volunteers will take place at regular intervals or as required. Volunteers are expected to make an on-going commitment.

There are restrictions on applicants.

Applications to The Administrator at the above address.

### Catholic Housing Aid Society

189a Old Brompton Road, London SW5 0AR. Tel: (01) 373 4961

The Society has 15 branches throughout the country. It helps anyone with a housing problem. The branches advise on landlord-tenant questions, council housing arrangements and problems with purchasing. The time at which advisory services are open varies from branch to branch, although most operate in the evenings. Volunteers are needed to work in the advice centres, to do administrative office work and to help with research work. Those working in the advisory centres need to offer a couple of evenings a month and the Society runs a number of in-service training programmes.

Those interested should apply to the above address or to their local branch.

### Centrepoint Night Shelter

57 Dean Street, London W1. Tel: (01) 734 2506

This is an emergency night shelter for young homeless people who are new to London and are felt to be at risk in the West End. Volunteers work as part of a team of about six one night a week under the supervision of a full-time worker. Their main function is to provide a welcoming atmosphere for clients and a sympathetic ear when required, as well as helping with practical chores e.g. cooking, washing etc. All nationalities are welcome but should be able to speak English, and preferably aged over 18. It is preferred also if volunteers can make a long term commitment i.e. at least six months.

For further information and application forms contact the Volunteer Administrator.

### Festival Welfare Services

347a Upper Street, London N1 0PD. Tel: (01) 226 2759

FWS member organisations provide voluntary welfare services at open-air music festivals throughout Britain, including first aid, emotional and drug counselling, legal advice, emergency and information services, fire-fighting, baby minding, lost property and supervision of sanitary facilities. Volunteers are needed to assist trained volunteers in providing these services and some administrative help is needed in the London office. Applicants should have some sympathy for the concept of open-air music festivals and the ability to work in rough surroundings with various types of people. Expenses are not usually paid but sometimes food is provided. A tent would be very useful.

Those interested in helping should contact Penny Mellor at the above address.

### Night Cellar Trust
57a St Clements, Oxford. Tel: (0865) 726303

The Trust operates a year-round emergency accommodation shelter in Oxford for 16 to 25 year olds. The shelter is staffed by volunteers on a rotation basis with more than 50 volunteers being needed annually. Volunteers have close contact with the young homeless and undertake all the practical tasks of running the shelter including cooking and writing in the log.

Volunteers must be in good health and prepared to work for a minimum of six months but no special skills are required. No accommodation or pocket money is provided.

Apply to the Chairperson at the above address.

### SHELTER, National Campaign for the Homeless
88 Old Street, London EC1V 9HU. Tel: (01) 253 0202

Shelter helps provide a housing aid service and aims to improve housing conditions all over the country. Volunteers work in the national headquarters and sometimes in the regional offices, of which there are around 30 around the country. The type of work that they do depends on their personal skills; for example, some may be able to type, which is always useful, while others may have a specialised knowledge of housing. But enthusiasm and conscientiousness can make a volunteer equally useful. In addition, many people help to finance the organisation with fund raising events. All are welcome to join local groups or become members of the campaign.

The amount of help which is given to Shelter depends on the volunteer her/ himself. Some people have helped for years, while others only do so for a week or two. Travel expenses are re-imbursed.

Applicants should contact the Administrative Assistant at the above address to discover the whereabouts of their local regional office.

### Womens Aid Ltd
P.O. Box 791, Dublin 6, Eire. Tel: (01) 961002

This organisation offers refuge to battered wives and their children, providing accommodation for approximately 10 families including 40 children. Volunteers can provide assistance on an on-going basis, mainly helping with the children, especially during school holidays when they take them on outings. There are no special requirements, but some experience with children would be an advantage. There are no restrictions of age or nationality.

Those interested should apply to the above address.

# The Sick and Disabled

For all its efforts, The National Health Service is unable to provide full support for all those who have chronic illnesses or permanent disabilities. The organisations in this section are able to help fill this gap because they have specialised knowledge of the condition and can provide appropriate support.

The range of activities of these organisations include protecting the patients' rights, carrying out research into their illnesses and disabilities, and, of course, helping the patients in their everyday lives, whether directly (e.g. arranging excursions) or indirectly (e.g. walking puppies for future training as guide dogs for the blind). The scope of volunteer activities within these organisations is equally large and includes direct contact with the patients either in their homes or in hospital, and indirect assistance such as research, fund raising, dictating books for the blind, etc. In many cases (e.g. British Association of the Hard of Hearing, Arthritis Care), there is a particular need for volunteers with the relevant disabilities or injuries. In other cases, able-bodied volunteers prove more useful.

Other sections dealing specifically with the sick and disabled include *Hospitals, Children and Youth* and *The Elderly*.

### Anorexic Aid
The Priory Centre, 11 Priory Road, High Wycombe, Bucks HP13 6SL

This organisation has 40 self help groups throughout the country which offer help and advice for people suffering from Anorexia and Bulimia Nervosa. Volunteers are needed to help with office duties, counselling, befriending new members, organising group meetings and manning the telephone.

Anyone interested in offering their help should contact the Secretary.

### Arthritis Care (formerly The British Rheumatism and Arthritis Association)
6 Grosvenor Crescent, London SW1X 7ER. Tel: (01) 235 0902/5

Arthritis Care was founded in 1947 by a young rheumatic sufferer who wished to help and encourage others. The organisation has remained an essentially self-help society. There are at present about 450 branches around the country (all the branch officers and helpers are volunteers) and around 40,000 members. Active branch members render indispensable help in running the branch meetings, which may be a housebound member's only contact with the outside world, and in organising fund raising activities. In addition, any assistance which can be given with transport is much appreciated. Volunteers are needed to visit the housebound on a regular basis.

Those interested in joining should contact the Secretary at the above address to be put in touch with their local branch.

## Association to Combat Huntington's Chorea

34a Station Road, Hinckley, Leicestershire LE10 1AP. Tel: (0455) 615558

Volunteers are always welcome to help the Association's work for sufferers from this incurable and fatal disease. Opportunities exist at the Head Office, the London Office and (especially) at the residential Care Home near Epping; also in any of the local branches around the country. Full details from the Executive Director at the above address.

## The Association of Swimming Therapy

4 Oak Street, Shrewsbury, Salop SY3 7RH. Tel: (0743) 4393

The Association encourages handicapped people to take part in swimming and water recreation and the formation of swimming clubs and swimming competitions for them. Instructors and helpers are trained within their clubs and at regional training courses. The AST works through regional associations to which local clubs can affiliate and on whose experience, advice and instructor training they can call. Many of the clubs engage in other activities besides swimming.

Between 600 and 700 volunteers are used annually as instructors, bathside keepers, safety helpers, dressers for males and females, time-keepers, social officers, doctors, administration officers, committee members and drivers for transporting handicapped members to and from the baths. Volunteers are selected after a period of attending swimming sessions to ascertain whether they are suitable for dealing with handicapped people. Volunteers should be in good health.

Further information can be obtained from the Honorary Secretary at the above address.

## National Back Pain Association

Grundy House, 31-33 Park Road, Teddington, Middlesex TW11 0AB. Tel: (01) 977 5474/5

The National Back Pain Association's objectives are to encourage research into the causes and treatment of back pain, to help to prevent damage by teaching people to use their bodies sensibly and to form groups which would help disseminate useful information, provide neighbourly help to sufferers, raise money and liaise with similar organisations worldwide. Volunteers are required to help in local branches and with office work in Teddington all the year round. Expenses and nominal fees are paid.

Applications should be made to the Executive Director at the above address.

## Birmingham Tapes for the Handicapped Association

20 Middleton Hall Road, Kings Norton, Birmingham B30 1BY. Tel: (021) 459 4874

The Association sends a monthly tape recorded sound magazine to handicapped people around the country. It also has a tape library which is free to members. Those interested should contact Mr Derek L. Hunt, Honorary Secretary, at the above address.

## Bristol Cancer Help Centre

Grove House, Cornwallis Grove, Clifton, Bristol BS8 4PG. Tel: (0272) 743 216

Opened in 1980, the Centre offers programmes which complement orthodox medical treatment for cancer patients. The patient receives medical supervision and counselling on nutrition, lifestyle and relaxation and meditation methods, as treatment is based on the principle that the whole person rather than just the disease should be treated. Approximately 20 volunteers are needed all year round to assist with postal queries (often the first contact patients have with the Centre), gardening, fund raising and clerical duties. Ideally volunteers work for a half or full day per week on an on-going basis.

Volunteers should be reliable, over 17 years old, and have a caring but humorous personality. A driver's licence is an advantage but not essential. Only in special circumstances will travelling expenses be paid.

Those interested should contact the Volunteer Co-ordinator at the above address.

## British Limbless Ex-Servicemen's Association (BLESMA)

185-187 High Road, Chadwell Heath, Romford, Essex RM6 6NA. Tel: (01) 590 1124

BLESMA operates two residential homes and a welfare service to make sure that limbless ex-servicemen and women (including widows) do not suffer hardship. The Association operates a regular Welfare Visiting Service through its branches across the country. Organised social activities are arranged and a general information and advice service is provided.

The Association is now in need of some 200 volunteers to help branches with committee work, welfare visits and fund raising. Individuals may undertake any or all of these tasks. The amount of time given is at the discretion of the individuals concerned. Possession of a driving licence would be advantageous and a motor mileage allowance can be paid.

For further details contact the Deputy General Secretary at the above address.

## British Paraplegic Sports Society

Ludwig Guttman Sports Centre for the Disabled, Harvey Road, Aylesbury, Bucks. HP21 8PP. Tel: (0296) 84848

The Society is involved with the promotion and encouragement of active sports among paraplegics and tetraplegics. Volunteers are needed to offer assistance at National and International Sports meetings. They may be needed for any period from one to ten days: accommodation is sometimes available. Applicants should write to the Chief Executive at the above address.

## The British Retinitis Pigmentosa Society

Greens Norton Court, Greens Norton, Towcester, Northamptonshire NN12 8BS. Tel: (0327) 53276

The Society was formed in 1975 and it aims to give relief to sufferers of RP in any way which may help them to live with, or overcome, their handicap, and to pursue measures towards finding the cause of RP and means of its treatment and cure. For further details of how volunteers can help with this please contact the Honorary Secretary at the above address.

## The Central Remedial Clinic
PO Box 697, Penny Ansley Memorial Building, Vernon Avenue, Clontarf, Dublin 3, Eire. Tel: (01) 332206

The Clinic is mainly concerned with the early assessment, education, training and employment of those with physical handicaps. It includes a special school for children with multiple physical handicaps that covers the usual school subjects and attempts to help each child to develop his natural powers and abilities. It has a Voluntry Corps of over 100 people who help to run the school, the pre-school nursery, the dining hall, the speech therapy department, physical education, the day activity centre and adult training workshop.

The Corps consists largely of both young school leavers, retired men and women, housewives and students on Work Experience Programmes. The hours for which they are needed depends on the jobs they undertake; the need for voluntary help is considerably reduced during the school holidays. Volunteers receive appropriate training where necessary. For further information contact the Development Officer at the above address.

## The Chalfont Society for Epilepsy
Chalfont St. Peter, Gerrards Cross, Bucks SL9 0RJ. Tel: (02407) 3991

The Centre, run by the National Society for Epilepsy, welcomes volunteers to assist their work with the care and rehabilitation of people with epilepsy. Volunteers are needed to provide caring assistance, raise funds, provide transport and act as escorts for outings, teach craft, help at social events, help with sporting activities and teach mentally handicapped residents etc. At present about 15 volunteers help the Society but any others are welcome. Help is useful at any time, but especially during holiday periods. Volunteers may stay for any length of time. No qualifications are necessary. Travelling expenses to and from the Centre are not paid, but outings and holidays are paid for.

Applications to Colonel D. W. Eking, Chief Executive, at the above address.

## The Chest, Heart & Stroke Association Volunteer Stroke Scheme
Manor Farm House, Appleton, Abingdon, Oxon OX13 5JR. Tel: (0865) 862954

The Volunteer Stroke Scheme is designed to help people who suffer from communication and associated problems as the result of a stroke. Volunteers are recruited to establish personal relationships with patients with the objective of helping them work towards improving their disabilities. This is done by using shared interests, games, puzzles and other simple methods to stimulate them and help the difficulties they have with language, memory and tasks such as the handling of numbers and money, telling the time etc.

Volunteers are well directed and advised and need no special qualifications apart from a wish to help and a willingness to make a commitment.

There are schemes in over 90 Health Districts in the United Kingdom, each run by a paid part-time organiser and co-ordinated by Regional Organisers. All schemes are under the direction of the National Administrator at the above address, from whom further information can be obtained.

### Community and Voluntary Services
Rehabilitation Services, Taberner House, Park Lane, Croydon CR9 2BA Tel: (01) 760 5640

Community and Voluntary Services recruit volunteers to help with its local Authority's services for disabled people. Volunteers from around the country and abroad are especially needed to help run Group Holidays away from Croydon for the disabled, which generally last for one week. The work to be done includes helping the holidaymakers dress, wash, go to the lavatory, etc., and escorting and helping them swim, dance, shop and take part in day trips. Besides the more relaxing seaside holidays, activity holidays are also organised which may involve walking, riding, rockclimbing and so on.

Volunteers must be aged between 16 and 70 and fit. They should be enthusiastic and conscientious: experience of nursing, medicine, or of voluntary work with the disabled would be useful. Free accommodation is provided. Volunteers are given pocket money and are helped with their travel expenses from home or their United Kingdom port of entry. Transport is provided from Croydon to and from the holiday venue. Applications to Mr C. Gray, Volunteer Organiser, at the above address.

### Cork Polio and General After-care Association
Bonnington, Montenotte, Cork, Eire

The Association operates a number of services for the mentally handicapped in Cork city and county, including care units, schools, training centres, hostels and a sheltered workshop. Voluntary help is needed in all of these areas, especially during the school holidays. For further details contact the Personnel Officer at the above address.

### Cystic Fibrosis Research Trust
Alexandra House, 5 Blyth Road, Bromley, Kent BR1 3RS. Tel: (01) 464 7211/2

The Trust has branches throughout Britain which give support to patients and their families. Volunteers are generally already familiar with cystic fibrosis and its problems, due to prior experience of the disease; however, outside volunteers within the local community may be of service.

Enquiries may be sent to the Director, at the above address.

### Down's Syndrome Association (DSA)
1st Floor, 12-13 Clapham Common Southside, London SW4 7AA. Tel: (01) 720 0008

The Down's Syndrome Association exists to give practical support, advice and objective information to children and adults with Down's Syndrome. In order that they may achieve their full potential, the Association also provides the vital help and information needed by their families, professionals and all those who work with them. In addition, they have an ongoing public information campaign, which is aimed at breaking down lingering prejudice. Underpinning all the activities is a London-based Resource Centre. Apart from holding an extensive range of specialist publications, it has been set up to provide practical learning aids and toys, audio/visual material, and is a meeting place for parents and children.

Those who are interested in offering assistance should contact the Information Officer at the above address.

## Friedreich's Ataxia Group
The Common, Cranleigh, Surrey GU6 8SB. Tel: (0483) 272741

This Group raises money for research into this incurable disease of the central nervous system. Volunteers are needed to do office work and to take sufferers out and occasionally act as helpers on overseas holidays.

For further information contact the National Organiser.

## Guide Dogs for the Blind Association
Alexandra House, 9 Park Street, Windsor, Berkshire. Tel: (0753) 85711

Help is needed by the Association in rearing its puppies until they are ready to be taken back for training. Anyone interested in becoming a puppy-walker should live near Bolton, Exeter, Forfar, Leamington, Middlesbrough, Redbridge or Wokingham. Most of the Association's brood bitches also live with families and there are occasional opportunities to help in this way.

Fund raising for the Association is organised through over 400 local branches that have been formed by volunteer supporters. Anyone who would like to help in these activities should contact the offices in Windsor.

## Jewish Blind Society
Golders Green Road, London NW11 9DN. Tel: (01) 458 3282

The Society is a national charity which helps the blind and partially sighted to be restored to independence and to remain in touch with the world around them. The Society maintains residential homes for the visually handicapped at Dorking, Surrey. There are residential and holiday homes at Bournemouth and Southport and community centres in London, Manchester, Leeds and Glasgow. It also provides welfare and financial aid for visually handicapped people and their families living in their own homes and for the younger physically disabled. Volunteers are needed either alone or in groups to work for short or long periods. The principal jobs performed by volunteers are making regular visits to our clients in their own homes and providing them with transport to and from the Society's day centres and clubs.

No particular skills are vital, although many can be useful. Those who will be working directly with the blind receive instruction. Expenses may be paid depending on the type of work done. Long term volunteers are given accommodation in residential homes.

Applicants should contact Betty Young, Volunteer Co-ordinator at the above address.

## MIND (National Association for Mental Health)
22 Harley Street, London W1. Tel: (01) 637 0741

MIND has over 200 affiliated local mental health associations in England and Wales which work for improvements in the care of people with mental health problems. They organise day centres, employment projects, social clubs, sheltered accommodation and facilitate self-help groups, all of which rely to a large extent upon voluntary help. Making friends with people in the community is often the most important step to rehabilitation for people with mental health problems. Volunteers are also needed in MIND groups' "Nearly New" clothing shops around the country, the proceeds of which are used to continue the work.

Although most of the tasks for volunteers require a long term commitment, occasionally short term projects are arranged. Depending on the resources of the local association, travelling expenses may be reimbursed. There are no restrictions on those wishing to volunteer. People who have experienced problems of mental distress in their own lives can bring particularly valuable insights to their voluntary work. Professional mental health workers, supporting and advising in a voluntary capacity also have an important role.

Inquiries may be sent to the Information Officer at the above address. There are also regional offices: WALES MIND, 23 St Mary Street, Cardiff CF1 2AA; NORTHERN MIND, 158 Durham Road, Gateshead, Tyne and Wear NE8 4EL; NORTH WEST MIND, 21 Ribblesdale Place, Preston, Lancs PR1 3NA; TRENT AND YORKSHIRE MIND, First Floor Suite, The White Building, Fitzalan Square, Sheffield S1 2AY; WEST MIDLANDS MIND, Princess Chambers, (3rd Floor), 52/54 Lichfield Street, Wolverhampton WV1 1DG; SOUTH WEST MIND, Bluecoat House, Saw Close, Bath, Avon BA1 1EY; SOUTH EAST MIND, 4th Floor, 24-32 Stephenson Way, London NW1 2HD.

## Multiple Sclerosis Society of Great Britain and Northern Ireland
25 Effie Road, London SW6 1EE. Tel: (01) 736 6267

The Society operates over 350 local branches throughout the UK to provide a welfare service to suffering members and to raise funds both for welfare and for research into the causes and cure of multiple sclerosis. Volunteers can be of service in raising the morale of MS sufferers and providing friendship by visiting them and by arranging and funding excursions.

Enquiries to the General Secretary at the above address will be forwarded to the appropriate branch office.

## Muscular Dystrophy Group of Great Britain and Northern Ireland
Nattrass House, 35 Macaulay Road, London SW4 0QP. Tel: (01) 720 8055

The Muscular Dystrophy Group raises funds for medical research into this inherited muscle-wasting disease and offers practical advice and support to those people (and those families) affected by it. There are over 450 branches and representatives throughout the UK and Northern Ireland, all of whom are anxious for local helpers to assist in their fund raising and other activities. Write to the Branch Officer at the above address for the details of local branches.

### National Deaf-Blind Helpers' League
18 Rainbow Court, Paston Ridings, Peterborough PE4 6UP. Tel: (0733) 73511

The League aims to give hope and encouragement to deaf-blind people by bringing them together through Regional Group activities and a quarterly magazine (in braille, moon and print), and by increasing public awareness of their condition within the community. Anyone with a genuine concern for people with the double handicap of deafness and blindness, and time and energy to spare to help promote these activities, should contact the Chief Executive at the above address.

### National Eczema Society
Tavistock House North, Tavistock Square, London WC1. Tel: (01) 388 4097

This Society aims to promote mutual support for individuals and families coping with eczema. Volunteers are required to assist with the day to day running of the National Office and they may find themselves working within any of the Society's departments. Help is required all the year round. Both travel and lunch expenses are paid.

Those interested should contact Andrew Craven, Office Administrator at the above address.

### National Library for the Blind
Far Cromwell Road, Bredbury, Stockport, Cheshire SK6 2SG. Tel: (061) 494 0217

The Library is the only large general library lending books in braille free to the visually handicapped in Britain and abroad. Many of its books are transcribed into braille by volunteers who work at home. At present around 150 volunteers do this work for 5-10 hours per week, but more are needed. The work consists of both transcribing from print into braille and typing from print on to magnetic tape for automatic brailling; equipment and training are provided. Volunteers need to be able to concentrate and be patient and accurate; the text typists should be good copy typists and experience with a word processor or electric typewriter would be useful. Those interested should contact the Director-General at the above address.

### PHAB
Tavistock House North, Tavistock Square, London WC1H 9HX. Tel: (01) 388 1963

PHAB works through social clubs and activities in which physically handicapped and able bodied people work together on an equal basis in membership, management and programme issues. PHAB also provides holidays and courses in which physically handicapped and able bodied people live, work and play together. Volunteers can help with all aspects of these programmes by joining a local club.

For further information and details of local clubs contact the Secretary at the above address.

## Parkinson's Disease Society of the United Kingdom Ltd.

36 Portland Place, London W1N 3DG. Tel: (01) 255 2432

The aims of the society are threefold: to help patients and their relatives with the problems arising from Parkinson's Disease; to collect and disseminate information on the disease; and to encourage and provide funds for research into it. Voluntary workers provide vital assistance in the achievement of these aims; they assist at the national headquarters and run over 100 local branches. Helpers are especially desirable if they can assist in the setting up of new branches, as at present many voluntary workers are relatives of sufferers from the disease who already have many demands on their time. Drivers are always welcome at local branches, and fuel costs are reimbursed where appropriate.

Enquiries should either be directed to the Executive Director or Development Officer at the above address, or to the Honorary Secretary of the local branch of the applicant.

## Riding for the Disabled Association

Avenue 'R', National Agricultural Centre, Kenilworth, Warwicks. CV8 2LY
Tel: (0203) 56107

The aim of the Association is to provide the opportunity of riding to disabled people who might benefit in their general health and well-being. There are Member groups throughout the UK, whose voluntary helpers are drawn from many sources: Pony Clubs, Riding Clubs, the British Red Cross Society, Rotary Clubs, the Police Force, older school children, or simply responsible members of the community.

Prospective volunteers should contact a local Member Group directly. The list of Member Groups and a leaflet about the activities of the Association are available from the Secretary at the above address.

## The Royal Association for Disability and Rehabilitation

25 Mortimer Street, London W1N 8AB. Tel: (01) 637 5400

The Association does not recruit volunteers directly, but does act as an information service for them. Among its activities is the publication of a list of organisations who seek volunteers to help with holidays for disabled people.

Those interested should write to the Holidays Officer at the above address.

## Royal Association in Aid of Deaf People (RAD)

27 Old Oak Road, Acton, London W3 7HN. Tel: (01) 743 6187

This association operates in the Greater London region, Essex, Kent and Surrey to promote the social, general and spiritual welfare of those who are deaf or both deaf and blind. RAD tries to enlarge their world by communicating ideas and knowledge to them which hearing people take for granted. Special work is also carried out for the deaf in psychiatric and handicapped hospitals. Social club meetings are held mainly in centres and clubs where special events such as bingo, billiards and drama evenings are organised. Volunteers help with special one-day excursions and longer holidays.

Volunteers need to be in good health and willing to undertake the process of becoming fluent in sign language.

Enquiries may be sent to the Director of Fieldwork at the above address.

### Royal National Institute for the Blind (RNIB)
224 Great Portland Street, London W1N 6AA. Tel: (01) 388 1266

RNIB is Britain's largest organisation helping blind and visually handicapped people, and needs volunteers in many different areas of its work. For instance, in fund raising, by organising or helping at local events in co-operation with your local appeals organiser. Help is also needed in RNIB's residential homes and holiday hotels for driving, shopping, visiting, etc. The schools need care/classroom assistants and qualified or experienced help with swimming, riding, outings, etc. The cassette library needs volunteer readers to record books at home or in the RNIB studios. Volunteers are also needed to read books to students at university or at home. The Braille Department needs volunteers to transcribe a variety of books into braille. Volunteers must pass an exam in braille proficiency, and will need to spend a fair amount of time transcribing each book. Talking books are recorded by professional readers, but volunteers are needed to service the playback machines loaned to members. No great technical knowledge is necessary.

Volunteers are recruited for an indefinite period of time. Expenses are paid. Applications should be sent to the Director General at the above address.

### Royal National Institute for the Deaf
105 Gower Street, London WC1E 6AH. Tel: (01) 387 8033

The RNID, generally speaking, does not employ volunteers since much of their work is specialised. However, some of the schools, hostels and homes for the deaf around the country with which it has connections do employ volunteers. The RNID has recently expanded their fund raising department and would welcome volunteer assistance with events at weekends. The Information Officer at the above address will supply addresses for those interested to contact.

### St. John Ambulance Brigade
1 Grosvenor Crescent, London SW1 7EF. Tel: (01) 235 5231

The St. John Ambulance Brigade is a body of 250,000 volunteers worldwide who give millions of hours of unpaid service every year providing first aid cover at public events and undertaking a variety of welfare work in the local community. Recruits are always welcome; the UK membership now numbers over 80,000. Children aged between 6 and 10 can join St John Ambulance as Badgers, and become Cadets from the age of 10 to 16 and thereafter adult members.

For further information about the Brigade, contact the local county office (details in local telephone directory) or the address above.

**Scottish Society for the Mentally Handicapped**
13 Elmbank Street, Glasgow G2 4QA. Tel: (041) 226 4541

The Society concerns itself with all aspects of the welfare of mentally handicapped people. The main thrust of the Society's voluntary work is the organisation of social and recreational activities through its local branches, of which there are at present 80 in Scotland. Most branches run clubs and similar activities and welcome volunteers able to give up some time on a fairly regular basis.

Opportunities for other forms of voluntary work are limited, and there are few opportunities to participate in holiday camps; these are organised through local branches. Those interested in the care of the mentally handicapped in Scotland are welcome to contact the Director at the above address for further information.

# Other Non Residential Opportunities

The following organisations have been included in the Short Term Residential chapter but they also welcome non residential support.

Conservation Volunteers
— Northern Ireland
Festiniog Railway Company
Grosvenor Museum Excavation
  Section
National Autistic Society

National Federal of City Farms
Queen Elizabeth's Foundation
  for the Disabled
The Simon Community (UK)
Stallcombe House

# The Volunteer and Unemployment Benefit

One of the basic principles behind the payment of unemployment benefit in Great Britain is that it must only be given to those who are free to take up a job if one becomes available. The Department of Employment used to argue that if someone was doing voluntary work then they were not available for work, and so should not receive any benefit. The official attitude has softened in recent years, as it has been realised that in times of high unemployment it does not achieve anything to bar those who have little chance of finding work from making constructive use of their time. Ultimately, what is permitted is at the discretion of the individual's Benefit Office, so people are advised to consult the sheet listed below for full details of membership.

The situation now is that volunteers can claim unemployment benefit, provided they meet a few basic conditions. They must remain available either for a job interview or to begin work at 24 hours notice. They are allowed to receive reasonable expenses, such as the payment of bus fares to wherever they will be helping. They can also receive pocket money of up to £2 per day except on Sundays, when there is no limit on how much anyone claiming unemployment benefit can earn. People who are following their former occupation — for example a printer operating a printing press in a community centre — are, however, not allowed to accept pocket money.

People who are unemployed can also continue to receive benefit if they take part in a voluntary work camp lasting for 14 days or less in Great Britain as long as they give their Benefit Office advance warning and the camp is run by either a charity or a local authority. The situation is less clear for those wanting to join a work camp abroad, as it is at the discretion of their Benefit Officer whether or not they will be allowed to continue claiming.

The same basic principles as those listed above apply for people claiming supplementary benefit, except that they can only receive up to £4 per week in pocket money. Further information on how volunteers can claim both supplementary and unemployment benefits is contained on *"Information Sheet 4: Welfare Benefits"*, which is available for 60p to people who send a stamped self-addressed envelope to the Volunteer Centre Information Unit, 29 Lower King's Road, Berkhamsted, Herts. HP4 2AB.

# Further Reading

Please note that many of the organisations featured in this book also produce their own literature: do not hesitate to contact them if you would like further information about their activities.

**Archaeology Abroad:** 31-34 Gordon Square, London WC1H 0PY. Produces three information bulletins a year on archaeological opportunities abroad for its members: send a stamped addressed envelope for details of membership.

**Central Bureau for Educationalll Visits and Exchanges:** Seymour Mews House, Seymour Mews, London W1H 9PE. Publish *Volunteer Work Abroad,* a directory of organisations that send volunteers abroad for medium and long term periods: available from them for £3.00 plus 50p postage.

**Christians Abroad:** 15 Tufton Street, London SW15 3QQ. Produce a series of leaflets about work abroad, especially voluntary work in the Third World: send a stamped addressed envelope for details.

**Co-ordinating Committee for International Voluntary Service:** 1, rue Miollis, 75015 Paris, France. Produce a leaflet giving brief details of organisations arranging voluntary workcamps around the world: available in exchange for 4 international reply coupons.

**Council for British Archaeology:** 112 Kennington Road, London SE11 6RE. Publishes several newsletters every year that give details of archaeological sites needing help from volunteers: the annual subscription in 1989 will be £7.50.

**The National Youth Bureau:** 17-23 Albion Street, Leicester LE1 6GD. Produces *Sparetime Sharetime,* a resource pack on voluntary work and young people that includes a directory of voluntary work opportunities in England and Wales: free, but send 50p to cover postage.

**Returned Volunteer Action:** 1 Amwell Street, London EC1R 5UL. Publish a pamphlet entitled *Thinking about Volunteering:* send £1 plus a large SAE.

**The Royal Association for Disability and Rehabilitation (Radar):** 25 Mortimer Street, London W1N 8AB. Publishes a list of holiday centres for the disabled in Britain requiring voluntary help: send a stamped addressed envelope to the above address.

**The State of Israel Department of Antiquities and Museums:** P.O. 586, Rockefeller Museum, Jerusalem 91004, Israel. Publishes an annual guide to archaeological digs in Israel requiring help from volunteers: send an international reply coupon to the above address.

**UCCS International Office:** 38 de Montfort Street, Leicester LE1 7GP. Publish a booklet entitled *Jobs Abroad* twice a year that contains details of current vacancies abroad of interest to Christians. Send £2.40 for a year's subscription.

**Vacation Work Publications:** 9 Park End Street, Oxford OX1 1HJ. Publish a range of books covering both voluntary and paid work in Britain and around the world, including: *the Directory of Jobs and Careers Abroad, the Directory of Work and Study in Developing Countries, Kibbutz Volunteer, the Directory of Summer Jobs Abroad, the Directory of Summer Jobs in Britain* and *Work Your Way Around the World.* Send a stamped addressed envelope to the above address for details.

**The Volunteer Centre:** 29 Lower King's Road, Berkhamsted, Herts. HP4 2AB. Produces a range of information sheets containing advice and information for both volunteers and voluntary organisations in Britain: send a stamped addressed envelope for a list of these sheets.

# Index of Organisations

# Vacation Work also publish:

The Directory of Summer Jobs in Britain ............................................ £5.95
The Directory of Summer Jobs Abroad ............................................... £5.95
Vacation Traineeships for Students ..................................................... £5.95
Adventure Holidays .............................................................................. £3.95
Work Your Way Around the World ...................................................... £7.95
The Au Pair & Nanny's Guide to Working Abroad ............................. £5.95
Working in Ski Resorts — Europe ....................................................... £5.95
Kibbutz Volunteer ................................................................................ £4.95
The Directory of Jobs and Careers Abroad ........................................ £7.95
The Directory of Work and Study in Developing Countries .............. £6.95
Travellers Survival Kit — Europe ....................................................... £5.95
Travellers Survival Kit — Soviet Union and Eastern Europe ........... £8.95
Travellers Survival Kit to the East ...................................................... £4.95
Travellers Survival Kit — USA and Canada ....................................... £6.95
Travellers Survival Kit — Australia and New Zealand ...................... £6.95
Hitch-hikers Manual Britain ................................................................ £3.95
Europe — a Manual for Hitch-hikers .................................................. £3.95
The Travellers Picture Phrasebook ...................................................... £1.95

# Distributors of:

Summer Employment Directory of the United States ........................ £7.95
Internships (On-the-Job Training Opportunities in the USA) .......... £12.95
Emplois d'Ete en France ...................................................................... £6.95
Jobs in Japan ........................................................................................ £9.95
Teaching Tactics for Japan's English Classrooms ............................ £5.95

Vacation Work Publications, 9 Park End Street, Oxford